THE TASK
of
NATIONS

HERBERT V. EVATT

DUELL, SLOAN AND PEARCE
New York

Copyright, 1949, by
Herbert V. Evatt

*All rights reserved, including
the right to reproduce this book
or portions thereof in any form.*

FIRST EDITION

PRINTED IN THE UNITED STATES OF AMERICA

THE TASK OF NATIONS

CONTENTS

I	General Assembly at the Palais de Chaillot	3
II	The Scope of the UN—Its Successes to Date	23
III	UN Policy and the Principles Which Guide It	33
IV	The Great, Middle, and Smaller Powers	43
V	Greece	55
VI	Berlin—Impasse among Great Powers	73
VII	Problems of the Peace Settlements	87
VIII	The Genocide Achievement and the Children's Aid Program	101
IX	Human Rights—The Unanimous Declaration	111
X	Palestine: The First Phase	121
XI	Palestine: The Second Phase	129
XII	Palestine: The Third Phase	147
XIII	Palestine: The Fourth Phase	165
XIV	Indonesia	175
XV	Atomic Energy—A Threat and a Promise	201
XVI	Peace and Welfare—A Common Interest	209
XVII	Churchill's Letter to Stalin	227
XVIII	One World—The Task of All Nations and All People	235
	Appendix—Charter of the United Nations	244
	Index	275

THE TASK OF NATIONS

I

GENERAL ASSEMBLY AT THE PALAIS DE CHAILLOT

The Paris Assembly

THE hopes and fears of all people were centered in Paris when the United Nations Assembly met there on 21st September 1948.

People everywhere were hungry for peace, and looked to their representatives to sweep aside the fears and gloomy prophecies of war which were again tormenting men.

It was a critical testing time for the United Nations Organization, to whom mankind had entrusted the great task of preserving peace on just terms.

Relations between the great powers were worse than they had ever been since the war ended. A deadlock had arisen on Berlin which was a symptom of the failure of these powers to agree on the peace settlements for Europe. Old disputes and situations such as Greece and Korea had persisted throughout the year and reappeared on the Assembly's agenda. The Atomic Energy Commission and the Commission for Conventional Armaments had suspended their work on the ground that no basis of agreement could be found at present.

The world seemed divided into two camps led respectively by the United States of America and the Soviet Union, and to some people it also seemed that this split was irrevocable and that nothing could be done by any individual country except to back one side or the other. There was certainly a drift in the direction of war. There were even some who went so far as to predict early hostilities.

But the third session of the General Assembly gradually demonstrated that this defeatist attitude would never dominate the practical work of the Assembly. As each item came up for discussion it was clear that a substantial number of members, particularly among the middle and smaller countries, were actively working to discover and broaden an area of agreement so long as it did not prejudice a just conclusion.

Nor did the great powers themselves fail to make important contributions, sometimes under pressure of the opinion of a substantial proportion of the other countries. In some of the most vital and difficult subjects, such as atomic energy, all the great powers made some concessions, even though final agreement was still not attained.

The Paris Session of the General Assembly had many achievements to its credit. Individual decisions and recommendations can be singled out and acclaimed as successes. But the biggest achievement of all was that the international atmosphere was improved. It became apparent to everybody that all nations wanted peace and that there was not going to be a world war in the near future. Representatives of the various governments continued the United Nations habits and routine of working together and discussing common problems around the table. The very act of assembling each day and working to a common agenda brought home to every representative that, though we came from different countries, we were also part of one Organization and came from one world.

PALAIS DE CHAILLOT

For the first time since New York was chosen as the permanent headquarters of the Organization, the General Assembly was meeting away from home—in the Palais de Chaillot at Paris. Many had prophesied great inconveniences, lack of adequate documentation, and other such problems. None of these forebod-

General Assembly at Palais de Chaillot

ings came true. The Assembly went smoothly and efficiently, which is a great tribute to Mr. Trygve Lie, Mr. Andrew Cordier, and the whole Secretariat for the skill with which they transferred the necessary staff and equipment, and also a tribute to the French Government for its hospitality and good management.

Paris proved an admirable site and though I think in principle the Assembly should not leave its permanent headquarters, particularly after the new buildings have been completed, it was valuable for delegates to see Europe in its efforts of reconstruction.

Paris is the center of one of the great world civilizations and cultures. It proved to be a particularly appropriate place for the third session, because here we adopted the Universal Declaration of Human Rights. France in the past has been the source of many historical movements for individual liberty, and was once the birthplace of another great declaration of human rights.

Just as happened in New York, the people of Paris came crowding to our meetings. The public seating space for plenary sessions of the Assembly and for some of the committees, particularly the political committee, was filled daily. Men and women came from all over Europe to see the United Nations—their organisation—in action. One of the many good results of having public meetings is that everyone can see exactly what is going on, and so get a sense of the real forces at work which cannot be obtained merely by reading documents reporting the decisions of the meetings.

Fifty-eight Nations

As I sat in the chair presiding over the General Assembly for three months, I looked down into the hall and saw the representatives of fifty-eight nations there, drawn from all six continents, from countries with widely differing political and social philosophies and systems and in different stages of economic and cultural development.

They were seated in alphabetical order so that these distinctions did not prevent the various countries mingling together. The U.S.S.R., United Kingdom, and United States sat side by side. Beside one another in the next row were Afghanistan, the Argentine, Australia, and Belgium.

This accident of seating does in fact have some influence upon relations between delegates. Representatives naturally get to know their neighbours best of all. Australia's relations with the Belgian delegation, for example, are always very close. This is partly because we have to a large measure common ideals and common ways of thought, and partly because of the close friendship established by our servicemen in the First World War. But it is also assisted by the fact that we sit next to one another in committees and we are able to exchange impressions and otherwise consult together. This applies to all countries. Sitting next to a representative in committee day after day one naturally strikes up a friendship with him, even if he is sometimes advocating a policy directly opposed to one's own.

All delegates usually get on very well together outside the conference room, when they meet in the lounges and elsewhere and can talk freely and frankly on a personal basis and can range beyond questions of foreign policy and get on to other matters of common interest. It is like our own Congress and Parliaments, where Republicans and Democrats, Conservatives and Labour, fight one another, sometimes bitterly, on the floor of the house but can be quite good friends outside. The same spirit exists in the United Nations. No matter how much we may differ on particular points, we are all part of one vast team engaged in working for peace and welfare for all mankind.

Looking down from the president's chair, I could also see some of the leading personalities of the world gathered here and meeting every day.

American Personalities

In the American seats, for example, was General Marshall, then Secretary of State, who had played so outstanding a part as a military leader in shaping the victory for all the United Nations in the Second World War. He was even then ill and had to return home not long afterwards. General Marshall used to confine his active participation in United Nations affairs to the plenary sessions of the General Assembly where he was a regular attendant, but he spoke only in the general debate at the opening of the session. His speech on that occasion was a short and restrained address, and by refraining from provocative remarks he helped to set the tone of the Assembly and allow it to proceed along constructive lines. In the committees and in the debates on particular items on the agenda, the United States position was put by other members of the delegation to whom the General gave a great deal of discretion as to the way in which they handled each matter, so as to carry out United States policy.

General Marshall's chief lieutenant was Senator Austin, a Republican who had had a long career in the United States Senate and who had done great service for his country and for the world by championing internationalism at a time when it was not always popular to do so. Senator Austin also became ill during the session and therefore was unable to attend committees after the first month. He has done magnificent service for the United Nations over the past two years in helping to establish the permanent headquarters in New York and in smoothing the many difficulties which have been continually arising in connexion with the new building.

The burden of leadership after both General Marshall and Senator Austin withdrew fell on Mr. John Foster Dulles, another distinguished Republican. He is one of the lay leaders of the churches in America, and is a man of great ability and with long experience in international affairs going back to the negotiations after the first world war. With Senator Vandenberg he was one of the big figures in forming the foreign policy of the Republican Party so that the United States would play a full role in international affairs and become a member of the United Nations. He has great capacity for mastering a problem and for lucid exposition, and is always a leading figure in any committee on which he serves.

One of the great personalities of the Assembly was another American delegate, Mrs. Eleanor Roosevelt. President Roosevelt probably did more than any other single man to bring the Organization into being. In fact it was he who coined the name "United Nations" and the Organization owes much to his great faith in the need and the possibility of the great powers working together and to his equally great moral purpose and genuine desire to live at peace with all countries. Mrs. Roosevelt did not have to rely solely on the deep admiration and affection which her husband had inspired. She earned her position by her own great merits, her own faith and enthusiasm for civil liberties and the advancement of the welfare of all mankind. Everywhere she went in France she was greeted with enthusiasm by the French people who would form themselves into crowds outside buildings that she was visiting.

Russian Personalities

The Russian delegation was again led by Mr. Vyshinsky, then Deputy Foreign Minister, who is one of the most picturesque figures of the United Nations. He is a man of great ability, with a keen intellect and a rapier-like skill at debating and argument. His keen sense of humour and lively manner make him at his best a most attractive speaker, and though he has been frequently in the minority he has played a big part over the past three years in shaping the course and the procedures of the

United Nations. Even his opponents admire his wit and venomous shafts, and indeed his occasional ferocity.

His chief deputy at the Third Session was Mr. Malik who is now the permanent head of the Soviet Mission to the United Nations. Mr. Malik also has a good sense of humour and a courtesy and persistency which often bring good results. He succeeded Mr. Gromyko whose name became almost a household word in other countries because it was he who, as the representative on the Security Council, was called upon to exercise the veto so many times. Mr. Gromyko also had a quiet manner and could usually keep a poker face and innocent air that made him even more enigmatic to the general public than most Russian representatives. But there are few people in the world who have mastered the Charter better than Mr. Gromyko, and he made many personal friends among the representatives of all other countries.

British Commonwealth Personalities

For most of the session the leader of the United Kingdom delegation was Mr. Hector McNeil, Minister of State, who is a shrewd and still young Scot who has served on most United Nations bodies over the past three years and has been a popular figure on them all. He has all the skill and ability in debate that one expects of a good House of Commons man.

One of the interesting things that one notices in United Nations meetings is the way in which nearly all representatives from the British Commonwealth have a skill in chairmanship, in grappling with questions of procedure so that business proceeds in an orderly manner, and in being able to speak on occasion without having to read their speeches. Some of the outstanding chairmen of the United Nations have come from the Dominions—Mr. Wilgress of Canada, Sir Carl Berendsen of New Zealand, and Sir Ramaswami Mudaliar of India.

This is probably attributable to the British parliamentary system which not only encourages those qualities but makes them almost a necessity for people in public life. It applies not only to the United Kingdom and the older Dominions: no finer speakers were present than the representatives of India and Pakistan. Of course I do not mean to imply that there are no representatives of other countries who possess equal skill in procedure and debating, but the uniformly high standard of the British Commonwealth representatives in this field invites attention.

The name of Mrs. Pandit is another that comes immediately to mind. She is the only woman who has so far led a delegation to the Assembly, and her dignity and sincerity have made a great impression on all members. She is the sister of the Prime Minister of India, Pandit Nehru, who is one of the great men of the world today—in fact he may prove to be one of the great figures of history—and I was happy to arrange for him to address the Assembly in plenary meeting when he paid a short visit to Paris after attending the British Commonwealth meeting in London.

Peter Fraser, the Prime Minister of New Zealand, made a welcome reappearance in the Paris Assembly after an absence of nearly three years. He played a big part at San Francisco in 1945 in making the Charter a more democratic instrument and in formulating the trusteeship provisions.

Sir Zafrullah Khan, the Foreign Minister of Pakistan, had one of the keenest minds and one of the strongest characters of the Assembly. He made a speech in the plenary session which will long be remembered, in which he defended religious liberty and expounded Moslem teaching in order to uphold this principle.

Mr. Mackenzie King of Canada was present at the opening session and delivered his country's speech in the general debate, thus making his final appearance at international gatherings before he laid down the burdens of Prime Ministership which he had borne for so long and in so distinguished a manner. He was one of the main architects of British Commonwealth development after the First World War, contributing greatly to the Dominions' emergence as sovereign states controlling their own foreign policy and relations.

South Africa was represented by Mr. Louw whose country was under heavy fire in the Assembly on both the questions of the future of South West Africa and the treatment of Indians in the Union. He had a difficult task to perform, and his earlier experience as a diplomat served him in good stead in explaining the South African point of view to the Assembly and in the equally important task of explaining the Assembly's views to his own countrymen. In the end the question of the treatment of Indians was postponed until the New York meeting in April.

Personalities from Other Countries

There were many big figures from the smaller countries. Outstanding among them was Paul-Henri Spaak, the Prime Minister of Belgium. He was a big man in every way, representing the best qualities of western civilization. He was the first President of the General Assembly, where he was called on to shoulder a difficult task in establishing the procedures of that body and in laying down precedents. How successful he was, can be judged from the effective working of the Assembly rules and machinery today. As the work of the Paris Assembly developed, he and his delegation played a leading part in the efforts that were made to find a satisfactory meeting ground for Eastern and Western Europe, and his good sense and fairness were especially valuable in his work as Chairman of the Political Committee of the Assembly.

There were many other notable figures: leaders of the Arab world like Faris el-Khouri of Syria, who had worked hard in the Security Council to further agreement between the great powers; leaders of Eastern Europe like Dr. Oscar Lange of Poland, one of the world's leading economists with a long record of liberal and socialist campaigning in Poland, a man who always argued his case in a reasonable and persuasive manner; leaders of Latin

America like Dr. Arce of the Argentine, a pertinacious and resourceful man who was not afraid to stand up to anyone and who had been President of the Special Session of the Assembly earlier in 1948; leaders of Western Europe like Joseph Bech of Luxemburg, civilized and urbane, with an inevitable cigarette forever drooping from beneath his moustache; and leaders of Asia like the representatives of Burma who were making their first appearance at an ordinary session of the Assembly and who were quickly establishing the position of their newly independent country in international counsels.

THE PRINCIPAL ORGAN

Under Article 7 of the Charter, the General Assembly is a principal organ of the United Nations. The record of the past three years shows that it is rapidly becoming recognised as *the* principal organ.

That is the role which many of us envisaged for it at the San Francisco Conference. One of the great achievements of that conference was to increase the powers and prestige of the General Assembly.

The General Assembly is the democratic core of the Organization. All fifty-nine members belong to it. There is no limit to the Assembly's right of discussion and no nation has a right to exercise an individual veto in order to prevent a resolution being adopted. Other principal organs of the United Nations—the Security Council, the Economic and Social Council, the Trusteeship Council, and the Secretary-General—report to the General Assembly every year. It is the body which elects the members of the other principal organs. It is the body which approves the budget for the whole Organization. Consequently the Assembly is the great focal point from which all other United Nations bodies draw their source and to which they must all look for ultimate guidance and support.

Reflection of Public Opinion

The Assembly is the great sounding board for the public opinion of the whole world. Representatives come along charged with instructions from their governments and often with predetermined views as to what the decision should be on particular matters on the agenda. But the Assembly always turns out to be something more than a mere instrumentality for recording votes that have been previously decided. Debates in committees and in the Assembly itself do have an effect on the opinions of the individual members. Time and again countries change or modify their attitude in response to arguments by other members and in response to the weight of opinion manifested in the Committee.

Equally we can see the effect on delegates of the reactions of the ordinary citizen, the man in the street, to the problems being discussed. World opinion is something which no representative dares to ignore.

An example of this occurred in the 1947 General Assembly when the Soviet representative, Mr. Vyshinsky proposed a resolution on war-mongering. This resolution was couched in offensive terms and, as it stood, had no hope of acceptance by other countries—indeed, it did not deserve to be supported in that form. But I felt that the problem which Mr. Vyshinsky had raised, that of war-mongering, was a real problem which deserved attention and should not be swept aside. I therefore introduced some amendments to the Soviet proposal which removed the offensive references and added some positive provisions of a peaceful and democratic character. Australia's position was subsequently supported by Canada and France who were thinking along similar lines, and the three of us introduced a joint resolution which in due course was unanimously adopted by the Assembly.

Some representatives at first resented Australia's intervention in this way because they would have preferred to throw out the

Soviet resolution completely and unceremoniously. But such a course was simply not possible nor was it desirable. It is always better for the Assembly to adopt a positive alternative than to ignore an issue altogether.

In this case the Assembly could not reject the Soviet resolution out of hand without its action being misunderstood by the people of the world. In a discussion which I had in the early stages of the debate with the representative of one of the leading Western European Powers, he told me that public opinion at home simply would not allow him to vote down the Soviet resolution without taking some positive action in the matter.

This, then, is the body over which I was chosen to preside— the principal organ of the United Nations, containing representatives of all the members of the Organization, with unlimited right of discussion, and reflecting and responsive to public opinion of the whole world. In doing me the great honour of electing me to this high office the Assembly was also imposing on me a great responsibility, together with a great opportunity to advance the purposes and principles of the whole Organization. Of this I was deeply conscious as I took my seat in the chair for the first time.

Presidential Election

The presidential election on 21st September was a tense business, as all such elections are. The previous year I had come within three votes of defeating Dr. Aranha of Brazil, and I knew that a large number of members wished me to be president for the Paris Session. However, a lot would depend upon the votes of the Latin American States who together numbered twenty out of the total membership of fifty-eight. These States in the past had always cast their votes as a bloc in elections and it therefore seemed that any candidate who did not have their support was unlikely to be chosen.

I knew that I would not have the support of the Arab States

General Assembly at Palais de Chaillot

who disagreed with my vote the previous year in favour of the partition of Palestine. I did not bear any personal resentment against the Arab representatives for this attitude, because I appreciated the deep emotions which the Palestine question inspires in them. Both before and after my election to the presidency I found it possible to co-operate with the Arab representatives on the many issues that came before the Assembly, and have never had any grounds to complain that they did not support me in the chair.

Various rumours circulated around Paris for some time before the election to the effect that one of the Latin American representatives would be nominated for the presidency. Such a suggestion encountered a lot of opposition, not only among other countries but also in the Latin American group itself. Dr. Aranha of Brazil had been president of both the special session and the ordinary session in 1947 and Dr. Arce of the Argentine had been president of the special assembly in 1948. There was a general feeling among other countries that the Latin Americans should not use their great voting power to elect yet another of their members to the presidency of the third session of the Assembly. This view was also held by some of the most experienced Latin American leaders, and found forceful expression in the meetings of the group when it met before the election.

The final discussions in the Latin American group was in a secret meeting on the day before the session began. The meeting continued until the early hours of the morning. Many members wished to support me, but others put forward the names of various Latin American representatives. In the end it was decided that Dr. Juan Bramuglia, the Foreign Minister of the Argentine, should be supported for the presidency, and it was expected that all the Latin American states would support him.

Nevertheless when the vote was taken when the General Assembly met, several of the Latin American States did not vote with the bloc but gave their votes to me in the first ballot. I secured twenty-five votes to Dr. Bramuglia's twenty-two, with a smaller number of votes going to Mr. Modzelewski of Poland and Mr. Bech of Luxemburg. A second ballot was therefore necessary and some other Latin American states transferred their support to me with the result that I got thirty-one votes to Dr. Bramuglia's twenty, and I was therefore elected. Subsequently several other representatives of Latin American countries told me that they also would have liked to cast their vote for me, but they felt morally bound to support the candidate from their group.

The result was, of course, very pleasing to me as it was a great honour and I felt it crowned my service to the United Nations beginning with the San Francisco Conference. Indeed some of my warmest supporters were those who had fought alongside me at San Francisco for many democratic and progressive principles in the Charter. I regarded my election as a further opportunity to work for the United Nations in a new capacity, particularly as I knew the success or failure of the Paris Assembly could determine the whole future of the Organization.

Latin Americans at the Assembly

The split in the Latin American vote was, I felt, a good thing for the Organization and for those States themselves. It demonstrated that the Latin American group was not a bloc which was slavishly bound to follow one line, and that its members did have and did exercise some discretion. It also meant that I did not owe my election as president to any bloc. I was completely free and did not feel tied by obligations to any group or country.

During the subsequent months Dr. Bramuglia and I got on very well together. He did not take a prominent part in the work of the Assembly because he had to preside over the meetings of the Security Council which at that time was concerned with Berlin. He had there a most difficult task which he carried out with great skill and judgment. He was pursuing in the Security Council the same general policy I was pursuing in the Assembly, that of trying to find and facilitate agreement among the nations and preventing deadlocks or open breaks. Subsequently, as I shall recount later, when Dr. Bramuglia's efforts did not prove successful, I acted with Mr. Trygve Lie to address a public appeal to the four great powers to renew their efforts to reach a settlement on Berlin and to co-operate to this end with Mr. Bramuglia. My efforts were intended to strengthen Mr. Bramuglia's hands and were understood by him as such, and when he laid down his office he publicly expressed his appreciation of my actions and support. It was a fortunate thing for the Organization that in these critical months the Presidents of the Assembly and the Security Council were working along parallel lines.

After my election I received the utmost support from all the Latin American leaders also. Old friends and devoted servants of the United Nations like Dr. Guillermo Belt of Cuba and Mr. Padilla Nervo of Mexico were as usual a tower of strength in the Assembly. Mr. Hernan Santa Cruz of Chile was another who gave invaluable service to the Assembly; he was the chairman of the Economic and Financial Committee, and we had worked closely together earlier at Geneva as members of the Economic and Social Council. Dr. Ricardo Alfaro of Panama was chairman of the legal committee and had been attending meetings since San Francisco days, and he too gave me full support.

Limitation of Speeches

As President it was my duty to remain loyal to the Charter of the United Nations and to do my utmost to see that the Assembly discharged its functions faithfully under that Charter. The President has great responsibilities in helping to steer the work of the Assembly so that it proceeds not merely efficiently but in a manner that allows all questions to be adequately and fairly discussed.

I am proud of the fact that throughout the whole of the Third

Session in Paris it was never once necessary to limit discussion in the plenary sessions. Every member was allowed to speak as long as he wished on each item of the agenda. It would have been possible under the rules to move that debate be closed on any particular item, and this was suggested on one or two occasions by some representatives. I always set myself steadfastly against such a course and preferred to rely on the commonsense and restraint of the individual members. That confidence was never misplaced.

If a debate is closed while some members still wish to speak, an impression is always left either with members themselves or with the general public that the whole truth has not been presented in the debate. This is particularly the case when on many matters there exists within the organization a small though clearly defined minority, which can always be overruled by sheer weight of numbers irrespective of the merits of the case. As Mr. Vyshinsky is so fond of pointing out, minorities have their rights and where there are only a few members to put a particular point of view long speeches from each of them may sometimes seem necessary.

There is a converse to this, that the minority should not abuse the tolerance of the majority. Sometimes in one's eagerness to defend the rights of minorities, one may forget that majorities also have their rights. On the last day of the Assembly I found it necessary to say to Mr. Vyshinsky: "I should like to recall to Mr. Vyshinsky that old Mongolian proverb—I believe it comes from Outer Mongolia—that the majority is not always wrong."

Fortunately the Soviet group did, in my opinion, co-operate in this respect and we were able to get through all our plenary meetings without having to muzzle anybody. This is an achievement when one considers the contentious nature of some of the problems that were each disposed of in one day or a little longer.

There was a move to close the debate on Korea which began just after midnight on the day scheduled for the final adjournment of the session in Paris. After the Ukrainian, Chinese, and Byelorussian representatives had spoken, some members began to make preparations for moving the closure of the debate. This became known to me and when the representative who was then speaking had finished, I immediately adjourned the session till next day. It was then two o'clock in the morning, and delegates were very tired.

The Assembly met again at three o'clock the following afternoon, which was a Sunday, when everyone was refreshed by a good night's rest and tempers were no longer frayed or on edge with weariness. We concluded our debate in a fairly short time without anyone being limited in the length of his speech. As a result nobody felt that the subject had not been adequately discussed, and both sides were given an opportunity to put their views properly. After the Korean item was disposed of, we had a short ceremony to thank the French Government for its hospitality and to mark the conclusion of the work done at Paris. The Assembly was thereby able to adjourn in a manner which did credit to its members and was worthy of its position and responsibilities in the world.

In justice to those who wished to close the Korean debate abruptly, I should state that they feared it might not be possible to get a quorum together on the Sunday, as some members had already made preparations to leave Paris. But I had a high opinion of the sense of responsibility of the members, and it was justified by the fact that we had a bigger attendance than usual for the closing debate.

Occasionally in the committees, debate was closed or, more often, speeches were limited in length. This sometimes occurred after the general debate on an item had been concluded and the committee was proceeding to debate particular points in a resolution. Quite often in these circumstances the limitation of speeches was not strongly opposed by anybody, as it was recognized to be a fair way of apportioning time, provided that the rule was interpreted flexibly when occasion justified. I never heard any serious complaint from anyone that debates in committees were unfairly restricted, nor could such a charge have been sustained.

The Record of the Paris Assembly

As I watched the Assembly working I could see it evidence a sense of unity. The Assembly, and the United Nations itself, is something greater than the sum of the individual nations who compose it. It takes on a life of its own. Just as in the House of Commons or in Congress there is a force which is greater than any single member, so too the United Nations Assembly has an existence apart from the members who compose it. It is a real instrument of international organization and not just a register of votes.

The Assembly met in Paris for 71 working days. It held 50 plenary meetings, compared with 49 the year before, and 568 meetings of committees and sub-committees, compared with 445 the year before.

This represents an enormous expenditure of time and effort. We cannot judge these merely by what goes on in the committees themselves. We must also take into account the even greater time and effort spent in preparing for the discussions and in formulating policy. There is no group of men and women in the world today who are more hard-worked than diplomatic representatives attending international conferences. They know no forty-hour week, nor do they pursue the somewhat dubious pleasures of "cookie-pushers," to quote a characteristically pungent phrase of the late Harry Hopkins. Cocktail parties are comparatively rare, and are often regarded by tired delegates as more of a nuisance or irksome official duty than as a pleasure. It is a tribute to the ideals and practical possibilities of the United Nations that so many people are prepared to devote so much of their lives to wearying but vital work.

When the Assembly adjourned on 11th December it had completed action on most of the items on its agenda, including most of the controversial political items. It had adopted a Universal Declaration of Human Rights and a convention to prevent and punish genocide. It had acted effectively on many items in the economic and social field. Above all it had demonstrated that the fifty-eight nations were able to work together and that there was at present no likelihood either of war or of the United Nations breaking up.

II

THE SCOPE OF THE UNITED NATIONS—ITS SUCCESSES TO DATE

THE primary objective of the United Nations is to preserve peace and promote fair dealing in international relations. It is on this basis that most people judge it. What have been the achievements in this direction by the Organization in the past three years?

Let it be said at once that its achievements are great. The United Nations must be judged not simply by the effectiveness of action which it has taken to settle disputes and situations after they have arisen, but even more by its success in preventing disputes from ever occurring. This is a matter which it is not easy to judge because we do not know how often nations have been deterred from aggression or unjust actions by the existence of the United Nations.

There are many sources of tension all over the world, and yet it is remarkable how often they have been kept the subject of discussion and not allowed to degenerate into open fighting. Matters which a few years ago would have been cause for at least a rupture of diplomatic relations are now turned into subjects of peaceful negotiation between the countries concerned.

The first success of the United Nations was in connexion with the Iranian question, which was raised in the Security Council on 19th January 1946. The Iranian delegation complained that a situation had arisen which might lead to international friction owing to interference by the U.S.S.R. through the medium of its officials and armed forces in the internal affairs of Iran, particularly in preventing the Iranian Government from exercising power in Azerbaijan. After hearing both sides, the Council asked the two parties to negotiate together.

On 18th March the Iranian delegation also complained that the U.S.S.R. was maintaining troops on Iranian territory contrary to treaty provisions which would have required their withdrawal on 2nd March. The Security Council considered the matter at some length and was informed of the negotiations between the U.S.S.R. and Iranian governments. Over the next few months the Council received various reports by the Iranian representative on developments inside the country. In due course Soviet forces were completely withdrawn and the Iranian Government re-established effective control over the province of Azerbaijan. After a certain stage the U.S.S.R. denied that the Security Council had any right to consider the matter further as the dispute had been settled, but the Security Council has remained seized of the question.

The Council's action in the Iranian case was to bring the two parties together and to keep the situation under observation. In this way the dispute was satisfactorily handled at that time.

Palestine is another question which has been handled justly and effectively by the United Nations. When the United Kingdom decided to surrender its mandate, a vacuum would have been created if there had not been an international body in existence whose determination could be accepted as valid by all the great powers. Considering the historical background of passion and enmity existing in this region over the Jewish question, it is surprising that the situation has passed off with so little fighting and that the new state of Israel has been born in so orderly a manner. The United Nations gave a decision based on an impartial assessment of the facts of the situation. The difficulties that have arisen have been mainly the fault, not of the United Nations decision, but of the failure of some countries to observe that decision. As time goes on the situation seems to have improved and ultimately peace and stability should be established on the basis of the United Nations decision.

The Balkan situation is another example of successful United Nations intervention. Here again there is a long historical background to the dispute based on old jealousies and rivalries among the Balkan states. This has been reinforced by an underlying struggle for influence in this region between the U.S.S.R. on the one hand and the United States and Britain on the other. It is a situation that could have been explosive. The United Nations has not finally solved it, but it has helped in several ways. The presence of its observers has been a deterrent to assistance to the guerrillas by the three northern neighbours. Its mediation functions have made it possible for the four countries concerned to talk together. It is no mean achievement that in the middle of these great disturbances representatives of the four countries should be able to meet amicably in Paris to discuss such matters as frontier conventions and the exchange of minorities, and that in the General Assembly Greek and Yugoslav representatives should participate in discussions on the problem of Greek children and join in voting for a unanimous committee resolution on that subject.

The Kashmir dispute is still another situation which will probably be solved successfully by the United Nations. Here also were explosive possibilities which could have involved a vast sub-continent in war with perhaps millions of men engaged in fighting. The solution to the dispute has been a slow process, but it now appears that both sides will be able to agree on a course of action including a plebiscite.

These are a few examples. In weighing the success of the United Nations it is not enough to ask what it has done. We should also ask what would be the position if the United Nations had not existed. Palestine would certainly have become the scene of great fighting involving all the Middle East and possibly involving great powers with interests in that area. In that case Palestine might easily have become the source of a third world war. Indonesia is another case where United Nations intervention put an end to fighting which could have cost untold lives. These are all examples of concrete successes by the United Nations.

The Scope of the Organization

The builders of the United Nations learned several lessons from the experience of the League of Nations, and the new Organization has several sources of strength which the League did not have.

The United Nations contains all the great powers. Neither the United States of America nor the Soviet Union were members of the League of Nations when it was established, and the United States never joined. This greatly hindered the effectiveness of the League. It might have been possible to secure adequate action against Italy at the time of the invasion of Abyssinia if the United States had been a member and could have participated actively in discussions on this subject.

The weakness of the League did not lie only in the fact that America was not bound morally or legally to observe decisions and recommendations of the League. The League also suffered greatly because America did not participate in the formulation of its decisions, and therefore the voice was absent of one of the great powers with enormous influence throughout the world. This was also true of the Soviet Union until it entered the League in 1934.

It is to be hoped that in due course every nation in the world will be a member of the United Nations. At present no fewer than fourteen nations have applied for membership but have not yet secured the approval of the Security Council. Five of these applications are over two years old. In addition there will eventually have to be room for the ex-enemy states of Germany and Japan, when the peace treaties have been concluded and they have proved themselves to be democratic and peace-loving states. This however is still a rather distant prospect.

Our ultimate objective must be universality and it is regrettable that so many countries which have declared themselves will-

The Scope of the UN—Successes to Date

ing to accept the obligations of the Charter should be excluded from membership. A most indefensible exclusion is that of Ceylon, which is a completely sovereign and obviously peace-loving state, and the admission of which is favoured by an overwhelming majority of the General Assembly.

Another great source of strength for the United Nations compared with the old League of Nations is the former's wide functions in the economic and social field. The League had certain responsibilities for these matters, but they were limited compared with the new world organization. The Australian delegation was one of those which led the fight at San Francisco to have the Economic and Social Council made a principal organ, instead of being a subsidiary body of the General Assembly as was originally proposed in the draft prepared at Dumbarton Oaks.

The Charter contains a pledge by each member to promote solutions of economic and social problems and also promote higher standards of living, full employment, and respect and observance for fundamental human rights. The entrusting of these functions to the United Nations shows an appreciation of the new importance of economic matters in international relations.

Many specialized agencies have since been created which have been brought into relationship with the United Nations. They include the Food and Agriculture Organization, the International Civil Aviation Organization, the International Bank and the International Monetary Fund, the World Health Organization, and several other bodies. The International Labour Office, which was established in 1919 as an autonomous institution associated with the League of Nations, has been made a specialized agency of the United Nations. The International Trade Organization has not yet been fully established but extensive preparatory work has been done and several agreements have already been completed by governments to give effect to some of the objectives and the work of its preparatory commission.

In this way there has been established an extensive network of economic and social co-operation. Constant contact between the technical and other representatives of the participating governments has helped to develop an understanding of one another's problems and has built habits of international co-operation.

Not enough attention is given to the influence on world peace and co-operation of the mechanics of discussing problems in the United Nations. The mere routine of having to come to a table and discuss a problem with representatives of other countries exercises a persuasive influence. In technical fields the representatives often develop a feeling of partnership which transcends national or political considerations.

In the case of disputes, the very routine of having to be at a conference table at a certain time each day and having to defend one's position brings a sense of responsibility, and sometimes puts incidents into their proper proportion against other world problems and the interests of other countries. Tempers are given time to cool. Added to this is the fact that no one is unmoved by discussion. Even a great power which feels convinced of the rightness of its case or the strength of its resources tends to be deterred by unanimous criticism of its policies. It may modify its actions. Sometimes this modification is not done publicly, for the desire to save face is not confined to countries of the Far East. Changes in policy may be made quietly and sometimes can only be seen by changes in attitude or actions over a period.

The effect of this routine of procedure and discussion was demonstrated in the Security Council in the Berlin dispute. Here was a situation where some discerned possibilities of war. Yet what happened? The Western Powers placed it upon the agenda of the Security Council and discussions began. Mr. Vyshinsky for the Soviet Union denied the Security Council had any jurisdiction but he remained present at the meetings of the Council and even intervened occasionally in an attempt to protect his position. The President of the Council, Dr. Bramuglia, with five other so-called "neutral" members, attempted to mediate between the two parties. Mr. Vyshinsky and representatives of the three Western Powers took part in these discussions with Dr. Bramuglia. The first stage of consideration of the item ended with the Security Council's being unable to make any decision because the Soviet Union exercised a veto.

Yet something was accomplished. Whereas at the beginning some people had mentioned the possibility of war, by the end of the period no one, on either side, regarded Berlin as a ground for war. Indeed, no one had ever wanted war, but Berlin was the sort of situation in which countries might blunder into war if the United Nations were not there to keep everyone on his best behaviour during the period when dangerous incidents might occur. The situation had to some extent been placed into perspective. Tempers had cooled, and Berlin was seen as part of a bigger problem. The forces working for agreement had asserted themselves and proved stronger than the recalcitrant elements.

Improvements in the Organization

No one would maintain that the present Charter is a perfect instrument. Like all political documents it is a product of compromise. It represents a text agreed upon by more than fifty nations at San Francisco. I have myself criticized some of its provisions, and at San Francisco fought hard to modify the principle of the veto. However, as loyal members of the Organization whose Charter we have all ratified, we must accept the Charter as it is. Efforts at reform must be made legally and within the Organization.

As I have often argued, there is a good case for giving the great powers a right of veto in important matters involving enforcement action, but the veto in its present form goes too far and has an unfortunate consequence upon the just and efficient working of the Organization. Nevertheless the veto in this form is the price we have to pay to have any Organization at all. If the veto had not been conceded at San Francisco, possibly neither the Soviet Union nor the United States would have become members of the Organization, and perhaps some of the other great powers would also have stayed out. In any case, whether other countries came in or not, the Organization without the Soviet Union and America would have been of little value so far as achieving its major objective of world peace was concerned.

At the Second and Third Sessions of the Assembly in 1947 and 1948 the representative of the Argentine attempted to circumvent the veto by having the General Assembly admit to membership of the United Nations countries whose admission had been vetoed by one of the permanent members of the Security Council. Despite arguments by the Argentine delegation to the contrary, such action would have been a clear violation of Article 4 of the Charter, which requires the Security Council first to recommend an applicant's admission. Therefore, although the Australian delegation considered that these countries should have been admitted because in its opinion they satisfied all the conditions of membership, the delegation nevertheless voted against the Argentine resolution, because Australia believes in strict adherence to the Charter even when such action conflicts with our desires in any particular situation.

The Charter of the United Nations, like nearly all constitutions, is a rigid document which is not easily amended. Any amendment, after approval by two-thirds of the members, requires subsequent ratification by two-thirds including the five permanent members of the Security Council. Thus the right of veto can be exercised to prevent amendment of the Charter.

But improvements can be made without a frontal attack on the Charter. The improvements and developments which have already taken place, often almost imperceptibly at the time, are considerable, and each year the Organization is better than it was the year before. The third session of the Assembly worked more smoothly than the second, just as the second worked more smoothly than the first. Secretariat members have gained experience, and lessons are learnt from the past, so that the life of the Organization is a continuous process of growth. I felt it a great responsibility but also a great opportunity of service that as president in this formative stage I was able to participate and give some guidance in the establishing of precedents which will help shape the future of the United Nations.

Members can co-operate in various ways also to make the Organization work more smoothly and effectively. For instance an understanding has grown up that an abstention from voting by a permanent member of the Security Council does not constitute a veto. That is just one example of the constant development and improvement that is going on within the United Nations itself.

Those who criticize the Charter in a destructive manner are performing no service to world peace. Those who are really interested in preserving peace give their full support to the Organization and attempt to improve it by constructive criticism, by supporting fair and peaceful policies on each question that comes before the Organization, and by trying to bring public opinion in each country to support those governments and leaders who are loyal to the United Nations and its principles and purposes.

The United Nations does not exist in a vacuum, nor is it a separate entity from the governments which comprise it. It can only be successful if the governments of the world give it their full backing. It was not the League of Nations which failed the world; it was the member governments which failed the League.

So, too, the United Nations depends upon the support of an informed and interested public opinion. The people of the world ultimately hold the fate of the Organization in their hands. Its future is assured if they support it and insist on their leaders doing so, too. The strength of the United Nations lies in the loyalty and steadfastness of the people of the world and their leaders.

III

UN POLICY AND THE PRINCIPLES WHICH GUIDE IT

AT the San Francisco Conference I represented Australia where since 1941—the year of Pearl Harbor—I have had the responsibility of being Australian Foreign Minister. The policies which Australian delegations have followed in United Nations gatherings during that period indicate the principles of policy and behaviour which I believe countries should follow if they are to be loyal to the Charter and make the United Nations work effectively.

ADHERENCE TO CHARTER

First and most important is strict adherence to the purposes and principles of the United Nations Charter at all times. The Charter is an internationally accepted code of conduct and statement of ideals for all nations. As long as all nations remain loyal to the Charter, there is a common purpose and a common measuring-rod. Consequently a basis of agreement already exists for every problem if it is judged according to that code and standard.

One of the most important articles of the Charter, Article 103, provides that, in the event of a conflict between the obligations of the members under the Charter and their obligations under any other international agreement, their obligations under the Charter prevail.

It is quite in accord with the Charter that its members should form and belong to other international bodies and associations. Regional organizations come within this category and are expressly contemplated by Chapter VIII of the Charter. Australia, for example, took the initiative in forming the South Pacific Commission to promote the interests of native inhabitants in the dependent areas of the South Pacific. Other examples can be cited, such as Benelux and the Organization of American States.

But, as I have pointed out, the Charter provides that all such obligations which individual members accept must be subordinate to, and in accordance with, those accepted in the United Nations Charter. Every member is pledged to the view that the United Nations is the supreme international body. It alone can give a common impetus and purpose to the efforts for peace made throughout the whole world. It alone can harmonize the activities of the various countries and international bodies. Worldwide security can be found only in a worldwide organization. That organization is the United Nations, and its purposes and principles are contained in the Charter.

Justice, Not Power

The great principle of the Charter is justice. The maintenance of international peace and security is the first aim of the United Nations, but the San Francisco Conference added to the Dumbarton Oaks draft the proviso that this peace and security should be maintained "in conformity with the principles of justice and international law." This is a most important improvement, and reflects the pressure of the smaller nations. Peace can always be secured if the small country gives way to the big one or if the peace-loving country gives way to the aggressor. But the smaller nations at San Francisco were concerned that in the new world organization disputes should be settled in accordance with the principles of justice and not according to the dictates of power.

That is the choice: justice or power. In the United Nations all nations are equal in the votes they exercise in the General Assembly and in other organs, though in the Security Council the five great powers have the right to exercise an individual veto.

The Assembly is, above all, the most democratic organ because not only has everyone an equal vote but all nations are represented in it. There is no nation so small that it is unable to exercise some influence on decisions, and no nation so great that it is completely unresponsive or indifferent to the views expressed by others.

It would be untrue to say that all nations are equal in fact just as they are equal in voting power. Such a conclusion is obviously absurd. In local politics in each of our countries, the principle of one-man-one-vote does not mean that all men are equal in the power and influence they exercise within the community. So, too, the different size and wealth of countries means that they exert a different influence in the family of nations. But size and wealth are not the only criteria. One of the remarkable lessons of the Assembly is that, if a small nation is represented by men of ability, vigour, and integrity and if its policies are just and directed towards peace, it can exercise an influence far out of proportion to its size and can give a leadership which even the greatest powers recognize and follow. If one were asked to name the leading delegations of the last General Assembly, one would not include all the great powers, but the representatives of some nations with small populations would be included.

Some may object that justice is only a word and that we do not carry the argument any further merely by saying that disputes should be settled according to justice. What is justice? That is a question which it is impossible to answer when it is put so abstractly. But in particular instances it is usually possible to see when justice is done and when injustice is done. The man in the street instinctively knows when an injustice has been perpetrated, and no legal haggling or obscuring of the situation with technicalities and details can erase that impression from his mind. Delegates to the United Nations react in the same way. In the Assembly the delegations whose views prevail are not those who move elaborately along lines of precedent or technicality, but those who go straight to the root of the matter and deal in realities and principles—in short, those who openly and frankly call and work for a just solution.

The Assembly must not only be responsive to public opinion, but it must act in such a way that the public understands what it is doing. Sometimes it may be necessary and unavoidable that for technical reasons, members must cast votes which, taken out of context, look unjustified. For example, a representative sometimes has to vote against a resolution with which he is in substantial agreement, because he intends at a later stage in the voting to support another resolution which he thinks is still better. But representatives have to be on their guard so that they will not be placed in a position where for reasons of expediency or bargaining or in an endeavour to out-manoeuvre another power, they vote against good measures and recommendations which are in accordance with the Charter without making clear the constructive course they support and intend to follow and also making it clear that they are in fact taking active measures to carry out such a just and constructive policy.

No Satellitism

It follows from this that each question must be judged on its merits. The question to ask is: "Is this right or is it wrong?" not: "Who is supporting this?"

Countries that attempt blindly to follow a leader frequently find themselves in difficulties. The great powers are not always consistent in their own policies. They chop and change in response to political conditions and pressures internally or what they regard as their immediate interests. Nations which attempt to follow them are frequently humiliated by having to change simultaneously. This was the case with some countries on the Palestine issue. The United States supported partition at the 1947 Assembly, but wobbled in succeeding months before it returned again to its original position. Those countries which attempted to follow the day-by-day alterations were frequently embarrassed.

If countries adhered to a policy determined by themselves according to the principles of the Charter they would not be placed in this position. No country can afford to cast stones at another for inconsistencies in policy. Changes occur, often very properly, for a number of reasons. Every country finds itself confronted from time to time with a new situation. Again, changes made in the light of debate, to facilitate agreement, to accord with the will of the majority, or to take account of new facts disclosed in the debate, can be entirely creditable. But even these changes, based on one's own judgment of the principles and interests involved, can sometimes be embarrassing enough.

Changes in policy made in response to turns by another power are a different matter, and adversely affect not only the influence of the country concerned but also the successful working of the Organization. Adherence to one's independent judgment and to the principles and purposes of the Charter is the only sound course —and the only safe course.

This does not mean deserting one's friends or abandoning one's ideals. Quite the contrary. Countries with a similar faith in democracy and countries with similar backgrounds and interests, tend to follow the same courses without having to resort to slavish methods of regimentation or imitation.

That is the case with the British Commonwealth. Its members, independent sovereign states, are completely free to pursue their own foreign policies. Nevertheless, in great matters they tend to act together, as their immediate and wholehearted participation in the Second World War from its very beginning indicated. In other matters they tend to follow similar courses. Their differences are usually concerned with means rather than ends. That is because all members have a similar faith and desire for peace and democracy, a similar wish to promote economic and social progress everywhere, and a respect for the rights and equal status of one another.

Related to this question is the tendency for countries sometimes to vote in blocs. No one could ever accuse the British Commonwealth of voting as a bloc, for its members differ frequently enough for such a charge never to have even the appearance of truth. There are other groupings inside the United Nations, such as the Soviet group of six, the Latin American group of twenty, the Arab group of six, and the Scandinavian group of four. These groups sometimes split into sub-groups, and sometimes are increased in size by kindred states. The extent to which these vote as a bloc differs markedly and varies according to the subject being discussed. It is natural that on some items certain countries should vote together and concert their policies, and a frank exchange of views among themselves is often beneficial.

The tendency towards bloc voting seemed to be greater at the second Assembly in 1947 than it was at the third Assembly at Paris. Rigid bloc voting is an impediment to the working of the Assembly, and where the bloc is big or can exercise a commanding position it is comparable to the veto. Important decisions of the Assembly require a two-thirds majority. Since the Latin American group contains twenty members out of the total membership of fifty-eight, these States can if they wish exercise a veto on any matter. Moreover in other questions they could form the solid core for a majority to be built on.

Usually the Latin American states have exercised their power with restraint, for their leaders are good supporters of the United Nations and are aware that their own standing depends on the sense of responsibility they show at these conferences.

METHOD OF INVESTIGATION

In order to render a just decision it is necessary to have the facts on which that decision can be based. Australia was a member of the Security Council for its first two years and worked in that body to establish the principle that on each problem brought before it the facts should be established before a decision was made, preferably by an impartial investigation.

The first occasion on which this principle was applied was in April 1946 in connexion with Spain where at the instance of the Australian representative a committee of five members of the Security Council was established to examine the facts and report back to the Council. The next occasion was in December 1946 on the Balkan situation, where a commission of inquiry was appointed to proceed to the Balkans and examine the situation on the spot.

This principle has now become standard practice in the Security Council, and is equally valid in the Assembly. When the question of the future of Palestine was first debated in the Special Session in 1947, the member which asked for the convening of the session, the United Kingdom, itself asked that a Commission should be sent to Palestine to ascertain the facts to serve as a basis for subsequent Assembly action.

Acceptance of United Nations Decisions

Another important principle is that each member should faithfully observe the recommendations and decisions of United Nations bodies. The effective and just working of the Organization depends on the acceptance of the wishes of the majority.

It is true that the Assembly can only make recommendations, which therefore are not legally binding upon the members. But a recommendation on an important matter requires a majority of two-thirds and the votes contributing to such a majority are not lightly given. The recommendation therefore should not be lightly ignored or defied.

This is the course which Australia has always followed. For example, in 1947 the General Assembly decided in the face of strong opposition from Australia and several other countries that the Third Session should be held in Paris and not at the permanent headquarters in New York. Some members wished to pursue their opposition to this, in direct ways and indirect ways, such as trying to prevent the necessary funds being voted. But I set my face against any such practice. The majority had expressed its will and we should accept that majority.

Another example occurred in the Interim Committee of the General Assembly which decided in March 1948 that the United Nations Temporary Commission on Korea should observe elections conducted in the southern zone only. The Commission, having been denied access to North Korea by the Soviet military authorities, was unable to observe elections for the whole of Korea, as specified in the original Assembly resolution defining its functions. Australia felt that the decision of the Interim Committee did not accord with the intent of the General Assembly when it adopted its resolution on Korea. Nevertheless Australia accepted the majority decision, and its representative participated fully in the work of the Korean Commission along the lines that the majority decided.

Many other examples could be adduced of occasions when Australia has accepted a majority decision. In fact, this is the only basis on which the United Nations can work. If every country felt itself at liberty to ignore or defy decisions of which it disapproved, the whole Organization would rapidly break up. Most countries recognize this and act accordingly. It is the democratic principle.

Some examples of refusal to accept majority decisions were provided by the Soviet Union and its associated states at the General Assembly in 1947, which might almost be called "the year of the great boycott." These six members refused to serve on the Balkans Committee, the Korean Commission, and the Interim Committee of the General Assembly. They maintained that these three bodies had been illegally constituted and that they represented an intrusion of the Assembly into the sphere of the Security Council. Their arguments were contested by other members, in my opinion, validly, and big majorities of the Assembly decided to establish each of the bodies.

In these circumstances the course for all loyal members of the Organization was to accept the Assembly decision and to serve on the bodies for which they were chosen. The failure of the Soviet Union to do so led me to draw again on my large imaginary stock of old Mongolian proverbs and to quote one in the plenary session of the Assembly: "You have got to be able to take it, as well as dish it out." It is not enough to attack other members and criticize their positions; one has to be prepared to accept the decisions reached by the majority as a result of the debate.

The Paris Session of the Assembly in 1948 represented a great improvement in this respect. Though the Soviet Union continued to boycott the three commissions whose validity it had challenged the year before, it did not extend its boycott to any other bodies.

Solutions not Resolutions

It should be the aim of each member of the United Nations to work for a solution of each problem brought before it. It is not enough simply to secure the passage of a resolution by the required majority. The counting of hands solves very little if the answer is not accepted and carried into effect by the countries concerned.

That is part of the principle behind the veto. It is futile and even dangerous to attempt to force upon one of the great powers a decision about which it feels so strongly that it is prepared to resist it by force if necessary. If the veto were merely a threat in reserve which a great power could use to safeguard its vital interests if forced into an extreme position, it would be less objectionable than at present. It would in these circumstances be a reserve instrument for inducing other countries to aim at a reasonable solution which would secure maximum agreement.

The securing of such agreement should be sought automatically and naturally at all conferences whether a veto exists or not. There is consequently a fallacy in insisting on a veto at a peace conference. A peace conference naturally attempts to secure a treaty to which all interested powers will adhere. Every country, great or small, has an ultimate power of veto at a peace conference because it can always refuse to ratify the final document. The fact that a great power did not have a formal right of veto at such a conference would not mean that its views would be irresponsibly overridden by a majority of the participants.

The need for finding agreement is also the reason why the so-called "mechanical majority" does not in fact exist and would be unsuccessful and self-defeating if it did exist. Those who try to push resolutions through by sheer force of numbers are inexperienced in international conferences, and misjudge both the usefulness of the resolution and the temper of their fellow representatives. If a country attempts to push through an extreme resolution in this way it usually happens that the vast majority, including those who are usually sympathetic to the sponsor, vote against the resolution or modify it so that it becomes more acceptable as a basis of agreement.

Similarly the United Nations should not take up matters and give decisions which it cannot take effective steps to carry out. Decisions which are impossible to implement or endorse tend to bring discredit upon the Organization and endanger its prestige. Resolutions which are vague and wordy and serve no useful purpose also help to discredit the body which passes them. It is of no service to clutter up a book with resolutions which are virtually meaningless or unnecessary.

In each matter brought before the Assembly the objective should be not simply a resolution but a workable and just solution to the problem.

IV

THE GREAT, MIDDLE, AND SMALLER POWERS

THE Charter of the United Nations was prepared and agreed upon by the nations at a conference at San Francisco in 1945. I represented Australia at that conference, and one of the principles for which I fought was to increase the effective role of the middle and smaller powers in the new Organization. In this Australia had the support of many other countries who felt as we did.

This fight was not waged in any spirit of captious criticism of the efforts of the great powers or in any desire to underrate their past contribution to victory. America, Britain and Russia had provided the bulk of the armed forces and supplies which had won the war. It was right and necessary that upon them should fall the leadership to establish and sustain the United Nations. It was they who would, in the event of future aggression, probably have to bear the brunt of any enforcement measures necessary to punish and repel the aggressor.

Contribution of Smaller Powers

At the same time, the contribution to victory made by the middle and smaller powers should not be underrated either. The record of the Dominions of the British Commonwealth is evidence of this. In the Pacific the effort of Australia was second only to that of the United States. Australia fought in all theatres of war, provided an essential base for the operations against Japan, won in New Guinea the first land victory against the Japanese, and extended her resources and manpower to the utmost. New Zealand, too, put an extraordinarily high proportion of her young men into the forces, where they served with great gallantry in the Middle East and Italian campaigns. Canadian troops formed a significant component in Field Marshal Montgomery's forces in the invasion of Europe. South African troops participated in all the African campaigns, playing a great part in the liberation of Abyssinia. Indian troops played an outstanding part on both the European and the Pacific fronts.

The smaller nations of Europe also made an essential contribution, hamstrung though they were by years of cruel occupation in the course of which millions of their citizens lost their lives. The sufferings of the people of Poland are beyond description, as first one army and then another swept across that unhappy country. Their capital city was blown to pieces, and masses of their people were deported or exterminated in concentration camps. The names of other countries also come immediately to mind as victims of Nazi occupation and brutality.

But it is not on their war record alone that the small powers lay claim to a significant voice in the conduct of international relations. Their contribution to the arts of peace has often exceeded in quality and influence the accomplishments of great powers.

Part of the difficulties which have arisen in the post-war world can be traced to the fact that international conferences and negotiations are too often dominated by the two titans, the United States of America and the Soviet Union. An international society where—instead of two giants standing alone—there were many members with real independence, would be far more healthy. For the past few years there has unfortunately been too great a tendency for international issues to be set out crudely in what is claimed to be black and white without adequate attempts being made to find an area of agreement between the two rival views. The middle and smaller powers have a special role to play in pointing out and working for a middle ground which satisfies not only the divergent views but, most important, is also based on just principles.

One of the most hopeful developments inside the Assembly of the United Nations, and particularly at the Paris Assembly, has been the increasing tendency of the smaller powers to assert themselves. Their influence has been throughout towards bringing the parties together and towards mediation. This has been the almost instinctive reaction of most leaders of these countries, and accurately reflects their public opinion. The people of Europe know —and this, I believe, applies to the people of Eastern Europe as well as those of the west—that in the event of trouble's breaking out between America and Russia, they will be in the middle, and that it behooves them to see that every effort is made to bring the great powers together so that everyone can live in peace.

It is in the light of this that we must view the rise of new nations, such as India, and the grouping together in their mutual interest of other nations, such as Benelux and some of the wider associations in Western Europe. Anything that reduces the predominance in the world of two or three powers is a good thing for peace, and hence too for the real interests of the great powers themselves. Thus one contribution of the Marshall Plan to world peace will be, not, as is sometimes alleged, that it will tie the countries of Europe more closely to the United States, but that it will make them more capable of standing on their own legs and exercising an independent voice.

Some of us at San Francisco saw that the apparent eclipse of the small powers was only temporary and that they still had a significant role to play in world affairs. Fortunately, several provisions were inserted into the Charter of the United Nations to give the middle and smaller powers the opportunity to exercise the role which was their right.

The Veto

The most striking provision of the Charter conferring special privileges on the great powers is Article 27. It provides that, except in procedural matters, all decisions of the Security Council require the concurring votes of the five permanent members, namely China, France, the Soviet Union, the United Kingdom, and the United States of America. The Security Council, which is one of the principal organs of the United Nations, has the primary responsibility for the maintenance of international peace and security. No decision can be made on any matter of substance unless each of the great powers concurs—and it has been the practice that even matters of procedure cannot be declared to be such except with the concurrence of all five.

Some countries have opposed completely the whole principle of the veto. Australia does not go as far as that. We agree that it is reasonable to allow the great powers to exercise an individual veto where enforcement measures are involved. But we regard it as utterly wrong and stultifying that this right should also be exercised to prevent peaceful settlement of disputes and to prevent decisions on matters that are of a minor nature.

I am not going to rehash the whole dispute at San Francisco or deal at any length with the struggle I waged on behalf of Australia associated with many middle and smaller powers. The fight against the veto which we conducted was not a fight against the Soviet Union. Primarily, the case for allowing a veto upon matters of conciliation as well as matters of enforcement was waged on behalf of the great powers by the United States and the United Kingdom delegates. The Russian delegates, for the most part, looked on and always voted the right way.

The great protagonists for the veto included Senator Tom Connally of Texas and Sir Alexander Cadogan and Professor Webster of the United Kingdom Delegation. From time to time, these

The Great, Middle, and Smaller Powers 47

advocates were assisted, and perhaps embarrassed, by reinforcements from their own delegations. Still, the main burden was borne by them; and they of course were not necessarily expressing their own opinion but carrying out the prior agreement made between Churchill, Roosevelt, and Stalin at Yalta.

After reading all the material and discussing the matter with most of the participants at Yalta, I am convinced that the significance of the veto on peaceful settlement or conciliation was never fully appreciated in the hurry and bustle of the Yalta Conference. However, the question was thrashed out to some extent by representatives of the great powers at a preliminary conference between them held at Dumbarton Oaks although I feel certain that there, too, if the case which was later put by us at San Francisco had been fully presented, we would have succeeded in obtaining important modifications of the Security Council rule of voting now contained in Article 27 of the Charter of the United Nations.

Our argument concerning the veto can be stated briefly. The great powers will probably have to provide the bulk of the forces and bear the brunt of any enforcement measures that might be decided upon by the Security Council. There is, therefore, a good case for requiring the consent of all of them to the employment of such measures. A still stronger argument is that if the United Nations ever has to use force against one of the great powers themselves, the Organization will probably have already been split to its very foundations and a major war, if it has not already occurred, would be the consequence of the use of such measures. The principle of the unanimity of the great powers on great matters involving enforcement measures is one of the rocks on which the United Nations has had to be built.

The peaceful settlement of disputes is quite a different matter. As it is now, any one of the permanent members of the Security Council can use its right to an individual veto so that it prevents the Council taking measures to mediate, to bring the parties together, or to call upon the parties to cease fighting. A permanent member can veto a resolution on the ground that it does not go far enough, and thereby it can produce the even more dangerous situation that nothing at all is done. Dangerous drift may be the consequence, during which time the Security Council is powerless to act, and ultimately the time for enforcement measures may indeed arise because the situation was not nipped in the bud while there was yet opportunity.

This is no fanciful speculation of what could happen. It is a true picture of what has often occurred over the past three years. In June 1946, for example, the Soviet Union vetoed a resolution on Spain, not because it went too far or was too drastic, but solely because it was not drastic enough. This veto had the somewhat paradoxical consequence that the Security Council was unable to take any action at all.

The use of the veto has not in practice been restricted to enforcement measures; it has not even been restricted to important matters connected with the pacific settlements of disputes. It has been used whenever it is the exerciser's wish to do so, and unfortunately the Charter makes such conduct permissible. The battle of the veto was won only in part at San Francisco by those who saw the perils and injustices which would flow from its unrestricted use.

Limitations on Effect of Veto

But nevertheless the San Francisco Conference did secure some abatement of the extreme position set out in the Dumbarton Oaks text.

It was agreed that the right to exercise a veto in the Security Council could not be used to prevent discussion—it was confined to the adoption of decisions. The powers of the General Assembly were also increased so that no limit exists to the Assembly's right of discussion of any matter. Even matters before the Security

The Great, Middle, and Smaller Powers 49

Council can be discussed, though no recommendation can be made on them except at the request of the Council itself.

It should also be remembered—and this is sometimes overlooked in popular discussion—that the veto does not exist outside the Security Council and its organs. There is no veto in the General Assembly, the Economic and Social Council, or the Trusteeship Council, or in other bodies such as the regional economic commissions and the specialized agencies.

The Conference at San Francisco took an important step to offset some of the ill-effects of the veto when it gave the General Assembly special functions in the field of international peace and security. Article 10 of the Charter gives the Assembly the general power to discuss and make recommendations on any matter within the scope of the Charter or relating to the powers and functions of any organ. International peace and security are specifically referred to in the following article, which allows the Assembly to discuss not merely general principles but any questions relating to the maintenance of peace and security, and to make recommendations to the states concerned and the Security Council. The Assembly may call the attention of the Security Council to situations which are likely to endanger international peace and security.

Article 14 of the Charter makes the position still clearer. It says that "the General Assembly may recommend measures for the peaceful settlement of any situation, regardless of origin, which it deems likely to impair the general welfare or friendly relations among nations, including situations resulting from the violation of the provisions of the present Charter setting forth the Purposes and Principles of the United Nations." The only qualification to these powers is that the General Assembly cannot make a recommendation with regard to a dispute or situation in respect of which the Security Council is exercising its functions, unless the Security Council so requests.

Thus in the field of international peace and security, the General Assembly has a concurrent jurisdiction with the Security Council.

The Security Council has primary responsibility in this field and should normally be the body which acts and to which disputes are referred. However, there will be some questions which the General Assembly will decide to consider. Normally it will be where the Security Council has been unable to act because of the exercise by one of the permanent members of its right to an individual veto. There may be other cases where it seems desirable to have a question discussed by all fifty-nine members of the Organization.

In such matters the powers of the General Assembly, compared with those of the Security Council, are limited in two ways.

First, though its right of discussion is unlimited, the Assembly cannot make a recommendation on a question if the Security Council is exercising its functions in respect to it.

Secondly, the Assembly does not have the Security Council's powers to impose enforcement measures. The Assembly can merely discuss and make recommendations to its members or to other organs of the United Nations. As Article 11 (2) of the Charter says, any question relating to the maintenance of international peace and security which is brought before the General Assembly, has to be referred to the Security Council, either before or after discussion, if action is necessary—that is to say, enforcement or mandatory action, as distinct from recommendations.

Against those limitations, the General Assembly has two great sources of strength.

The biggest is the great moral weight which attaches to a recommendation arising out of the deliberations of fifty-nine sovereign states. No nation can with impunity ignore a decision reached by such a body. The weight of world opinion is far greater than the legal power of the Assembly to enforce its recommendations.

Moreover, the Assembly is able to reach a decision without being frustrated by exercise of individual vetoes. The vote of each nation is equal and the only limitation is that in important matters a majority of two-thirds is required.

Some signs of improvement can be discerned. Probably in the light of experience more restraint will be shown in the exercise of the veto. In relation to the fighting in Palestine and the fighting in Indonesia, the Soviet Union, although at times quite dissatisfied with certain points of the successful resolutions, did not destroy them by recording a vote in the negative.

At the same time, a new rule of practice has sprung up in the Security Council by which the abstention of a permanent member from voting is not regarded as negativing the resolution before the Council. As to this, I need only say that, although this new practice may be difficult to reconcile with the technical wording of Article 27, the practice is a most beneficent one and offers a way of escape for a permanent member to record an attitude of dislike or scepticism in a particular case without destroying the positive proposal which is in fact acceptable to seven out of the eleven members of the Security Council.

The Smaller Powers at the Third Assembly

The position may be summed up as follows. As a result of the strenuous efforts of Australia and other countries at the San Francisco Conference, the original draft for the world organization which had been prepared by the great powers at Dumbarton Oaks was considerably amended to give a more effective role to the middle and smaller powers. The essence of these changes was to increase the power and influence of the General Assembly, thereby affording an opportunity for all members to participate to the utmost in the work of the Organization.

The Paris Session of the General Assembly showed the smaller powers exercising a greater influence than ever before. As each of the political items on the agenda came up for discussion, strenuous efforts were made by the middle and smaller powers, and sometimes by the bigger powers themselves, particularly France, to overcome or to ease the deadlocks.

In their efforts the smaller powers tried to prevent a breakdown or cessation of talks on any subject on the ground that present failure to agree was permanent and irremediable. They tried to conciliate between opposing views in an attempt to find an area for a just agreement. The result was that time and again discussions were kept going, concessions were secured, and agreement was brought closer.

Representatives of the Soviet Union have invented the phrase "mechanical majority" to describe a process whereby, it is said, the United States and United Kingdom can drum up a majority sufficient to carry any resolution they want in the General Assembly, Security Council, or other organs. The veto is claimed to be the counterpart to this.

It would be idle to deny that sometimes majorities are secured by pressure rather than argument. I have always deplored bloc voting and satellitism whatever the source may be. Australia has always exercised an independent position.

But analysis of voting in the General Assembly at Paris shows that real independence was exercised by the smaller countries, and that frequently the United States was defeated or obliged to make concessions on an item. The fact that in the final resolutions the majority did take up a position in which the United States concurred was due to the real identity of views on the policy involved and to the fact that some measure of agreement had been hammered out during the debates.

Members were yearning for signs of concessions and approaches from the Soviet Union. When such signs were given they were eagerly seized. The whole trend of activity on the part of the vast majority of members was to avoid having to back either Russia or the United States, but rather to bring the two together, provided that the terms of agreement were just.

Hence the extraordinary position arose that, whereas at San

Francisco it was hoped that the great powers would give a lead to the others, now on the contrary it was the smaller and middle powers who were attempting to bring the great powers together and settle their differences.

V

GREECE

THE problem of Greece has been before the United Nations continuously since December 1946, when the Greek Government asked the Security Council to consider a situation leading to friction between Greece and her northern neighbours, Albania, Bulgaria and Yugoslavia. The three latter states were accused of supporting guerrillas rebelling against the Greek Government.

As a consequence the Security Council established a Commission of Investigation consisting of representatives of all eleven members of the Council to ascertain the facts relating to the alleged border violations and to report as soon as possible to the Council on these facts, together with any recommendations it might wish to make for averting a repetition of the violations and disturbances.

The Commission visited Greece and also Bulgaria and Yugoslavia, and it had field teams in all four Balkan States. It submitted a majority report, with only the U.S.S.R. and Polish representatives dissenting from the finding that Yugoslavia and, to a lesser extent, Albania and Bulgaria had supported the guerrilla warfare in Greece. The Commission recommended to the Security Council a series of proposals designed to establish good neighbourly relations, prepare new frontier conventions, and regulate questions of refugees and minorities. It also recommended that the Security Council establish a new body to investigate any future frontier violations and to use its good offices to settle controversies and otherwise to assist in solving difficulties arising between the four Governments.

This report was presented to the Security Council in June 1947, but the Council was unable to take appropriate action because the

Soviet Union exercised its veto to prevent the adoption of resolutions substantially endorsing the findings of the Commission. No resolutions based on other principles were acceptable to the majority of the Council. It therefore became impossible, or at any rate most unlikely, that any effective Security Council action could be expected at that stage.

The Greek question was therefore taken up by the second session of the General Assembly in September 1947, after it had been removed from the agenda of the Security Council.

The mounting crisis between Greece and its northern neighbours as rebel action in Greece became more intense, was (unlike the rebellion itself) an international dispute causing friction and likely at all times to cause open breaches of the peace between the four nations concerned.

Behind the dispute lay one of the deepest tragedies in connexion with the second world war and the attempted liquidation of that war.

No country fought harder against Mussolini and against Hitler than did Greece. No people sacrificed more. Yet, when the day of liberation arrived for Greece, the people were almost immediately torn by internal dissension. The struggle for power was violent and has never yet completely ceased.

I speak very feelingly of Greece because of the special relationship between the peoples of Greece and of Australia. In the crucial months of 1941, Australian and New Zealand troops were in the forefront of the terrific struggle waged by the Greek people in resisting the armoured might of Hitler as he swept down towards the Aegean. The peerless valour associated with historic centres like Marathon and Thermopylae was repeated as the soldiers from the Southern Pacific once more co-operated to help defend the peoples of Europe against a newer and even greater tyranny than that of the Persians during that earlier great war.

A great deal has been written and said about the military enterprise involved in the despatch from Africa of these warriors from Australia and New Zealand, who had already proved their fighting qualities in North Africa and had materially helped to destroy the Italian armies.

It has been argued that the enterprise was successful because, as a result of it, the German attack on Russia, which commenced on 21st June, 1941, was delayed to some extent. On the other hand, it has been argued from a military point of view that the nature and size of the forces with inadequate air and land support made effective resistance to the German forces practically impossible.

Judgment on this need not be pronounced here. As it was, the forces of Greece, of Australia, of New Zealand, and of the United Kingdom, were beaten back and heavy losses were encountered. Withdrawals were carried out which led to further fierce fighting against great odds in Crete.

Despite the military setback in the expedition to Greece, the people and the soldiers of Greece fully appreciated the remarkable character of the resistance which had been put up in conjunction with their own Greek forces. A warmth of feeling between the peoples was engendered which, in my opinion, will always remain.

Assembly Action in 1947

For these reasons, Australia took a very firm attitude at Lake Success in 1947 when the Assembly was asked to establish its own special commission on the Balkans because the Security Council's commission had ceased to function as a consequence of exercise of the veto in the Council by the Soviet Union.

Two diametrically opposed proposals were submitted to the political committee.

On the one hand the United States submitted a draft resolution finding that Albania, Bulgaria, and Yugoslavia had supported Greek rebels in contravention of the principles of the Charter and calling upon them to desist from giving this support. The draft resolution recommended that the four Balkan Governments establish normal diplomatic and good neighbourly relations, formulate frontier conventions, settle refugee problems, and study the practicability of an exchange of minorities. It also proposed the establishment of a Special Committee of eleven members appointed by the General Assembly to observe the compliance of the four governments with these Assembly recommendations and to be available to assist them in carrying them out.

The Soviet Union on the other hand introduced a proposal declaring that the Greek authorities were guilty of provoking incidents on the frontiers. It said that the internal situation in Greece was the main cause of the dispute and that this situation was the result of foreign interference. The Soviet Union wished to establish a Special Commission to guarantee that foreign economic aid to Greece was used solely in the interests of the Greek people.

Thus the Greek question was turned into a battle ground for a clash between the Soviet Union and the Western Powers.

This debate on Greece and the Balkans at Lake Success in September and October 1947 was one of the fiercest at which I have ever been present. Mr. Vyshinski fought brilliantly and almost desperately against the attempt by the General Assembly to exercise its jurisdiction.

He argued against the legality of the proposed Commission of Investigation to be established. On this legal argument I am convinced that he was completely wrong. John Foster Dulles and I put the case upon the plain wording of the Charter and there was no real answer given to our argument.

On the wisdom of General Assembly action, Mr. Vyshinski's case was somewhat stronger. He pointed, with telling effect, to several instances of statements made to the Security Council Commission which brought forth evidence which, to say the least of it, was most unreliable. Nonetheless, there was a substantial body of evidence that practical aid in some respects was being furnished to the Greek guerrillas from the territories of Yugoslavia, Albania, and Bulgaria.

Mr. Vyshinski's interposition had this effect, that the Commission as established was required not merely or even primarily to investigate cases where aid to the Greek guerrillas seemed to have been furnished from across the northern borders. At the instigation of France, which in all these difficult disputes has taken a positive stand in favour of reconciling parties for the future rather than condemning some of them for what has taken place in the past, the resolution of the Assembly also made very clear that the Commission should direct portion of its efforts towards conciliation rather than a complete concentration upon the investigation of frontier disputes.

The Assembly eventually adopted by a big majority a resolution based on the American proposal. It eliminated those references which attributed blame to the northern neighbours, and substituted for them a factual statement based on the report of the Security Council's Committee of Investigation.

The 1947 debates of the General Assembly on Greece remained very bitter to the end. The Soviet group would not recognize the legality of the Assembly's decision. The U.S.S.R and Poland, who were chosen as members of the new Balkans Committee, refused to send representatives, continuing to argue that its establishment was contrary to the Charter which laid the responsibility of preserving international peace and security on the Security Council.

Report of Balkans Commission

The United Nations Special Committee on the Balkans (commonly known as UNSCOB) reported to the General Assembly in 1948 that, while the Greek Government had co-operated with it, the Governments of Albania, Bulgaria, and Yugoslavia had refused all co-operation. Greek guerrillas in the frontier zones had been largely dependent on external supply, had frequently moved at will in territory across the frontier for tactical reasons, and had frequently retired safely into the territory of Albania, Bulgaria, and Yugoslavia. The Special Committee also recommended its own continuance.

Australia was a member of the Commission and the attitude of its representatives had sometimes been misunderstood. Australia believed that the functions of the Assembly Committee were essentially different from those of the earlier Security Council Commission. The specific task of the Security Council Commission was to investigate the situation in order to obtain facts on which the Security Council could act. The facts obtained by that Commission were before the Assembly in 1947 when it made its own decision to establish a committee.

The function of the Assembly Committee was more positive. It is true that it was required to observe the compliance of the four Balkan Governments with the recommendations of the Assembly, but it also had a role of mediation and of good offices in settling differences between the Balkan countries. Australian representatives, both in the Commission itself and in the later Assembly debates, attached particular weight to this role. It may fairly be said that the Australian delegation thought that UNSCOB had not given adequate attention to the vital function of conciliation, which might have removed the main cause of the border disputes which arose from time to time.

Australia also insisted on rigorous standards of evidence being applied to all reports that came before the Special Committee. The Australian representatives therefore dissented or abstained from categorical conclusions based on the presumption of observers. This critical approach came largely to be accepted by the Special Committee.

In the debates in the political committee of the Assembly the most active member of the Soviet group, Mr. Bebler, the Deputy Foreign Minister of Yugoslavia, roundly criticized the nature of the evidence that was put before UNSCOB and ridiculed it very effectively—at least his attack sounded very effective until it was pointed out by other representatives that the evidence which

Mr. Bebler was quoting was evidence which had been rejected by UNSCOB itself because of its flimsy nature.

Some of the countries which had thought that Australia was being unnecessarily scrupulous in the early stages of UNSCOB's work came to me during the Assembly debates and expressed their thankfulness that such an attitude had prevailed in UNSCOB. We knew that UNSCOB's conclusions would be carefully examined and criticized in the Assembly. Therefore, if these conclusions were to stand searching criticisms, a critical approach was necessary. As a result of this approach prevailing, the final factual conclusions unanimously approved by UNSCOB accurately reflected conditions along the northern frontiers of Greece and were not successfully challenged in the political committee of the Assembly.

Assembly Action in Paris

In the political committee in Paris the arguments of the previous year, to some extent, were repeated when the UNSCOB report came up for consideration. The leader of the Slav group was the Yugoslav representative, Mr. Ales Bebler. The rest of the Soviet group took a less prominent part than the year before and were not so heated in their language. Mr. Bebler did not, however, abate his vigour and in the opinion of many people he over-played his hand in the committee debates. He is a very able man who speaks several European languages fluently and has great energy and resourcefulness. He read three prepared statements, each of which occupied three hours or more, and made several impromptu interventions of lesser length.

The arguments of the Soviet group fell into three categories. First, they denied the charges that the northern Balkan neighbours had assisted the Greek guerrillas. Secondly, they strongly attacked the Greek Government as the source of the trouble in the

Balkans, and did not conceal their opinion that its reactionary policy was responsible for the disturbances in the Balkans and that no improvement could be expected until it was replaced by a more democratic regime. Thirdly, they alleged that the troubled situation in Greece was the result of foreign intervention, particularly United States military and economic infiltration which had made the country an American satellite.

The delegates of the United States, United Kingdom, France, and China introduced jointly a resolution which was the basis of most of the discussion in the Committee. This resolution, after reciting the conclusions of UNSCOB concerning the aid and assistance which the Greek guerrillas on the frontiers had received from the northern neighbours, considered that this aid endangered peace in the Balkans and was inconsistent with the United Nations Charter. It called upon Albania, Bulgaria, and Yugoslavia to cease this aid and assistance and to co-operate with Greece and UNSCOB. It also continued UNSCOB in being.

The Australian representative set out the position of the Australian Government as it had been developed in UNSCOB. Rather apprehensive at the prospect that UNSCOB might continue as little more than a chronicler of the Greek tragedy, he urged that UNSCOB concentrate on a positive effort to find some solution to the Greek problem. The Greek people had suffered grievously for many years, and had the right to be left alone by their neighbours so that they could reconstruct their country and live peaceful lives. Australia rejected the Slav arguments and the resolutions based on them, and supported in principle the four-power resolution. However, Australia proposed four amendments designed chiefly to place more emphasis on UNSCOB's mediation role and also to clarify the text.

Many other amendments were introduced during the debate by El Salvador, Lebanon, the Dominican Republic, South Africa, and Greece. Some of these were intended to toughen the resolution and in the end were either defeated in the committee or withdrawn. The Australian amendments were all carried, with the support of the four powers which introduced the resolution. The resolution as amended was then adopted by a big majority.

Though a majority of members were in agreement with the resolution put forward by the four powers there was a general feeling that its adoption would not in itself solve the situation and that it needed to be supplemented by other measures of a more positive nature. The Australian delegation felt that it was more important to seek for a permanent and just solution of the problem than to fix blame or mete out punishment for what had occurred in the past. Logically we supported the continuance of UNSCOB for another year, with emphasis on its functions of conciliation and arbitration, but in our judgment this was not enough.

Accordingly Australia introduced another resolution which asked myself as the President of the Assembly and the Secretary-General to convene immediately in Paris a meeting of representatives of the Governments of Albania, Bulgaria, Greece, and Yugoslavia. The president and rapporteur of the political committee itself (Mr. Spaak of Belgium and Mr. Sarper of Turkey) were added to the talks. This resolution was extraordinarily well received by all the great powers and by the Balkan states themselves. It was particularly warmly greeted by some of the middle and smaller powers, who were alarmed by the acrimony which had been engendered by the main debate and at the deadlock into which the Greek problem appeared to have fallen. There were some representatives who doubted the possibility of reaching agreement but none who doubted the desirability of trying to do so.

The Australian proposal was adopted unanimously. This was the first occasion in the United Nations handling of the Greek question that a resolution had secured unanimous acceptance. This precedent was followed almost immediately in the discussion of Greek children.

Greek Children

The question of Greek children was a matter which had aroused great feeling. Many children had been removed, mostly from guerrilla-controlled regions in the north of Greece but also from other places during guerrilla raids, and they were now in various states in Central and Eastern Europe. The representatives of the Balkan countries admitted the presence of Greek children within their borders, but stated that they were there with the consent of their parents and in order to protect them from what was pleasantly termed the "monarcho-fascist" government of Greece. Mr. Bebler hired a public hall to show a film of these children, who were pictured as being happy and well-fed and attending schools.

The Greek delegation had originally proposed an amendment to the main four-power resolution calling for the return of the children. The Chairman of the Committee, Mr. Spaak, wisely suggested that this question be considered separately from the four-power resolution and accordingly postponed its discussion. After the main resolution had been disposed of the Belgian and Australian delegations took the lead in drafting a resolution which was more concrete than the rather vague proposal of the Greek delegation and which might result in the early return of some of the children.

As a result a resolution was formulated which secured unanimous acceptance both by the political committee and by the General Assembly. The Assembly recommended the return to Greece of Greek children at present away from their homes when the children, their father or mother, or in his or her absence, their closest relative, expressed a wish to that effect. It further instructed the Secretary-General to request the International Committee of the Red Cross and the League of Red Cross and Red Crescent Societies to organize and ensure liaison with the national Red Cross organizations of the States concerned with a view to empowering the national Red Cross organizations to adopt measures in the respective countries to implement that recommendation.

The effective carrying out of this resolution will depend largely on the sincerity of the countries to which the children have been taken and on the extent to which the facts of each case can be impartially ascertained, in particular as to whether the real wish of the parents and relatives can be made known. However, the adoption of this resolution without dissent was welcome. It provided a clear statement of principle to which all countries adhered, and it also provided a practical way of taking up the case of each individual child who was known to have been removed. I am happy to say that, as a result of this resolution, some children have already been returned.

Domestic Jurisdiction

The Greek question is part of the whole Balkan situation, with a long historical background of wars and rivalries. The tension between Greece and Albania, for example, is intensified by a dispute as to the ownership of northern Epirus, and in particular about territory which has belonged to Albania since 1912. Minorities of long standing in each of the four countries help to bedevil relations between them.

The internal Greek situation is also a key factor in the problem. The guerrilla fighting is a challenge to the composition and functions of the present Greek Government. Some observers maintain that the rebels would collapse if they ceased to receive aid from other countries. Others deny this, and point to the strong guerrilla activity far south of the border where there could be no close contact with other Balkan countries; these observers maintain that the only solution is sweeping reform of the Greek Government and the admission of more liberal and left-wing elements. The poverty of the people and maldistribution of goods is another factor making for discontent and rebellion.

In justice to the present Greek Government, however, it should be recognized that the need to combat a large-scale rebellion automatically requires stringent regulations to maintain law and order and censorship. In any emergency the hands of the more extreme elements in a Government tend to be strengthened, and the democratic elements set back. The repressive measures in Greece are more the result than the cause of the present disturbances, but a vicious circle has been established. As conditions, political and economic, get worse disaffection grows. Efforts to promote economic recovery and development of the country are being continually disrupted by warfare and by guerrilla raids which destroy villages and bridges and capital equipment and often destroy stocks of food, clothing, and other goods which the guerrillas cannot carry away. In these circumstances the Greek people have never had an opportunity to rebuild their country and develop their democratic forms of government.

This internal situation of Greece, which lies at the root of the problem, is at present outside the sphere of the United Nations. It is essentially within the domestic jurisdiction of the Greek Government and is therefore a matter in which the United Nations is specifically forbidden by Article 2[7] to intervene.

But the United Nations can act to check the actions of other states which might endanger the peace by their own intervention in the internal situation of Greece. It is quite within the terms of the Charter for the United Nations to try to prevent the three northern neighbours from assisting the guerrilla forces. The Soviet Government has in its turn attempted to secure a United Nations recommendation that the American and British Governments should cease their present forms of assistance to the Greek Government economically and militarily.

It is true that both the northern states and the Anglo-American powers have been giving some measure of assistance to Greek nationals. But there is this important distinction. American and British assistance is given to the legal government of the country, which has been recognized by all members of the United Nations, is still recognized as such by them all, and has a seat in the very committee of the General Assembly where these discussions were proceeding. The original purpose of the American economic assistance—though this may have been somewhat subordinated later to military aid because of the fighting—was the economic reconstruction of a country which had suffered so heavily from Italian and German warfare and occupation. The assistance granted by the Americans and British was at the request of the legal government of Greece and therefore does not constitute interference in the internal affairs of that country of a nature of which the United Nations should take cognizance. Aid to the guerrillas on the other hand is given to rebels who have received recognition as belligerents from no country.

Therefore, while it was proper for the Assembly to condemn assistance to the guerrillas, the Assembly was right in refusing to condemn American assistance to the Greek Government. There is nothing in the Charter which forbids one country to assist another—in fact mutual aid is the whole spirit of the United Nations, provided it is given in such a way as not to conflict with the purposes and principles of the Charter.

Appeal to Save Trade Unionists

During the debate in the political committee it was reported that a number of Greek trade-union officials had been sentenced to death and that they would be executed on the 8th November. Many trade-union leaders in other parts of the world made representations to their governments to make efforts to have the executions stayed.

Two days before the executions were, according to this report, due to take place, the matter was raised in the political committee by the Czech representative who asked that the committee intervene to save their lives. There was some discussion on this matter, many representatives expressing horror that the executions should take place. There was great doubt, however, as to what action the committee could take. The committee did not have all the facts before it and they could not be furnished at such short notice. In any case it seemed that the execution of these men was a matter falling within the domestic jurisdiction of Greece and therefore not one in which the United Nations could officially intervene. A resolution declaring it to be outside the competence of the committee was in fact carried by the committee, with only the Slav group dissenting.

But the overwhelming majority of members of the committee obviously felt that the executions should be deferred so that the whole matter could be reconsidered by the Greek Government. Feeling in the committee ran fairly high, and it was only because of the wise and moderate behaviour of the Greek representative (Mr. Pipinelis) that this episode passed off successfully. Mr. Pipinelis expressed his willingness to consult with the chairman of the political committee concerning the executions and a resolution was immediately passed by the committee confirming this procedure.

As soon as possible after I was informed of this, I sent personal communications to the King of Greece and to the Prime Minister of Greece. After drawing their attention to what had happened I said:

"I earnestly hope that as a result of these conversations some means may be found of arriving at a satisfactory result. In the meantime, I would beg you most earnestly to suspend the sentences which have been imposed on the ten men.

"In my personal judgment the execution of the sentences at this juncture would seriously interfere with the attempts of conciliation which may result in lasting benefits to Greece and the people of Greece."

It will be seen from the wording that I acted unofficially because I was not going to interfere unconstitutionally in a matter of domestic Greek jurisdiction. I therefore put my appeal on a personal basis. But I felt that if the executions had taken place it might have damaged irrevocably such prospects as existed of securing agreement in the Assembly on the Greek issue. The executions did not occur and the Greek Government informed me that it was reviewing the sentences. In this way the Greek Government made a real contribution to a peaceful settlement in the Balkans.

Greek Mediation Talks

The work of the Conciliation Committee was commenced immediately and was adjourned only after the end of the Assembly on 14th December. Greece was represented by Mr. Panayotis Pipinelis, Bulgaria by Mr. Theodor Vladigherov, Yugoslavia by Mr. Ales Bebler, and Albania by Mr. Theodor Heba. The feeling between the Greek representatives on the one hand and those of the three northern neighbours on the other was so difficult that, after a preliminary meeting under my chairmanship, we thought better progress would be made by interviewing the representatives separately in order to get some basis for progress.

Accordingly, I suggested a programme merely as a basis of discussion. The programme consisted of eight points:

Diplomatic Exchange:

1. Immediate agreement between Greece on the one hand and Albania, Bulgaria, and Yugoslavia on the other for the full exchange of diplomatic representatives at the highest level.

Frontier Regulations:

2. Immediate agreement in principle to draw up new frontier conventions or revise existing ones.
3. The four Governments to patrol their frontiers to ensure that no aid or assistance was received from across the border by dissident elements in an adjoining State.
4. Conventions to be implemented by frontier commissions, which would be assisted by a group of U.N. guards or U.N. observers.

Territorial Claims:

5. Agreement by all four Governments to accept present frontiers as definitive, and in the case of Bulgaria and Greece to carry out the relevant terms of the Treaty of Peace.

Greek Children:

6. Special machinery to accelerate the return of the Greek children who have been removed from their homes across the border.

Refugees and Minorities:

7. Agreement in principle to regulate questions of refugees and minorities once normal diplomatic relations had been established.

Body of Mediation:

8. A small body of mediation or of good offices consisting of, say, three outstanding persons of international prestige selected for their individual qualifications, who would assist in the carrying out of the foregoing points.

In the above list, point No. 5 suggested the possibility of an agreement by all four governments "to accept present frontiers as definitive." On the other hand, point 4 proposed a frontier commission which would be assisted by a group of U.N. guards or U.N. observers.

One relevant or possible application of point 5 was that Greece might accept the existing de facto boundary of Albania as definitive. To this Greece objected, largely upon the ground that the matter should be taken up through diplomatic channels and not dealt with by the Committee of Conciliation. Then, with regard to point 4, objection was taken by the three northern neighbours of Greece, particularly Yugoslavia, which raised strong objection to the supervisory functions which might be exercisable by U.N. guards or U.N. observers. This smacked too much, in Yugoslavia's opinion, of UNSCOB, the findings of which they regarded as completely wrong and unjust.

I will not deal any further with the programme, except to make the point that, when towards the adjournment of the Committee

Greece

in December, Albania insisted that Greece must treat the existing de facto boundary between the two countries as definitive and the Greek Government maintained its refusal, the representative of Albania tried to use the mere programme, which was, in effect, a provisional agenda, as evidence that a definite offer had been made to accept the present frontiers as finally fixed. Of course this was not so.

The difficulty of conciliation was increased by public statements on the matter released through the press and attributed to the Governments of Yugoslavia and Bulgaria. Equally embarrassing were several statements which purported to come officially from the Information Department of the Greek Government.

The conciliators met with the representatives of the four countries at a very large number of consultations and conferences aggregating nearly sixty meetings averaging an hour each. This work had to be sandwiched in between other heavy work of the conciliators and it was very strenuous indeed.

We held on to our objective and we very nearly reached agreement between the four governments on questions of exchange of diplomatic representatives, frontier conventions, patrol of frontiers, handling of frontier incidents and breach of international law in the frontier zones, the establishment of mixed frontier commissions, and allied matters.

The one point on which the committee could not get final agreement was the formal request of Albania that Greece should agree to treat the existing boundaries between that country and Albania as definitive. It was almost heart-breaking when finality was nearly reached to have the whole agreement held up on such a point. Strictly speaking, the boundary question should have been deferred, because existing boundaries between the two countries have long been recognized de facto and neither Greece nor Albania has the slightest intention of attempting to alter them by force.

I am saying nothing whatever as to who is to blame for the final hold-up. I assume that both parties acted in perfect good faith.

The point seemed to me of such tiny importance that Albania did not need to press it but, equally, Greece hardly needed to resist it. However, the representatives no doubt had trouble with public opinion at home.

Finally, on behalf of the committee I publicly expressed thanks to all four countries concerned for their co-operation, and postponed the resumption of committee work until the resumption of the General Assembly in April at Lake Success, New York.

At New York I proposed an amended draft agreement between Albania and Greece which reproduced all the clauses of the agreement which the representatives of the two countries had been willing to sign at Paris, but added phrases which made it plain that there would be a substantial acceptance by both Albania and Greece of the existing boundaries. In my opinion this should, in the circumstances, have been sufficient assurance to Albania as well as to Greece. The Greek Government accepted the formula in substance. The Albanian Government did not reply though adequate time was allowed; however its representative insisted that his government had not rejected the amended draft. I was of the opinion that the replies of Bulgaria and Yugoslavia would be favourable provided that Albania accepted the new draft.

When the General Assembly completed its session, the Conciliation Commission was unable to function in its existing capacity. But the good offices of the United Nations remain available to the four Balkan Governments. Having regard to the progress which the Conciliation Commission made, and the very close approximation to final agreement reached, an early attempt to complete its work might well be successful. Both at Paris and New York, the spirit displayed by the representatives was good, but, of course, they had no plenipotentiary authority. The situation was complicated by Mr. Gromyko's attempt to find a formula to end the Greek civil war. I believe that all aspects of the question could be solved by an impartial arbitrator and that the long nightmare of Greece could be ended on just and honorable terms. The United Nations jurisdiction is not unlimited but it is very wide. The United Nations attempt to conciliate should never be abandoned.

VI

BERLIN—IMPASSE AMONG GREAT POWERS

WHEN the Assembly met on 20th September, the four powers occupying Germany had been discussing for some months the blockade of Berlin by the Soviet Union. The question was in fact brought before the Security Council not long afterwards.

The Berlin dispute was serious not only in itself but even more so as a symptom of the disagreements between the great powers. It hung like a pall over our deliberations in the early days of our meetings in Paris. Fortunately United Nations intervention was not without good effect in this field also.

Background of the Problem

The Council of Foreign Ministers met at the end of 1947 to try and reach agreement on the future of Germany. But no agreement was reached. The three Western Powers—the United States, the United Kingdom and France—then began discussions of their own in March of 1948 on the subject of Western Germany, and invited representatives from Belgium, the Netherlands, and Luxemburg to attend.

Russia maintained that the holding of these discussions involved a breach by the three Western Powers of the Yalta and Potsdam Agreements contemplating four-power government of Germany during the occupation period. Accordingly, on 20th March, the representative of Russia on the Allied Control Council withdrew from a meeting of the Council. This withdrawal from the Allied Control Council was followed by the intense application of restrictions on communication between Berlin and the western occupation zones of Germany.

On 6th June, 1948, the six-power discussions finished and recommendations were made, including a recommendation for the establishment of a government of Western Germany. These recommendations were submitted to the six participating governments, were accepted by all of them and were immediately denounced by the Soviet radio and press, which described them as an "illegal departure" from the principles and spirit of Yalta and Potsdam.

The area of disagreement was soon extended to include that of currency reform. In the absence of agreement upon a uniform method of introducing a new currency throughout Germany, the Western Powers introduced a separate currency in their zones of occupation on 20th June. The Russian authorities immediately cut rail, road, and canal communications between the western zones and Berlin. The grounds given for such action were to prevent smuggling of currency into the Russian Zone and also "technical difficulties" with the railway system.

Russia followed this action with the issue of a new currency for their own zone in Germany and for Berlin. The Western Powers indicated they would have had no objection to the new Soviet currency for Berlin if the Russian authorities had made its issue in Berlin subject to four-power control. This the Russians refused to accept, whereupon the Western Powers declared the new Soviet currency illegal in the Western sectors of Berlin and issued a new conversion of the Western currency for those three sectors.

At the end of June, an exchange of letters took place between General Robertson, United Kingdom Commander-in-Chief in Germany, and Marshal Sokolovsky, the Russian Commander-in-Chief. The former demanded the immediate lifting of the blockade for humanitarian reasons. Marshal Sokolovsky in reply emphasized that the only reasons for the blockade were, as stated above, the prevention of currency smuggling and "technical difficulties" with the railways.

On 3rd July the Soviet Governor agreed to a meeting of all four Governors. Marshal Sokolovsky, in defending Russian policy, linked the maintenance of the Berlin blockade with the results of the earlier discussions between the three Western Powers.

This meeting in Berlin having failed to resolve the deadlock, the three Western Powers sent separate notes to the Russian Government emphasizing in clear, convincing terms their juridical rights in Berlin and their implied right of access to Berlin for the purpose of armistice arrangements. The Western Powers demanded the lifting of the blockade and offered, if the blockade were lifted, to discuss further questions affecting Berlin.

In reply, the Russians emphasized an infringement by the three Western Powers of four-power decisions in relation to Germany and Berlin, such infringement being proved, it was alleged, by first, separate monetary reform, second, the separate currency of the Western sectors of Berlin and, third, the policy of dismembering Germany. The note also pointed out that the Western Powers had not offered to negotiate on the subject of Germany as a whole.

The British and United States Governments were determined to exhaust the full possibilities of negotiation. Conversations were begun at Moscow. It was then made clear by the Western Powers that the Soviet proposal for four-power talks on Germany as a whole would be acceptable if satisfactory agreement could be made on Berlin. Agreement was reached for the lifting of the blockade; the application of Soviet Zone currency to the whole of Berlin providing this was under four-power control and safeguarded the holders of Western marks; and the holding of four-power meetings on Germany as a whole at a later date.

The four Military Governors of Berlin were supposed to formulate a directive indicating the procedure to be followed in order to carry out this Moscow Agreement. However at Berlin it became clear that Marshal Sokolovsky did not accept the Moscow decisions as being more than a general direction, and he would not accept the implications of four-power control of Berlin currency.

Once again talks were resumed in Moscow, but Marshal Sokolovsky's attitude was confirmed.

In this impasse, the United States, the United Kingdom, and France sent a note to the Russian Government restating their position on the points at issue and formally requesting the Soviet Government to lift the blockade and provide a basis for the renewal of discussions. On 27th September the three powers indicated, after receiving the Soviet reply, that they intended to place the Berlin dispute before the Security Council of the United Nations. These notes complained of Russian "illegal and coercive measures" to secure political advantages by attempting "to reduce the status of the three occupying Powers in Berlin to one of complete subordination to Soviet rule."

On 3rd October, the Soviet Government replied, attributing the blame to the action of the Western Powers in repudiating the concept of four-power control of Germany as a whole. The note suggested that the matter might go to the Council of Foreign Ministers which could examine not only the situation in Berlin but the question of Germany as a whole in accordance with the Potsdam Agreement.

Security Council Action

However, the matter was referred to the Security Council, it being alleged that a threat to the peace within the meaning of Chapter VII Article 39 of the Charter had been committed by Russia. Despite resistance, the matter was admitted to the agenda of the Security Council, Mr. Vyshinsky of the U.S.S.R. and Mr. Manuilsky of the Ukraine objecting.

The next stage of this grave affair was a resolution submitted to the Security Council by Argentina, Belgium, Canada, China, Colombia, and Syria acting jointly. It will be observed that these

Berlin—Impasse Among Great Powers   77

six powers excluded the four great powers directly involved in the dispute and also the Ukraine. The powers sponsoring the resolution came to be called "neutral" powers for the reasons I have given. Certainly they were not parties to the dispute.

The amazing position had arisen that the Charter of the United Nations was now being used for the purpose of settling great power differences despite the oft-reiterated declaration at San Francisco that the veto principle was entirely justified on the ground that great power unanimity was the basic conception of the United Nations. In a sense, this position was reversed. Great power dispute had reached a critical stage and all the great powers involved—four of them—had been close allies in the war against Hitler.

But the veto did not cease to be operative merely because the initiative was being taken by the six powers mentioned. In other words, it was known from the very beginning of reference of the matter to the Security Council that no resolution on the subject of Berlin could be declared carried in the event of active Russian opposition. This was so whether the action proposed was taken by way of Chapter VII (which speaks of threats to the peace) or Chapter VI (pacific settlement of disputes).

Here let me interpose a word or two of explanation. A great deal of discussion often occurs in the Security Council as to whether a question concerns a situation which is likely to endanger peace or whether it concerns a threat to the peace. This distinction is not merely one of words. Chapter VI of the Charter covers the pacific settlement of disputes and of situations which might lead to international friction or give rise to a dispute. The powers of the Security Council in such situations are to seek solutions by negotiations, enquiry, mediation, and other peaceful means. Chapter VII of the Charter covers action with respect to threats to the peace, breaches of the peace, and acts of aggression. In these cases the Security Council is not limited to peaceful solutions but can order enforcement measures, including economic sanctions and military action. It is therefore a decision of real substance whether a situation is a threat to the peace or is one likely to endanger the maintenance of international peace and security.

If the Berlin matter were treated as arising under Chapter VII, Russia, although party to the dispute, was entitled to vote as laid down in Article 27 of the Charter. Being entitled to vote, Russia could also by voting in the negative, prevent a resolution being adopted, as laid down also in Article 27. On the other hand, if the matter had been treated as arising under Chapter VI, then none of the four powers directly concerned could have voted, as once more laid down in Article 27. That would have left seven only of the members of the Security Council eligible to vote, with the Ukraine certain to support the position of Russia. Therefore, as seven votes were required for any affirmative vote, action under Chapter VI was also impossible. Thus it was clear from the beginning that no resolution could be adopted in the face of Russian opposition.

As it was, the matter was treated as arising under Chapter VII, with a view to preventing an aggravation of the situation in Berlin which was described as "grave" by the resolution proposed by the six "neutral" powers. The four occupying powers were, by the resolution, to be called upon to put into effect simultaneously, first, the immediate removal of all restrictions on communications, transport, and commerce imposed after 1st March 1948, and, secondly the convening of an immediate meeting of the four Military Governors to arrange for the unification of currency in Berlin on the basis of the German mark of the Soviet Zone. This was to be arranged by the four Military Governors in accordance with the Moscow directive of 30th August and to be carried out under the control of the four-power financial commission described in that directive.

The proposed resolution in substance was the lifting of the embargo or blockade by Russia at once, that is on the date of the notification of the resolution of the Security Council, and the complete fulfilment of the unification of currency in Berlin by 20th November.

The resolution also proposed that, within ten days after 20th November, the four powers should reopen negotiations in the Council of Foreign Ministers on all outstanding problems concerning Germany as a whole.

The resolution was opposed by the Soviet Union on the ground that it did not provide for the actual introduction of the new unified currency in Berlin simultaneously with the lifting by Russia of the restrictions on communications. On 29th October, the voting in favour of the resolution was nine against two, namely the Soviet Union and the Ukraine. Accordingly, the resolution was rejected.

The Mexican Resolution

In order to make very clear the attitude taken by the Secretary-General and myself on 13th November in relation to the Berlin deadlock, I now turn to the situation brought into existence in the General Assembly.

The delegate of Mexico, Dr. Padilla Nervo, had suggested, at an early stage of the opening debate in the General Assembly, that a resolution should be drafted calling upon the great powers to renew their efforts in the making of peace and to associate with them middle and smaller powers who had also made contributions to the winning of the war against Hitlerism and Fascism. Dr. Padilla Nervo is one of the most distinguished representatives from Latin America with a long record of service to the United Nations and its ideals and with experience on several of the principal organs of the Organization. Throughout 1948 he was chairman of the Interim Committee of the General Assembly and filled that office with great dignity and efficiency. His action in proposing this resolution to the Assembly was prompted by his sincere desire to make the United Nations work successfully by bringing about greater co-operation of the great powers and by establishing the peace settlements whose absence is so important a factor in the present difficulties.

I immediately drew the attention of the General Assembly at the public sitting to the importance of the suggestion made. The Berlin situation was most threatening and the complete stalemate between the four powers was a continuing and serious obstruction to the work of the Assembly.

I also called a special meeting of the General or Steering Committee, of which I was Chairman, where I again emphasized the importance of the Mexican resolution of Dr. Padilla Nervo. At my suggestion, the General Committee immediately added the item to the agenda of the Assembly.

The next stage in the matter was the introduction by Dr. Padilla Nervo of his resolution to the Political Committee. There was widespread relief and approval at the proposed resolution, and all the great powers spoke in favour of its adoption.

The recommendation of the Political Committee came before the Plenary Assembly on 3rd November and was adopted by the overwhelming vote of fifty votes in favour with none against.

The terms of the resolution were very striking. It made the point that the United Nations cannot fully attain its aims so long as the peace treaties after the Second World War have not been concluded. The resolution added that, after three years, peace had not been made on the initiative of the great Allied powers and that this disagreement between the powers "is at the present time the cause of the deepest anxiety among all the peoples of the world." The General Assembly in the resolution recalled the Declaration of Yalta of 11th February, 1945, by Churchill, Roosevelt, and Stalin proclaiming that "only with continuing and growing co-operation and understanding among our three countries and among all the peace-loving nations can the highest aspiration of humanity be realised—a secure and lasting peace."

The General Assembly endorsed these declarations and expressed its conviction that the great powers would conform to the spirit of the declarations. It recommended them to redouble their efforts "in a spirit of solidarity and mutual understanding to secure in the briefest possible time the final settlement of the war and the conclusion of all the peace settlements." Finally, the Assembly recommended the great powers to associate with them "in the performance of such a noble task" the States which, by becoming parties to the Washington Declaration of 1st January, 1942, had joined the ranks of the United Nations in the war against Hitlerism and against Fascism.

There is no doubt that the failure of the great powers to reach agreement on Berlin through the instrumentality of the Security Council—evidenced by the Soviet negative vote of 29th October—had created considerable anxiety amongst all the middle and smaller nations at the Assembly. The situation of tenseness which had existed at the opening of the Paris Assembly on 20th September had been aggravated by the failure to agree when it was certain that only by four-power agreement, as I have explained above, could any resolution be adopted.

EVATT-LIE APPEAL ON BERLIN

What therefore was to be done with the solemn and compelling resolution of the Assembly of 3rd November, 1948? That resolution called upon the great Allied Powers to forget past failures and renew their attempts to settle differences with a view to the making of a just peace in order to fulfil the highest aspirations of humanity. Mr Lie and I felt that the time had come for further intervention. The Chairman of the Security Council (Dr. Bramuglia) and his five colleagues responsible for the Security Council resolution had worked untiringly, but by 12th November it was obvious that no active steps by way of Security Council action were being taken to revive the Berlin question with a view to its speedy settlement.

Mr. Lie as Secretary-General of the United Nations is vested with great powers and discretion under the Charter. He had already set in motion a study of the implications of the financial and currency problems in Berlin on which the Security Council had broken down because the Russians refused to lift the embargo except simultaneously with the unification of the currency in Berlin.

A study of the terms of the Security Council resolution makes it absolutely clear that the lifting of the blockade by Russia was not a proposal separate from the proposal to unify the currency in Berlin on the basis of the Soviet unit of currency. On the contrary, the two matters were integrally connected in the resolution supported by nine members of the Security Council including the three great Western Powers. Putting it in another way, it was quite illusory and indeed untrue to suggest that if Russia had accepted the resolution of the Security Council, the Russian embargo would have been lifted unconditionally. Such a statement is quite the reverse of the truth. The embargo would have been lifted, not unconditionally but conditionally upon the carrying out within several weeks of all the arrangements for the unification of currency in Berlin on the basis of the German mark of the Soviet Zone. Within that short time, the currency measure had to be completely fulfilled. Nor was this all. Within ten days thereafter, the whole problem of Germany had to be reopened in the Council of Foreign Ministers unless another date was mutually agreed upon between the four Governments.

Stating it positively, the three great powers disputing with Russia had indicated unequivocally by their adherence to the proposal of the Security Council that, providing the blockade was immediately lifted, they would complete and carry into effect arrangements desired by Russia with regard to Berlin currency and would also accede to Russia's request to discuss Germany as a whole in the Council of Foreign Ministers.

Therefore, it is completely inaccurate to say that the three Western Powers were insisting on the lifting of the embargo as a condition precedent to considering Russian demands upon other topics. On the contrary, they insisted upon the lifting of the embargo and in return unequivocally indicated their acceptance of two Russian demands, each of which was to be carried out within a comparatively short time after the lifting by the Russians of their embargo. I stress this point because, later on, a number of persons suggested that the appeal of the Secretary-General and myself of 13th November invited the three Western Powers to take an attitude different and less firm than the attitude which they adopted in the Security Council by supporting the resolution of the six "neutral" powers.

The Secretary-General and I consulted with Dr. Bramuglia and on 13th November we decided to make a communication to the four powers who were signatories to the Moscow Agreement. On the very night that the appeal was issued and later on, upon his relinquishing his duties as Chairman of the Security Council for the month of November, Dr. Bramuglia paid a tribute to Mr. Lie and myself, generously referring to our efforts as a striking and noble contribution to the cause of a lasting peace.

I mention this because an attempt was made in certain quarters to suggest some degree of hostility or lack of sympathy between Mr. Lie and myself on the one hand and Dr. Bramuglia on the other. Such a suggestion was absolutely false. All three of us were in the closest touch at all relevant times.

Our action also had the full support of Dr. Padilla Nervo who regarded it as a practical step to carry out his resolution and as the sort of action he had had in mind in preparing it.

Accordingly, the appeal was issued. It was based, and that was the direct motive for my action, upon the remarkable resolution of the General Assembly of 3rd November, 1948, properly described as an "appeal to the great powers to renew their efforts to compose their differences and establish a lasting peace." The letter of Mr. Lie and myself was short. It represented considerable care and thought before its issue. We pointed out that, as all the great powers voted for the Assembly resolution, "they have accepted the recommendation and the world rightly expects them to take active steps towards carrying it out without delay." We indicated our belief that the first step was the Berlin question, that it was still pending before the Security Council, that it could be solved, and that the precedent of the Security Council's efforts at mediation should be fully and actively supported. The letter also urged upon the four governments to undertake immediate conversations and all other necessary steps to solve the Berlin question, thus opening the way to a prompt resumption of negotiations for the conclusion of the remaining peace settlements for Germany, Austria, and Japan.

I have not quoted every word of the letter, but the substance and purport of it have been given. It was completely justified in the circumstances and, before the Assembly finally adjourned, Dr. Bramuglia had again taken the initiative with a view to a technical study of the currency question. Some persons actually suggested that we should make a demand that the Russians first of all lift the embargo. This, in our view, was a matter for negotiations either direct between the four powers concerned or through the agency of the Security Council itself, which, as I pointed out, was prepared to associate with the lifting of the embargo by the Russians the concession of two important points for which they had asked, namely, the unification of the currency of Berlin on the basis of the Russian currency and the resumption of talks on the question of Germany as a whole before the Council of Foreign Ministers.

In truth, we were acting solely with a view to keeping negotiations alive in accordance with the letter and spirit of the appeal to the great powers for peace decided upon by the General Assembly of which we were the servants and agents.

My own belief is that these efforts of mediation made through the Security Council by powers which were not directly participating in the dispute over Berlin and also by the fifty-four nations in the Assembly which were not directly parties to the dispute were of considerable value. They were expressions of the anxieties and hopes of the peoples of all the world that steps should be taken to heal the differences between the Allied powers of the Second World War. As a result, the tension existing at the beginning of the Assembly was substantially eased when the Assembly adjourned in mid-December.

In this improved atmosphere developments led to the lifting of the blockade. Marshal Stalin, in replying on 30th January to some questions asked him by Kingsbury Smith, the brilliant I.N.S. correspondent, made no mention of the currency question in his references to Berlin. Since this has been a key point in the dispute, Mr. Jessup of the United States took an opportunity on 15th February to comment on this omission to the Russian representative (Mr. Malik). This was the first of a series of talks between the two representatives to the United Nations. From their conversations emerged an agreement whereby the Soviet Union and the Western Powers lifted the restrictions which each had imposed on communications, transport, and trade in Germany as a result of the Berlin dispute. It was agreed that the Council of Foreign Ministers would meet eleven days after the lifting of the blockade to consider questions relating to Germany and the problems arising out of the situation in Berlin, including the question of currency in Berlin.

This represented agreement on one point only. The big question of the German settlement as a whole remained. But the lifting of the blockade of Berlin was a notable contribution to peace and international understanding, and in its achievement the United Nations had played a worthy part. It illustrated, too, the importance of obtaining specific areas of agreement, even when the zone of disagreement is much wider. The problem of the future of Germany raises questions of principle, closely akin to those of the future of Japan. It would be dangerous indeed to regard Germany and Japan as mere by-products of the disagreements between Russia and the West. No one knows this better than France and Britain, in the case of Germany—or Australia, India, Pakistan, New Zealand, and the Philippines, in the case of Japan.

VII

PROBLEMS OF THE PEACE SETTLEMENTS

I EMPHASIZE once more to the resolution proposed by Mr. Padilla Nervo of Mexico, calling upon the great powers to renew their efforts to compose their differences and to establish a lasting peace.

The resolution contained a principle which it was useful to have reaffirmed by all nations, namely, that the making of the peace settlements should not be exclusively a function for the great powers and that the middle and smaller nations should be associated in an appropriate manner. The resolution itself did not specify the manner of their association but during the debates, principally arising out of discussion in committee initiated by the Australian representative, it was made clear that the consultation should give particular weight to the powers directly concerned, and especially to active belligerents.

During the war and afterwards, it used to be argued that the chances of agreement would be increased if the initial discussions of the peace treaties were limited to the great powers, since agreement would be easier to reach among a few than among many. The experience of the last three years conclusively disproves that thesis. On the contrary in the United Nations it has been shown that it is the presence of many interested nations which provides the greatest chance of settlement. Where there are only two contesting views, neither side is willing to budge. But a third party can point out alternative lines of approach and explore common ground. Where there are many participants, the inducement and pressure on conflicting parties to come together is correspondingly increased.

Moreover representatives of the smaller nations often have special qualities which fit them to be catalysts in these discussions. The representatives of great powers do not have a monopoly of the intelligence, imagination, and wisdom of the world. Indeed, the very fact that the great powers can often hope to rely on their power rather than on their arguments to get their way, tends to make them insensitive to the opinion of others and blind to opportunities of reaching agreement. Unless pressure is exerted by their friends and by neutrals, they may dig their toes in unnecessarily and refuse to budge. This is neither surprising nor altogether to their discredit. It is only by the presence on the spot of the representatives of other countries that world opinion can be made known and the interests of everyone demonstrated.

The reactions of other countries are not always easy to foretell, even by the most experienced, and the only sure way of ascertaining them is to give their representatives an opportunity to express their own views. I remember during the Paris Session a distinguished representative of one country showing me a resolution which he proposed to introduce and telling me that he "had everything sewn up" because he was certain most countries would support it. He went as far as to name those countries, including Australia. His proposal was certainly not acceptable to my delegation, and after it was tabled it was roundly criticized and torn apart by most other representatives, including many of those on whose support he had so confidently counted in advance. His proposal, therefore, had to be withdrawn for some very necessary repairs. Eventually agreement was reached on this subject. But agreement was promoted by the fact that the opinions of many were obtained, reflecting views based on a wide range of considerations. A rebuff from one country alone would rarely be enough to deter a determined man. It is the presence of all interested parties which promotes agreement.

Nevertheless in the making of the peace settlements some members of the United Nations have greater obligations and greater rights than others. The active belligerents in the war earned a special place for themselves because it was they who bore the brunt of the struggle for victory. It is they who in many cases have had to keep troops in occupation of enemy territory after the war has ended. In many cases, too, they have a closer interest in preventing future aggression by Germany or Japan because they have already been at least once, and sometimes more often, directly involved in war by such aggression and in the event of its recurrence they might again be called upon to provide forces to resist it or be exposed again to the dangers of occupation and devastation. It follows that when peace settlement problems do come into the Assembly, the active belligerents should have special weight given to their views by the other members of the Assembly.

Absence of Peace Settlements

The Mexican resolution called for the early conclusion of the peace settlements with Germany, Austria, and Japan. The settlements with Italy, Bulgaria, Roumania, Hungary, and Finland had been drawn up in 1946 and have now been ratified by nearly all the victorious powers.

There were some unsatisfactory features about those 1946 settlements, in particular the undemocratic methods by which they were concluded. The four great powers—United States, United Kingdom, France, and U.S.S.R.—drew up a draft as a basis of discussion for the peace conference, and agreed among themselves that no subsequent changes should be accepted without consent of all four. Therefore, when the Paris Peace Conference met, the smaller nations found that their effective voice was greatly limited and several clauses were inserted into the treaty which very few even among the great powers could be found to defend.

Nevertheless, it was clear then, and subsequent events have only served to confirm it, that it was right to draw up the peace treaties at that stage and right for them to come into force despite their faults. The faults are the price that has had to be paid for agreement. The result today is that the international relations and the internal policies of these ex-enemy countries are established on a firm basis of internationally accepted treaties, and the development of friendly relations throughout the world is thereby assisted. In contrast, in two of the most important areas of the world, Central Europe and Eastern Asia, no such basis of international agreement yet exists, since the settlements with Germany, Austria, and Japan have not yet been concluded.

When the Charter of the United Nations was drawn up at San Francisco it was assumed that the peace settlements with the major belligerents would have been concluded before now. The United Nations was set up to maintain peace, but in these key regions peace has not been established. Those areas are still in a twilight between war and peace. Unfortunately that uncertain atmosphere and its consequences tend to spread outside and to involve the United Nations as a whole.

The Charter was drawn up before the war with Japan was ended; the German armies surrendered during the conference. The Charter clearly contemplates that the task of making the peace should in the normal course of events not be done by the Organization itself.

The separation of the Organization from the peace treaties was largely at the instance of President Roosevelt, who had learnt a lesson from the set-backs suffered by President Woodrow Wilson in the United States after the first world war. The Covenant of the League of Nations had been made a part of the Versailles peace treaties and consequently when the United States Senate refused to ratify the treaties the United States also automatically decided not to become a member of the League. Conversely, the intense opposition of some senators to the League led them to vote against the peace treaties themselves, so that neither treaties nor American membership of the League were approved.

President Roosevelt felt that this time the great conception of a world organization for peace and welfare should not be tied up with peace treaties lest, once again, both might fail together. There is no doubt that President Roosevelt was right. The fact that all belligerents in the war against fascism, including all the great powers, became members of the new organization proved the wisdom of the President's strategy.

But at the same time Woodrow Wilson had also grasped a great truth when he tried to link the League and the peace treaties. The world organization exists to establish peace and international relations and it is hamstrung if in important areas something approaching anarchy in international relations exists and if large regions are virtually excluded from the influence of the organization. The absence of agreement on Germany lies at the root of some of the wider disagreements between the great powers.

As the past three years have gone by, the systems of Allied control over the enemy countries have come under increasing strain and in some cases the disagreements between the victorious powers have been so great that they have endangered peace. It has also become obvious that in certain important and urgent matters the great powers themselves are quite unable to reach agreement among themselves without outside assistance.

In these circumstances the matters have had to be brought before the United Nations. Though the United Nations is not the body which was intended to make peace it nevertheless has power to act if it feels it necessary to intervene. This right of intervention should, of course, be used very sparingly and only as a last resort.

The fact that it has been found necessary to refer some of these questions to the United Nations is at once a tribute to its vitality and capacity, and a confession of failure by the great powers themselves.

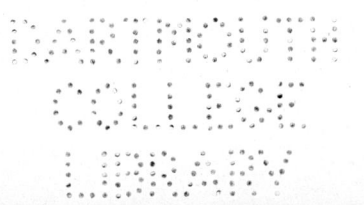

So far three matters arising from the last world war have come into the United Nations. The first was the question of Korea which was brought before the Assembly at the end of 1947 and was considered again at the Paris Assembly; the second was the future of the Italian colonies, brought before the Third Session of the General Assembly in 1948; and the third was the question of Berlin, brought before the Assembly in October 1948, which I have already discussed.

KOREA

Korea is a good example of the problems arising out of the war. The Cairo Declaration of 1943 by the United Kingdom, United States, and China declared that "in due course Korea shall become free and independent." Later that declaration was confirmed, first in the Potsdam Declaration which was accepted by Japan when she surrendered, and subsequently in December 1945 at the Moscow Conference of the Foreign Ministers of the U.S.S.R., United Kingdom, and the United States of America. The conference set up a Joint Commission of United States and Soviet Union representatives to assist in the establishment of a provisional Korean Government and declared that Korea should be placed under a four-power trusteeship for a period of up to five years.

These provisions were never put into effect. The United States and Soviet Union representatives did not reach agreement on even the initial stages of the Moscow agreement, and Korea remained under military occupation and sharply divided into two zones.

When Japan surrendered, as a matter of military convenience the United States forces accepted the surrender of the Japanese as far north as the 38th parallel and occupied that portion of Korea. Soviet forces accepted the surrender of the Japanese troops north of that parallel and occupied that portion of the country. This was never intended to be the basis of permanent political action, and yet this division of Korea has persisted for over three years. Contact and intercourse between north and

Problems of the Peace Settlements

south has become less and less, and today there are two regimes exercising control in the two zones.

The Koreans are one people in race, language, and culture. Economically Korea is one country, with the North dependent on the South for food and the South dependent on the North for industry, power and minerals. For over forty years of Japanese domination, the Korean people never lost their hope of independence and fought for it both at home and abroad. Several rebellions occurred against Japan and were ruthlessly put down. Now that the Japanese have been driven out it is a bitter blow to them that their country is divided and their national aspirations not yet achieved.

The question of Korea was first brought before the Assembly in 1947 by the United States of America. I represented Australia in the discussions on that question and appealed to the representatives of the United States and the Soviet Union to resume direct conversations during that session in a further endeavour to secure agreement. Neither country showed any enthusiasm for this suggestion, probably feeling that the experience of their talks in Korea itself did not give any hope of settlement. However, their reaction demonstrates this: that the Korean question which is still unsolved arises out of the failure of the two great powers to agree, and it is their continued failure which has made it impossible for the United Nations to take final action on this question.

The debate at the 1947 session was a fierce one. Mr. Vyshinsky challenged the right of the United Nations to intervene at all in questions arising out of the peace settlements, but he agreed to the matter being discussed by the Assembly. The Soviet Union charged the United States with terrorist activities in its zone of occupation and with putting into power a puppet regime dominated by undemocratic elements.

The United States representative, Mr. Dulles, on the other hand contended that there was no evidence that the Communist regime in Northern Korea was representative of the people. He proposed that a United Nations Commission should be sent to

Korea with power to visit all parts of the country and to observe the establishment of a national government elected on the basis of adult suffrage and by secret ballot from both zones of Korea, with the number of representatives from each voting area or zone proportionate to the population. The Commission was to be asked to arrange with the occupying powers after the establishment of the National Government for the complete withdrawal from Korea of their armed forces as early as practicable and if possible within ninety days.

A resolution substantially along the lines suggested by the United States was eventually adopted by the Assembly and a Commission proceeded to Korea. It was given every possible assistance by the United States authorities in the southern zone but the U.S.S.R. military authorities refused to admit members to the northern zone, or indeed to co-operate in any way with the Commission. The Commission therefore went ahead and supervised elections in the southern zone, as a result of which a Government was established having effective control and jurisdiction over that area.

Paris Assembly Action on Korea

The question of Korea came before the Paris Session of the Assembly. The position had not changed markedly over the past year except that there was now established a government in the Southern area whose election had been observed by a United Nations Commission which had reported that the election was a valid expression of the free will of the electorate. A great quantity of factual information had been assembled by the Commission on conditions and events in Southern Korea and all this was available for everyone to read.

In the north, on the other hand, there was no independently obtained and verified information of any sort. Some members of the political committee charged that conditions of terror and totalitarian dictatorship existed in the north, charges which were denied by the Soviet representatives but which could only be conclusively disproved by permitting independent observers to check them. This, however, the Soviet Union was not prepared to do.

Australia, as a Pacific power, and as a country which had made a decisive contribution to the war against Japan, was keenly interested in the future of Korea, and joined with the United States and China in introducing a draft resolution to the Assembly. This resolution took note of the establishment of the Southern Korean regime, which it declared to be a lawful government having effective control and jurisdiction over that part of Korea where the United Nations Commission was able to observe and consult and in which the great majority of the people of all Korea resided, and that this government was based on elections which were a valid expression of the free will of the electorate of that part of Korea and which were observed by the United Nations Commission.

The drafters of the resolution were careful not to go beyond the facts, and though some countries regard the South Korea regime as the legal government of the whole country, the resolution confined itself to the factual statement that its effective control existed in the south. The resolution established a new United Nations Commission, with emphasis upon the positive tasks of lending its good offices to bring about the unification of Korea and of seeking to facilitate the removal of barriers to economic, social, and other friendly intercourse caused by the division of Korea.

This joint resolution was eventually adopted by an overwhelming majority. Many of the arguments used at the previous session were again produced, the Soviet group once again bitterly attacking the southern regime as undemocratic and the creature of the American authorities. These charges were not sustained by the United Nations' own commission on the spot, which had itself actively intervened during the past year to improve conditions, for example by easing censorship and encouraging reforms in the Korean police system.

But, though it may be possible for the two regimes to continue side by side for the time being, partition is not a final or stable solution. Korean unity is only a matter of time, and we should bend all our efforts to see that when unity does come, the new state will be truly democratic and genuinely independent.

Those are the three great principles that should guide us—independence, democracy, and unity for the Korean people. Those are their right and they have shown themselves prepared to work and fight for them. The Korean people should be able to go about their ordinary business of life and move freely throughout their country without fear of aggression, arbitrary arrest or political dictatorship, and with steadily rising standards of living and welfare. Throughout the discussion of the Korean question, both before the matter came to the United Nations and ever since during the past year when it has been before the Organization, I have felt that the dominating consideration for us should always be the interests of the Korean people themselves.

Great changes are occurring in that region of the Far East today and the future of Korea cannot be regarded separately from the events in China and the role of the United States in the Far East. The Korean question is essentially part of the Japanese settlement, too. But whatever happens, the principles that should determine the future of the Korean people are clear and should not be denied for reasons of expediency. The Koreans should be allowed to determine their own future, and the task of the United Nations is to try and ensure that conditions are established whereby they are given a free choice.

ITALIAN COLONIES

Under Article 23 of the Italian peace treaty, Italy renounced all right and title to her territorial possessions in Africa, namely Libya, Eritrea, and Italian Somaliland. These possessions were to continue under their existing British administration until their final disposal. Their final disposal was to be determined jointly by the governments of the Soviet Union, United Kingdom, the United States of America, and France within one year from the coming into force of the peace treaty (that is, by 15th September 1948).

The four powers concerned made a formal declaration which was appended to the treaty that if they were unable to agree upon the disposal of any of these territories in the time allowed, the matter should be referred to the General Assembly of the United Nations for recommendation. The four powers agreed in that event to accept the recommendation, and to take appropriate measures for giving effect to it. They also agreed that the final disposal of the territories and the appropriate adjustment of their boundaries should be made "in the light of the wishes and welfare of the inhabitants and the interests of peace and security, taking into consideration the views of other interested governments."

On 15th September, 1948, the four powers informed the Secretary-General of the United Nations that they were unable to agree. The question of the future of the Italian colonies was therefore placed on the agenda of the Third Session of the General Assembly. The matter was not reached before the Assembly adjourned and was postponed until April.

When the General Assembly resumed its third session in New York on 5th April, 1949, the question was considered by the political committee. Work was very slow and most representatives were obviously perplexed as to the proper course of action. The principles for determining the settlement were contained in the Charter of the United Nations and also in the four-power declaration which stressed the wishes and welfare of the inhabitants and the interests of peace and security.

Many countries, including in particular the Latin Americans, wanted generous treatment to Italy, even the return of the former colonies to Italy under trusteeship. Opponents of this course pointed to the wrongs suffered by some of the people of these regions at Italian hands, particularly the Ethiopians and the Senussi Arabs. On the other hand it was recalled that the Italian people had thrown off the yoke of fascism in 1943 and that many Italian partisans and servicemen had fought for the Allied cause. A democratic Italy had a great contribution to make to the further progress of civilization and to the United Nations.

The Australian representative urged that a special committee of enquiry should be established by the Assembly to examine the question of Italian colonies and report to the fourth session of the Assembly in September. Such a committee would have been able to evaluate the information available and might have enabled a generally acceptable solution to be reached by the end of the year. Voting on the Australian proposal was deferred in order to give the committee an opportunity of reaching an agreement during the third session.

The committee heard representatives of the inhabitants of the territories. Many countries, including in particular the Arab representatives, strongly opposed the return of Italy to North Africa and the division of Libya into two or more parts. Several members of the committee wanted some form of collective trusteeship. Opponents of this course pointed to practical difficulties. The deadlock was finally broken by an agreement reached in London between the British Foreign Secretary (Mr. Bevin) and the Italian Foreign Minister (Count Sforza). This agreement formed the basis of proposals which were thereafter adopted by the committee, not without criticism from some representatives both as to their content and the manner in which they had been reached outside the United Nations.

Under these proposals, Libya was to be divided into three parts. Of these Cyrenaica was to be given as a trust territory to Britain; the Fezzan was to be given as a trust territory to France; and the remaining portion, Tripolitania, was to be retained under British administration until 1951 when it was to become a trust territory of Italy. The whole of Libya was to be given independence in ten years. Italian Somaliland was to be divided into two, the major portion being transferred to Ethiopia with suitable provision for

Problems of the Peace Settlements

the protection of minorities (mainly Italian). No agreement was reached on the remaining portion of Eritrea, though it was the wish of the United Kingdom and the United States and most of the Arab states that it should be incorporated in the Sudan. It was proposed that the former Italian colony of Somaliland should be returned to Italy as a trust territory for an indefinite period.

These proposals as a whole received a two-third majority in the political committee but the part relating to Tripolitania failed to secure two-thirds. In the three days that elapsed between the adoption of the recommendations and their consideration in the plenary session, there was intense lobbying and speculation. The whole matter hinged on the votes of one or two countries. By Tuesday night, 17th May, neither the supporters nor the opponents were confident of the result.

The Assembly began by rejecting an Iraq proposal to give immediate independence to Libya, and then began voting on the committee's recommendation. The proposal to transfer Cyrenaica to British trusteeship was carried by 36 votes to 17 which was the necessary two-thirds. Transfer of the Fezzan to France was approved by 36 votes to 15, which was also the necessary two-thirds. Then came the crucial vote on Tripolitania: 33 in favour, 17 against, with 8 countries abstaining. The proposal therefore failed of adoption by one vote.

The transfer of a portion of Eritrea to Ethiopia was adopted by the big margin of 37 votes to 11. But Italian trusteeship for Somaliland failed to secure two-thirds, 35 voting for it and 19 against.

The proposals as a whole were heavily defeated and it became clear that no decision could be made during its third session. It was finally decided to defer further consideration until the fourth session by which time the countries could re-examine the whole question and come fresh to the problem in September. There was no need for despondency. After all, the Great powers took three years over the question and failed to settle it, and the differences within the Assembly represented a grappling with the problem in the spirit of the United Nations.

It seems reasonably clear that the proposals rejected by the Assembly will require modification. However, there is no reason why the claims of the indigenous peoples for self-government cannot be satisfactorily met by the Assembly which will recognize the new Italy's special concern in North Africa. The case of the Italian colonies before the Assembly illustrates that the primary concern of the United Nations must always be for the principles of justice and fair dealing, not merely the political expediency of the moment—surely, very shifting sands in an international organization.

VIII

THE GENOCIDE ACHIEVEMENT AND THE CHILDREN'S AID PROGRAM

THE Third Assembly secured a great deal of agreement on the many economic and social matters which came before it. Great publicity was given in the press to differences on political items and to the stormy debates and vituperations which sometimes occurred in the political committee. It is natural that this should be so: disagreements and disturbances are always news, whereas smooth orderly running is not. But any attempt to assess the value of the work of the United Nations must take account of the wide area of agreement that is so often reached in non-political fields.

COMMITTEE ORGANIZATION

The Assembly has six main committees:

First Committee	:	Political and Security
Second Committee	:	Economic and Financial
Third Committee	:	Social, Humanitarian and Cultural
Fourth Committee	:	Trusteeship
Fifth Committee	:	Administration and Budgetary
Sixth Committee	:	Legal.

In addition the Assembly may, if it wishes, appoint ad hoc committees when circumstances justify it. Thus in 1947 an ad hoc committee was established to consider Palestine. This very important item on the agenda was so complicated and contentious that as chairman I found it necessary to spend many weeks on the job before we reached the "partition" solution. In 1948 an ad hoc political committee was established in the middle of the Paris Session because the first committee was making slow progress in disposing of its agenda—unavoidably because of the nature of the items before it—and some means had to be found of handling expeditiously some of the remaining items.

These two ad hoc committees contained a representative of each of the members of the Assembly. It is also possible to establish ad hoc committees which consist of only a few selected members, and the committees themselves frequently appoint subcommittees. As a rule, however, this occurs only when the matter involved is non-controversial or is chiefly a question of drafting. It is a good principle that in all other cases every one of the fifty-nine members should be able to serve on the relevant committee.

It will be observed that most of the work of the Assembly is not devoted to political and security matters at all. Five out of the six main committees are concerned with economic, social, trusteeship, administrative and legal matters.

It would be untrue to suggest that unanimous agreement is the rule in these five committees, but it is true that the differences are rarely of a bitter nature, that agreement is often reached, and that debates are frequently of a reasoned and moderate character.

I shall take three examples of the work of the Paris Assembly in the economic and social fields. One, the Universal Declaration of Human Rights, is sufficiently important to deserve a chapter to itself. The other two are genocide and the United Nations work in connexion with children.

Genocide

In a field related to the Declaration of Human Rights, the Assembly unanimously recommended for ratification by all members a convention to prevent and punish genocide.

The Genocide Achievement—Children's Aid

Genocide is the international crime of destroying a whole group of people on such grounds as national, racial, or religious origins or beliefs. It is a crime as old as history itself, but most people until recently believed that it had disappeared forever from civilized nations. Unfortunately it reached a new peak after the rise of Hitler to power in Germany. He killed literally millions of Jews and Poles and other peoples in the most barbarous fashion, solely on account of their religion or race.

Genocide was one of the crimes with which the leaders of the Hitler regime were charged at Nuremberg. The word itself was coined by Dr. Raphael Lemkin, a professor of law at Yale University, many of whose own family had suffered grievously from this crime. After the war he devoted himself with a single-minded purpose to securing international action to outlaw genocide and provide effective measures to punish it if it ever occurred again. He showed indomitable faith and energy both in spurring on other people and in making concrete suggestions of a practical nature, and the final adoption of the convention is a great tribute to him.

The first action taken by the United Nations in regard to genocide was a resolution adopted by the General Assembly in December 1946 affirming that genocide was a crime under international law and asking the Economic and Social Council to undertake necessary studies with a view to drawing up a draft convention. Things went rather slowly from then on, not altogether avoidably, and the matter passed between the Assembly and the Council and a Sub-committee until August 1948, when it again came before the Economic and Social Council at Geneva.

The Council had before it a draft prepared by a sub-committee. Many countries had raised objections to it on one ground or another, and to some people it might have appeared that the chances of an early decision were very slight. Perhaps the most important of the objections which had to be faced was that of the United Kingdom, New Zealand, and the Netherlands who doubted whether any convention was necessary at all, since the Nuremberg indictment specifically included genocide and the General Assembly had also adopted a resolution in 1946 affirming genocide to be a crime under international law. They thought that in any case the matter should be referred to legal experts for further elaboration.

This course would have involved a great deal of delay. The work of the Nuremberg tribunal was not a sound reason for delaying the preparation of a convention. What was needed was a statement which was not merely the dictate of conquerors to a defeated people but was an agreement freely entered into by sovereign states and declaring genocide to be a crime even if committed in time of peace.

Again, as further examples of the difficulties and objections to be overcome, many countries felt that the general principles were admirable, but it was difficult to define them without including matters which might otherwise prove embarrassing. In particular, provisions relating to cultural genocide raised objections because they included not only the destruction of churches and monuments but might give minorities the right to use their own language, thereby perhaps making it more difficult for a country to absorb immigrants. Some countries, in particular some of the Latin American states and the Soviet group, opposed the inclusion of political groups, feeling that such a clause might be interpreted to stifle political change or progress. Yet another stumbling block was a suggested provision for an international tribunal to try those who were accused of genocide; the principle of any international criminal jurisdiction was unacceptable to many countries.

I was attending the August 1948 meeting of the Economic and Social Council as the Australian representative, and in opening the general debate on the draft convention I strongly urged that final action on the convention should be taken at the coming meeting of the Assembly in Paris. I stated that while it might not be possible at that stage to obtain agreement on all points, this should not prevent the United Nations from adopting a convention. The convention should cover everything on which general agreement had been reached and the United Nations could then go on at a later stage to draft a supplementary convention which could cover the points which were still left open.

This proposal met with a great deal of support and came to form the basis of the Assembly's subsequent action. The debates in the legal committees of the Assembly were very protracted. Once again attempts had to be resisted which would have referred the convention to the International Law Commission for further study, or would have substituted a declaration for it.

But it was clear from the beginning that though acute differences existed on some of the points mentioned, there was no dissent from the basic idea that genocide should be outlawed. In the end complete agreement was reached on the whole text of a convention. The controversial clauses relating to cultural and political groups were dropped for the time being. Jurisdiction by an international penal tribunal was made to apply only to those states which accepted its jurisdiction, and the whole question of an international judicial organ to try persons charged with genocide or other crimes was referred to the International Law Commission for study.

The adoption of this convention by fifty-five votes to none marked a definite step forward. It is easy to say that no civilized man would want to commit genocide, but the fact remains that one modern highly civilized race, the Germans, did commit it on an enormous scale. In setting their faces firmly against this foul crime, all the members of the General Assembly were united.

Aid to Children

Some of the most effective work of the United Nations has been its aid to children. It falls into two parts: the International Children's Emergency Fund, which is responsible for distributing aid to children and which depends for its funds upon the contributions of Governments; and the United Nations Appeal for Children, which is a voluntary movement to raise funds from private citizens to assist children.

This aid to children is inspiring work. Children were victims of a war and of economic conditions in whose creation they played no part. The future of the world depends upon the children of today, and we have a duty to see that they can grow up to be healthy in mind and body.

The Children's Fund was established by the Economic and Social Council in September 1946 as one of the means of continuing necessary international economic assistance after the termination of UNRRA. Its purpose was primarily to assist children and other adolescents of countries which were the victims of aggression. All supplies and other assistance are given on the basis of need, without discrimination because of race, creed, nationality, status, or political belief. The Fund has operated with great efficiency and effectiveness in many countries of Europe and Asia.

So far the Fund has received from the Governments of the world the sum of $77,000,000. Of this the most has come from the United States of America which has contributed so far 56,-000,000 dollars. The United States Congress has agreed to give $72 for every $28 subscribed by other countries up to a total of 100 million dollars. This munificent act is both a great source of relief for the children of the world, and a stimulus to other countries to give assistance. The second biggest contributor is Australia which has made three instalments totalling 8,000,000 dollars. Canada, Switzerland, and Uruguay then follow in that order.

The United Nations Appeal for Children was established at the end of 1946 by the General Assembly, largely at the instigation of Mr. Aake Ording of Norway who conceived the idea of appealing to everyone in the world to give one day's pay to assist needy children. Mr. Ording was appointed Director of the Appeal and carried out his difficult task with magnificent zeal.

The Appeal was a great success. In 1948 over 34 million dollars was raised. A lot of this did not go to the United Nations or its agencies, because many private and long established bodies are doing good work in the international field of assistance to children and it would have been unfair to ignore them or to cut off any of their established source of funds. It was left to each country to decide for itself what proportion, if any, of the funds it raised should be given to the International Emergency Fund for Children. Some countries, for example the Scandinavian countries and Switzerland, gave nearly all their proceeds to private agencies for international relief of children. The world's five biggest contributors to the United Nations Children's Fund out of the proceeds of the Appeal were all members of the British Commonwealth, namely Australia, Canada, South Africa, New Zealand, and the United Kingdom in that order. All together, the Children's Fund benefited from the Appeal to the extent of $13,000,000.

Though the Appeal proved a great success in 1948, the Economic and Social Council in August decided to terminate it at the end of the year. I strongly opposed this decision which was only adopted by the narrow margin of eight votes to seven. The opposition to continuance of the Appeal based itself in the debate chiefly on two arguments: first, that it was not a proper function for the United Nations to continue making appeals to private individuals for relief purposes, and secondly that a big central organization was unnecessary and expensive. Part of the opposition on the second ground could be traced to internal jealousy within the secretariat and other United Nations bodies. Another principle about which there was some difference of opinion was whether it was right for the United Nations to sponsor an appeal when part of the proceeds might go to bodies which were not part of the United Nations organization.

In addition, there was some confusion in the final voting, because the resolution finally adopted by the Council was not clearly worded. One representative afterwards told me he voted for the resolution terminating the Appeal under the impression it would keep it in existence! That crucial vote determined the day. So vague was the resolution that after it was carried the chairman had to give a ruling on its interpretation, and ruled that it meant the termination of the Appeal.

In urging the continuance of the Appeal I pointed out the great and continuing needs of children throughout the world and the value of the Appeal in supporting the International Children's Emergency Fund. In view of the success of the Appeal up to date, it was almost incredible that anyone would wish to put an end to it. In addition to the money which it raised the Appeal had done a great service in making people all over the world aware of the purposes and activities of the United Nations itself. This goodwill already produced for the United Nations was an asset which should not be recklessly squandered. The Appeal had resulted in countless numbers of people feeling a sense of direct participation in the work of the United Nations, and it was furthermore in the interests of friendly international relations that people everywhere should work together to assist needy children in all countries regardless of politics.

I also pointed out that August was far too early to estimate what the final results of the Appeal would be. Some representatives pooh-poohed this suggestion, and appeared to believe that most of the money had been received already. Yet by the time the Assembly considered the subject, four months later, the total receipts had doubled!

The six other countries which supported Australia in the Economic and Social Council were Chile, Denmark, the Netherlands, Peru, Poland, and Venezuela. I received particularly strong support from the countries which had been devastated, and from Mr. Santa Cruz of Chile who rightly felt that the needs of children in underdeveloped areas were being overlooked by some representatives. After the result of the Council's vote had been announced I said that Australia would appeal from the decision

The Genocide Achievement—Children's Aid 109

to the General Assembly, and would place upon the agenda of its Third Session the question of continuing the Appeal.

During the period between the decision of the Economic and Social Council and the meeting of the General Assembly, public opinion began to make itself felt. In a large number of countries many private citizens and organizations protested against the decision and urged their representatives to continue the Appeal. The matter was raised, for example, in the British House of Commons. Countries which were not represented in the Economic and Social Council indicated their resentment at the Council's decision.

As a result, when the matter came up in December for discussion in the third committee of the Assembly, the principle of continuing the Appeal had already been won, so much so that a resolution to this effect was tabled by a number of countries headed by the United States which had been one of the leaders at Geneva of the opposition to continuing the Appeal.

The discussion in the third committee consequently revolved around the conditions in which the Appeal should be held. However, to avoid any ambiguities in interpretation in future, Australia introduced an amendment in the plainest terms which continued the Appeal. This was carried on a roll-call vote. The committee also decided that the proceeds of the Appeal in each country should go entirely to the Children's Fund and that administration should be entrusted to the Fund.

This decision to continue the Appeal was a great victory for world public opinion. It also imposes an obligation and duty on every citizen to support the Appeal again in the coming year. No one would grudge his contribution if he could see the happiness and health which the International Children's Fund brings to great numbers of needy children throughout the world. It is one of the forces that bind nations together, and build world peace and co-operation.

IX

HUMAN RIGHTS—
THE UNANIMOUS DECLARATION

ONE of the great achievements of the Third Session was the adoption, without dissent, of a Universal Declaration of Human Rights. It is a land-mark in world history, comparable to Magna Charta and the Bill of Rights in the history of the British Commonwealth. Here for the first time are set down clearly by representatives of nearly all the countries of the world the basic rights and freedoms to which everyone is entitled in all countries of the world.

The Charter of the United Nations itself set the dominating principles when it declared that one of the purposes of the Organization was to promote and encourage respect for human rights and fundamental freedoms for all, without distinction as to race, sex, language, or religion. The adoption of this Declaration is the first step forward from there by stating in detail what those rights are.

Preparatory Work

The work of the United Nations in the field of human rights began with the establishment by the Economic and Social Council at its first session in 1946 of a Commission on Human Rights. It was charged with submitting proposals, recommendations, and reports regarding an international Bill of Rights; international declarations or conventions on civil liberties, freedom of information, and similar matters; the protection of minorities; the prevention of discrimination on grounds of race, sex, language, or religion; and other matters concerning human rights.

The preparation and basic drafting of the Declaration of Human Rights is the first major achievement of the commission. But the commission and sub-commissions established by it have done a great deal of work on other matters within its terms of reference and the results will become apparent at future sessions of the Assembly.

Mrs. Franklin D. Roosevelt was chairman of this commission and performed outstanding service in steering the discussions and in providing moral inspiration. The commission was also fortunate in its other officers.

The vice-chairman was Dr. P. C. Chang of China who had a firm grasp of the principles involved and worked hard to secure a clear and practical document which would not only set out the rights of man but do so in a manner that would capture men's imagination.

The rapporteur was Mr. Charles Malik of Lebanon who, in 1948, was also chairman of the Economic and Social Council. He is an outstanding Arab leader with a genuine belief in the liberties of the individual and in the possibilities of international action in this field. He made the piloting of human rights matters his special interest in the Economic and Social Council and fortunately he was able as chairman of the social committee of the General Assembly in 1948 to take the Universal Declaration through its final stage.

The Commission on Human Rights did a great deal of patient and detailed work and in 1948 presented a draft of the Declaration to the Economic and Social Council. At its August meeting the Council passed the draft without detailed discussion to the Third Session of the Assembly.

The long and detailed debates in the third committee of the Assembly served to make clear how excellent was the work performed by the Commission of eighteen members. It is a tribute to them that the final Declaration approved by the Assembly is so close to the commission's recommendation. Many countries put forward amendments in the Assembly and some amendments were adopted, but usually it was found that the original commission text was the best, with possibly minor amendments.

The main criticisms on the substance of the commission's draft came from the Soviet Union and other states of Eastern Europe. These states have a somewhat different conception of democracy from countries of Western Europe and in accordance with their philosophy they wished to place restrictions upon the exercise of the rights set out in the Declaration. They also wished to introduce certain duties of the state towards the individual, but the majority of the committee felt this went beyond a declaration on the rights of the individual and should be considered as a separate matter.

The third committee spent longer on the Declaration of Human Rights than was spent on any single item by any other committee of the Assembly. A real enthusiasm gripped all the members. Even those who began their work rather sceptical of the possibilities of action in this field were before long caught up in the spirit of the undertaking and began to take an active and genuinely interested part.

In drafting an international Declaration of Human Rights it was inevitable that there should have been considerable differences of opinion as to the nature and extent of the basic rights in question. Different countries, with their different political, social, legal, religious, and cultural backgrounds, naturally approach the problem of human rights from different points of view. Again, the degree of importance which they attach to particular rights varies. The Declaration adopted therefore represented the highest common measure of present agreement between member States, both as regards its form and its substance. Some delegations would have preferred a shorter draft of clearly stated fundamental principles; other delegations would have preferred an even more detailed elaboration than the final draft. These differences of view were ironed out after two months of exhaustive debate. In view of the differences of opinion apparent during the committee debates, the adoption of the final document by an overwhelming majority of the members of the United Nations is a remarkable achievement.

The Universal Declaration of Human Rights consists of a preamble and thirty articles. In its last paragraph the preamble proclaims the Declaration as "a common standard of achievement for all peoples and all nations, to the end that every individual and every organ of society, keeping this Declaration constantly in mind, shall strive by teaching and education to promote respect for these rights and freedoms and by progressive measures, national and international, to secure their universal and effective recognition and observance, both among the peoples of Member States themselves and among the people of territories under their jurisdiction."

During the debate, many delegations emphasized the fact that the declaration would have moral but not legal force, and in support of this view they quoted that last paragraph in the preamble. A few delegations, however, suggested that the Declaration merely "spelled out" the provisions of the Charter of the United Nations dealing with human rights and they implied that, as the Charter was binding upon all members of the United Nations, so the Declaration itself might have automatic and binding legal effect. No decision was taken by the Assembly on this point, and it was the clear view of the majority of countries that the Declaration imposed only moral obligations upon Governments.

My own view accords with that of the majority. The Declaration does not, in my opinion, impose direct obligations upon Governments. In order to do that it will be necessary to have a document which is more precise in detail and contains specific provisions for its implementation. The preparation of such a document is the next important stage in the United Nations work in the field of human rights.

Australian representatives have constantly emphasized the need for action in the field of implementation. As leader of the Australian delegation to the Paris Peace Conference in 1946 I put forward several proposals there which were designed to guarantee human rights in the countries concerned. I proposed the establishment of an International Court of Human Rights to which individuals or groups or States might have recourse, subject to certain safeguards against abuse, if essential human rights were violated. These proposals were unfortunately not accepted by the conference and we have in consequence witnessed cases where some of the ex-enemy states have acted in violation of the human rights provisions of those treaties.

The Australian representatives on the Human Rights Commission have tried to keep the question of implementation in the forefront of the Commission's work, and have already elaborated the proposal for an International Court in some detail. When I first proposed such a court at the Paris Peace Conference, many countries regarded it as too advanced a move, but since that time there has been evidence of increasing and substantial support for the idea. France in particular has espoused this cause and in the work of the United Nations has fully lived up to her past great traditions in the field of human rights.

In the Commission on Human Rights some progress has already been made towards completing a Covenant which will include measures of implementation. Some countries would originally have preferred the Assembly to delay the passage of the Declaration itself until a Covenant could be passed simultaneously. But undoubtedly the right decision was made to go ahead with the Declaration and secure the widest measure of agreement at that stage before going on to the next. The Assembly passed without dissent a resolution that the Commission on Human Rights be asked to continue to give priority in its work to the preparation of a draft Covenant on Human Rights and draft measures of implementation.

But the importance of the Declaration itself is not affected by the fact that it is not legally enforceable, or by the fact that the rights do not yet exist in practice in some countries. The Declaration has a moral power which is of enormous weight and influence. The statement of the rights represents a goal or a standard to which every man can look and with which he can compare what he in fact enjoys. The fact that no country was prepared to vote against the Declaration indicates its compelling moral force.

Declaration Provisions

Article 1 of the Declaration sounds the key-note, containing the fundamental concepts of the whole document. It sets out the general principle of brotherhood:

"All men are born free and equal in dignity and rights. They are endowed with reason and conscience and should act towards one another in a spirit of brotherhood."

Article 2 indicates unambiguously the universal character of the document:

"Everyone is entitled to all the rights and freedoms set forth in this Declaration, without distinction of any kind, such as race, colour, sex, language, religion, political or other opinion, national or social origin, property, birth, or other status."

The thirty articles of the Declaration are all of vital significance in establishing a standard of world conduct. They cover a wide field.

One group of articles relates to the liberty and security of person, and provides that no one shall be held in slavery or subjected to torture. Another group relates to rights before the law, and lays down that all are equal before the law. No one shall be subjected to arbitrary arrest, detention, or exile; everyone is entitled in full equality to a fair and public hearing; everyone charged with a penal offence is presumed innocent until proved guilty.

Another important Article declares:

"The family is the natural and fundamental group unit of society, and is entitled to protection by society and the State."

Freedom of Information

Articles 18 and 19 set out fundamental concepts in the field of freedom of thought and publication. Article 18 says:

"Everyone has the right to freedom of thought, conscience and religion; this right includes freedom to change his religion or belief, and freedom, either alone or in community with others and in public or private, to manifest his religion or belief in teaching, practice, worship and observance."

Article 19 says:

"Everyone has the right to freedom of opinion and expression; this right includes freedom to hold opinions without interference and to seek, receive and impart information and ideas through any media and regardless of frontiers."

The latter article enunciates one of the basic principles of democracy—the right of free speech. It also contains a second great idea which is fundamental to democracy and international understanding—the right of free access to information and opinion of other persons and other countries. The future of the United Nations and of democracy depends upon an informed public opinion. That means that everybody should be allowed to put forward his views and everybody should be allowed to subject them to critical analysis.

The United Nations has been undertaking other important work on freedom of information. The Commission on Human Rights established a special Sub-Commission on Freedom of Information and of the Press. In March 1948 a conference on freedom of information was held at Geneva, which was open not only to all members of the United Nations but to other countries also.

This conference approved three draft conventions: a convention on the gathering and international transmission of news; a convention concerning the institution of an international right of correction; and a convention on freedom of information. The first of these was revised by the Economic and Social Council in August 1947, and all three of them were placed on the agenda of the Third Session of the General Assembly. The social committee of the Assembly did not find time to consider them in Paris because of the long consideration which it had to give to the Declaration of Human Rights.

The draft conventions were therefore postponed for the consideration of the adjourned meeting of the Assembly in April in New York where they formed the most important part of the nonpolitical work. Long and careful discussion took place in the third committee, under the chairmanship once more of Mr. Charles Malik of Lebanon. Very important parts were played by distinguished press representatives, such as Mr. Cannon of the *Christian Science Monitor* and Mr. Campbell of the *Melbourne Age*. Eventually a convention on the international transmission of news and the right of correction was adopted by a plenary session of the Assembly by 32 votes to 6, the minority being the Soviet Union and the other Eastern European states. This convention amended and combined the first two recommended by the Geneva conference.

Consideration of the third convention, on freedom of information, was postponed by the Assembly to its fourth session in September. Since the conventions are so closely related, it was decided that the first should not be open for signature until the Assembly had taken definite action on the second convention.

Economic and Social Rights

An important series of Articles of the Declaration deals with economic and social rights. Article 23 says, in part:

"Everyone has the right to work, to free choice of employment, to just and favourable conditions of work, and to protection against unemployment."

That statement breaks new ground in international declarations. It flows naturally from the provision in the Charter under which each member of the United Nations pledged itself to promote full employment. This article is both complementary and supplementary to that pledge. Each person is not only entitled to expect that employment will exist for everyone, but if he is honestly unable to obtain work he is entitled to appropriate protection and assistance.

Article 24 says that everyone has the right to rest and leisure, including reasonable limitation of working hours and periodic holidays with pay. Article 25 declares in part:

"Everyone has the right to a standard of living adequate for the health and well-being of himself and of his family, including food, clothing, housing, and medical care, and necessary social services, and the right to security in the event of unemployment, sickness, disability, widowhood, old age, or other lack of livelihood in circumstances beyond his control."

Those extracts and comments will serve to illustrate the scope and spirit of this declaration. The rights of man is one of the great battle-cries of history. One of the biggest problems confronting mankind today is how to preserve the essential freedoms of the individual in the face of the inevitable demand for the State to assume greater responsibilities in planning the economic life of the entire community.

It is a healthy sign that during the crisis of 1948 the nations of the world were prepared to grapple with the task of declaring solemnly what the rights of the individual are. That so wide an area of agreement was found is a great step forward.

X

PALESTINE: THE FIRST PHASE

THE story of Palestine is a fascinating example of United Nations principles and procedures.

At first sight the problem appears to be too complex for clear statement and general understanding. Yet seen in perspective Palestine is a convincing illustration of the gradual triumph of United Nations principles even when enforcement action lags far behind decision.

The Palestine question first came to the General Assembly of the United Nations at a session specially convened in April 1947. As a result of that Assembly's decision a Special Committee on Palestine (UNSCOP) was appointed. That Committee visited Palestine and other relevant territories—and brought back a report to the regular meeting of the Assembly in New York in September, 1947.

At New York an Ad Hoc Committee was appointed to examine the report of UNSCOP and make recommendations for the plenary General Assembly. This Ad Hoc Committee consisted of representatives of every one of the fifty-seven nations. It made recommendations to the Assembly in favour of establishing a separate Jewish state in Palestine and also a separate Arab state.

Recommendations were also made to establish a special United Nations trusteeship for the Holy City of Jerusalem and Bethlehem and for a plan of economic co-operation and union between the two new states.

Subsequently a further special Assembly was held at Lake Success in April 1948 consequent upon the Arabs' defiance of the United Nations' decision and Jewish insistence upon its being carried out.

The only result of this Special Assembly was the appointment of a United Nations mediator to try to bring about a truce under Security Council auspices between the Jewish and Arab peoples in Palestine. The Special Assembly was really called to suspend or set aside the partition decision of 1947 but that attempt completely failed.

Subsequently the Security Council was instrumental in making truce arrangements over which it is still exercising jurisdiction. Count Bernadotte worked ceaselessly towards this end and his lamented assassination was a great blow to the cause of conciliation in the Middle East.

The recent Assembly meeting in Paris has refused to alter the basic arrangements of the United Nations Assembly decision of 1947. Subsequently the Security Council has again intervened to obtain a truce and Mr. Ralph Bunche as acting mediator worked hard to bring peace in this region.

At first glance, therefore, the summary narration of all these steps seems to arouse a feeling of disappointment and frustration. In January 1949 further fighting between the state of Israel and Egypt was complicated by a tragic incident, involving United Kingdom aircraft, which seemed at first to threaten a general upheaval in the Middle East. But that danger has been averted by restraint and common sense.

Moreover when the main features are seized upon, they clearly fit into a pattern which is extremely creditable to the United Nations and especially to its General Assembly.

It must always be remembered that there was never a choice between United Nations intervention on the one hand and settled peace in Palestine on the other.

The United Nations had nothing whatever to do with creating the Palestine problem. A mandate for Palestine had been established by the League of Nations, acting under the authority of the Treaty of Versailles of 1919. Palestine was part of the territory surrendered by Turkey after its defeat by the Allies during the First World War. The United Kingdom became the mandatory power and the terms of the mandate contemplated that, without prejudice to the Arabs, Palestine would also become a national home for Jewish people in accordance with what was called the Balfour Declaration. That declaration was based on the fact of Jewish assistance to the Allied cause and the deep association of the Jewish people with the Holy Land.

The territory of Palestine has always been of special interest to Australia since its famous light horsemen took a very prominent part in the fighting against Turkey and in the liberation of the whole of Palestine from the Ottoman Empire.

At the San Francisco Conference in April 1945 there was no automatic transfer to the United Nations of mandated territories. Therefore, the United Kingdom continued to administer the mandated territory of Palestine after the United Nations Charter came into operation late in 1945.

UN Assumes Jurisdiction

How then did the United Nations come to assume jurisdiction over the Palestine problem? Despite the long period of United Kingdom administration and despite the improvement in the economic and physical life of the people of Palestine, under the United Kingdom mandate, the administration became, in the opinion of the United Kingdom as mandatory power, almost impossible. No plan of agreement for its future government commended itself to Jews and Arabs alike.

Therefore, on April 2, 1947, the United Kingdom Government as a last resort asked the United Nations General Assembly to place the question of Palestine on its agenda with a view to making recommendations for its future government.

The Palestine question was thrown into the United Nations Assembly jurisdiction in order to obtain a decision on a question of obvious international concern which was likely to impair friendly relations between several nations.

Here is a further point. It was not to be expected or even hoped that the Jews and the Arabs who outside the United Nations refused to come to an agreement as to the future government of Palestine would reach an agreement within the United Nations. Neither Arab nor Jew proposed to make the task of the mandatory power easier or to smooth over the period of surrender of the mandate.

The Arab point of view was clear and explicit. It was to the effect that the people of Palestine were entitled to a declaration of their independence and the termination of the United Kingdom mandate.

This Arab attitude explains quite clearly the Jewish opposition. There had been a remarkable increase in the number of Jews in Palestine since the mandate was originally established. None the less, the Arabs were in a substantial majority. Therefore any system of government providing for majority rule would mean the handing over of the Jews in Palestine to the control of the Arabs in Palestine, with disastrous results for Jewish migration and development and with the practical certainty of Palestine's ceasing to remain a national home for the Jews in accordance with the Balfour Declaration.

These were the competing points of view at the outset of the special Assembly called at the United Kingdom request. What was the United Nations Assembly to do?

The United Kingdom had come to the conclusion that, because of Arab and Jewish conflict, the mandate was no longer workable. Obviously they contemplated the withdrawal of British forces from the territory at the end of British mandatory administration.

The Assembly acted fairly and judicially; it heard the cases both for the Arabs and the Jews. It was decided to establish a Special Committee with the widest powers for investigation of all matters relevant to the problems of Palestine, especial regard being paid to the religious interests in Palestine of the Christian churches as well as those of Islam and Judaism. On Australia's initiative the five great powers were excluded from the Committee, which consisted of the representatives of Australia, Canada, Czechoslovakia, Guatemala, India, Iran, the Netherlands, Peru, Sweden, Uruguay, and Yugoslavia.

The primary function of the committee was to ascertain the facts and make a recommendation to the regular General Assembly, which was to meet in New York in the following September.

Assistance was given to the Committee by the United Kingdom Government and the Jewish Agency but the Arab Higher Committee declared a boycott of this United Nations agency. None the less, the Committee finished its report by August.

Certain recommendations were agreed to unanimously. All agreed that the mandate would have to be terminated and Palestine given independent government. No one suggested continuance of any form of mandate or trusteeship, it being obvious that, whether Arab or Jew, the peoples within the territory were capable of self-government.

This is an important point because at a later stage the United States suggested a form of trusteeship.

Upon the main issue there were two competing recommendations placed before the General Assembly by UNSCOP.

The majority plan was for the partition of Palestine into two political units, namely, a Jewish state and an Arab state. It was recommended that such political partition should be accompanied by an economic union of the two new states.

A minority consisting of three members of the Committee recommended an independent federal state of Palestine. In the legislature of this state, representation would have been given to Arabs as well as Jews, but inasmuch as the Arabs outnumbered the Jews, the Jews would have had no effective control within any portion whatever of the proposed federal state. Migration of the Jews could, and no doubt would, have been terminated or been drastically restricted by the Arab majority with the result that the Jews would have become a permanent minority in Palestine with serious repercussions, and disaster to all their hopes of national survival.

This second part of the United Nations handling of the problem of Palestine was the logical sequence to the first. The special committee was established; a large sum of United Nations money, exceeding one million dollars, was spent to enable the Committee to arm itself with all relevant information. The facts were collected and recommendations made in preparation for the United Nations Assembly meeting in September 1947.

Reactions to UNSCOP Report

But the Arab reaction to the majority report of UNSCOP was one of uncompromising and intransigeant hostility.

The Political Committee of the Arab League met in Beirut during September. Threats of economic sanctions against the United Kingdom and the United States (in accordance with the so-called Bludan secret decisions) were accompanied by threats of war.

A communique dated 19th September stated that the Arab League would "resist with all practical and effective means the execution of these (UNSCOP's) proposals, as well as of any other measures which do not ensure the independence of Palestine as an Arab State. The Arabs of Palestine would never accept any arrangement which would do away with the unity and independence of their country, but would wage war, in which no quarter would be shown, to repel aggression against their country and more particularly so because they know that all Arab countries would stand behind them, support them, and supply them with money, men, and equipment to defend their existence."

At the same time, the Committee enjoined each of the participating Arab governments to address individual notes, along the lines of the communique, to the Governments of the United Kingdom and the United States. For example, Iraq sent a formal note to Britain and America indicating that Iraq would fight for the full independence and security of Palestine if the United

Nations decided in favour of partition. Iraq would join the other Arab League States in helping the Palestine Arabs with money, arms, and men if partition was decided.

In this way was the pattern being formed of Arab reaction to the constitutional recommendation of the United Nations agency.

First of all there was the boycott of the Committee. Yet the Committee worked hard and reported fully. There was a plain intimation that the Arabs in Palestine would "wage war in which no quarter would be shown" against any decision to partition, and it was clearly intimated that all Arab countries should join in such a conflict.

These threats of violence were quite opposed to the letter and spirit of the Charter of the United Nations and were obviously aimed at intimidating the delegates to the Assembly so as to prevent their deciding in favour of the majority report supporting political partition.

On the 20th September, 1947, the United Kingdom Government announced its decision to withdraw from Palestine:

"Our immediate attitude," it said, "is that we are not prepared to accept the responsibility of imposing a settlement in Palestine by force of arms against the wishes of either or both parties, and that, failing a settlement to which both Jews and Arabs consent, our only course is to withdraw. . . . His Majesty's Government has therefore decided that, in the absence of a peaceful settlement, they must plan for an early withdrawal of British forces and of the British administration from Palestine."

This announcement of the United Kingdom Government introduced an element of extreme urgency into the Palestine question. But it did something more. It was a clear intimation that no positive enforcement of a United Nations Assembly decision would be undertaken by the United Kingdom unless both Jews and Arabs consented to a settlement.

It was in the highest degree unlikely that such an agreed settlement could be obtained from the Arabs and Jews who could not agree outside the United Nations. The very purpose of submitting the question to the jurisdiction of the United Nations Assembly was to ascertain what was the fair and just solution of the problem quite irrespective of whether that just solution would be accepted by both parties directly interested. As well ask a court of justice to decide a case in a way which would be agreed to by both sides!

It can easily be imagined how explosive an atmosphere was produced at Lake Success, New York, in September 1947, first by the Arab threats of warlike action in the event of the Assembly accepting the majority report of UNSCOP, and second, in view of the British Government's intimation that the early withdrawal of British forces would take place unless Arabs and Jews agreed upon a peaceful settlement.

XI

PALESTINE: THE SECOND PHASE

The United Nations Assembly was really being put "on the spot." Would the Assembly yield to the threats and wash its hands of all responsibility or would it go straight ahead, finish the work already commenced, and carry out its duty according to the letter and spirit of its great Charter?

The Arab States even opposed the establishment by the plenary Assembly of 1947 of the Special Ad Hoc Committee to consider the Palestine question for the purpose of making a suitable recommendation to the Assembly.

Here let me introduce a personal note. A large number of delegates who had been my fellow delegates to the San Francisco Conference in 1945, had requested me to become a candidate for the Presidency of the Assembly in 1947. I felt that the activities of the Australian Delegation in the United Nations since San Francisco, where we had worked extremely hard to improve the draft Charter, fairly warranted my standing.

Dr. Granados of Guatemala has told the story of this election of 1947 in his book *The Birth of Israel*. The Latin Americans met in caucus and agreed to throw their bloc vote in favour of Dr. Aranha of Brazil. In the first ballot Aranha received twenty-six votes and I received twenty-three and Jan Masaryk of Czechoslovakia six. These six votes obviously represented the eastern bloc votes. On the second ballot the eastern bloc votes were either deliberately marked informal or went to Dr. Aranha, with the result that he was duly elected.

For the moment I was disappointed at the result. But I had not been able to attend any prior meeting of the General Assembly and there were many delegates at New York who had taken no part whatever in the conference at San Francisco. The Presidency of the Assembly is the highest office which can be granted by the United Nations and when I subsequently came to know Dr. Aranha very well, I was deeply impressed with his splendid gifts and his loyalty to United Nations ideals. We became close friends.

Chairmanship of Palestine Committee

It was Dr. Aranha who suggested to me that I should accept the chairmanship of the Ad Hoc Committee for Palestine. This Committee, like the Political Committee itself, was to be a committee not of any limited character but comprising every one of the fifty-seven nations. Accordingly its decisions would probably determine the final United Nations Assembly vote on the Palestine question and indeed this proved to be the case.

Dr. Aranha pointed out these matters to me and I naturally asked him what the Latin American bloc had decided to do. So far all they had decided to do was not to put forward any candidate for any official position in connection with the Palestine Ad Hoc Committee. He assured me they all were anxious that I should accept the responsibility. "I tell you most sincerely that the future of the Assembly depends on the success of the Palestine Committee and in the interests of the United Nations I ask you to do the job." I told Dr. Aranha that I had also important assignments to carry out as leader of the Australian Delegation, particularly on the Political Committee, including such problems as Korea, Greece, War Propaganda, The Little Assembly, and Admission of New Members, and that I would have to carry out my duties under this arrangement as well. Dr. Aranha said there need be no clash. Accordingly I accepted nomination and was unanimously elected chairman.

I was also alive to the fact, and Dr. Aranha did not attempt to conceal it from me for a moment, that the Palestine job was the "hot potato" in the Assembly and that quite a few of the delegates were expressing the opinion, perhaps the hope, that the proceedings of the Committee would end in deadlock and the whole problem be returned once more to the doorstep of the United Kingdom which had borne the heavy responsibility for more than a generation.

I was greatly impressed by Aranha's point of view. He was tremendously keen upon the success of the 1947 Assembly. It seemed to me that if the United Nations could reach a fair and just solution of the Palestine question, it would greatly increase its own power and prestige, it would make history well worth making.

The attitude of the Australian Government on the question had been clear, firm, and consistent. Australia took the initiative at the Special Assembly in the appointment of UNSCOP. I had always insisted, right from the first meeting of the Security Council in London of 1946, that, where there were disputed questions before a United Nations body, a proper foundation or basis for any recommendation must be discovered. It was therefore essential that the relevant facts should be declared authoritatively after the fullest investigation by an impartial committee or commission. We had also contended that full publicity must be given to all the findings of any such committees or commission.

Australia's point of view was pressed forward repeatedly in connection with Security Council disputes in relation to Iran, Greece and many other subjects. The practice of enquiry and investigation had become fairly well settled.

Accordingly when Australia was elected to UNSCOP our delegates, John Hood and S. L. Atyeo, joined in the full report of the facts without committing Australia at that time to any firm decision in relation to the majority or minority recommendation of UNSCOP.

Palestine Committee Begins Work

The Committee work commenced at Lake Success. We had before us in true form not only the majority and minority reports of UNSCOP but a proposal by Saudi Arabia and Iraq for the termination of the mandate and the simultaneous recognition of Palestine as a unitary state.

All these matters were, at my suggestion, given over to general debate before the committee. This was of the most comprehensive character and no less than seventeen meetings took place.

We also decided, at my suggestion, that the Arab Higher Committee and the Jewish Agency should be allowed to participate on an equal footing in its deliberations.

The representative of the Arab Committee completely rejected the majority proposal of the Committee and advocated one Arab State for the whole of Palestine which would (he claimed) sufficiently protect the rights and interests of all minorities. On the other hand the Jewish Agency indicated their acceptance of the UNSCOP majority plan subject to further discussion of constitutional and territorial provisions.

From the beginning, the debate sometimes trespassed into the inadmissible area of warnings or threats as to what would happen in the event of a decision of the Committee in favour of political partition. One or two representatives from the Arab States frequently offended in this respect.

I had some difficulty in adjusting the order of speaking and reply as between the Arab Higher Committee and the Jewish Agency. Naturally enough, each group wanted both the first word and the last word. In the end this matter worked out smoothly enough because if, at one stage of the proceedings, one group got the advantage I always tried to balance this by reversing the order on the next occasion.

Whatever complaint the Arabs had about the decision of the

Palestine: The Second Phase

Committee they could never complain that their case was not fully heard to conclusion. Their spokesman was Jamel Husseini. He spoke with dignity and poise.

On the Israel side we had Dr. Weizmann (now President of Israel), Dr. Silver, and Mr. Moshe Shertok (now Foreign Minister of Israel). Dr. Weizmann's eyesight was so bad that special lighting arrangements had to be made to assist him in speaking; Silver was equally eloquent. Shertok always spoke in a direct business-like manner and with a complete knowledge of the changing situation in Palestine.

As I have already suggested, I entered upon the work of the Committee without prejudices in favour of any particular solution. However, I carefully studied all the relevant documents and listened with the greatest of attention to all the arguments. Proceedings of the Committee tended to revive, in relation to Palestine, "old unhappy far-off things, and battles long ago."

One argument, for instance, dealt with the question whether the Balfour Declaration was legally justified; and proposals were actually made to refer the question of its legality to the Court of International Justice. The truth was that the Balfour Declaration was a statement made on behalf of the British Government as to the future disposition and control of a portion of the territory of Turkey which that country would be required to cede to the victors of the First World War. In essence, the Balfour Declaration was a pronouncement of a political character. Undoubtedly the right of the nations to dispose of the territory of Turkey under a treaty of peace could be determined only by reference to the conditions of the various treaties of peace and the decisions of the League of Nations.

Over and over again it was sought to relate the question of the future government of Palestine to the world problem of Jewish refugees and displaced persons. The real suggestion was that the Committee's function was to find a general solution to relieve the tragedies caused by Hitler's base treatment of the Jewish people.

But UNSCOP had pointed out, and it was indeed incontrovertible, that the question of the future government of Palestine should not be regarded as the ultimate solution of the Jewish problem in general. However, the matter having once been introduced, it sometimes appeared plausible to suggest that all countries should take their fair quota of displaced persons so that Palestine should not be the sole place to which displaced Jews from Europe might migrate.

In the end the Committee's decisions satisfactorily distinguished between the one matter before it, that is, the question of Palestinian government, and the many matters which had some bearing upon the fate of the Jewish people in the rest of the world but which were not strictly relevant to the Palestine question.

The general debate was at times somewhat repetitious. However I felt it imperatively necessary that no attempt should be made to impose any restriction whatever at this stage upon the speeches of delegates. No doubt the representatives of Arab States felt their responsibility very keenly. Accordingly they were heard in full. By the time the general debate was closed there was hardly any aspect of the Palestinian problem whether historical, religious, philosophical or legal which had not been fully elaborated.

One notable feature in the debate was the complete absence of any support for the minority proposal of UNSCOP, that is, the establishment of Palestine as a federal state. Instead of that, the Arab States, and those who supported them, advocated the establishment of a unitary state for Palestine. This made the real issue somewhat clearer.

Next came a crucial stage in the proceedings of the Committee. The general debate was closed; what was the next step? The recommendations of UNSCOP did not contain anything more than a general outline of the future method of government of the territory. The general debate suggested that fourteen delegates had expressed themselves in favour of proceeding in accordance with the basic principles of partition as proposed in the majority

UNSCOP plan; on the other hand eight had favoured the establishment of an independent unitary Arab state. No support whatever was forthcoming for the minority UNSCOP suggested plan of federation for Palestine.

It was becoming apparent to me that many delegates would remain uncommitted till the latest possible moment, some hoping, no doubt, that it would be unnecessary to give a decision.

The figures I have mentioned, fourteen in favour of partition and eight against, also foreshadowed that it might have been very difficult to obtain a two-thirds majority in the Plenary Assembly when the recommendations of the Ad Hoc Committee went forward for its approval. From the past it was clear that the question of Palestine would be deemed one of importance requiring the special majority of two-thirds provided for in the Charter.

Some of those who supported partition also argued in favour of the necessity of the establishment of enforcement machinery to carry out any recommendations of the Assembly.

As a matter of fact this now appeared to me to misconceive the true functions of the General Assembly. Under the Charter, the General Assembly is a recommending body, but it possesses no executive authority apart from its power to regulate its internal administrative machine. It can recommend the adoption of a course of action by all or some of the members especially those directly concerned, and it can also make recommendations to the Security Council.

In truth the force of Assembly recommendations is not physical power. It rests upon the tremendous moral force of its decisions having regard to the general obligations of members of the United Nations to act in accordance with United Nations principles, purposes, and procedures. This question of enforcement always threatened to cause and nearly did cause a deadlock before the matter was ended.

Preparing Detailed Proposals

But the next immediate step before us was the determination by the Committee of its method of proceedings.

I told the Committee that the general debate had covered an enormously wide field, that no delegation had been restricted in putting forward the case, and indeed that one or two Arab states had spoken three times during the general debate.

I emphasized that the general debate was over and that we must come closer to the business of decision. I pointed out that UNSCOP had worked hard on the problem before us but it would be essential to bring before the Committee one or more comprehensive detailed schemes for the future government of Palestine.

The moment I called for a discussion on the point of procedure there was considerable manoeuvring for position.

First of all there were those who had completely committed themselves in favour of the partition scheme. They wanted the Ad Hoc Committee to do all its work solely upon the basis of the majority report of UNSCOP without any further consideration of the alternative view presented by the Arab states that there should be a unitary government of Palestine.

I thought that this summary disposal of the matter would be fatal to the just consideration of the problem and I strongly opposed it from the chair. I pointed out to the Committee that we were there to make recommendations for the General Assembly. I said it was their bounden duty to do everything that was reasonably necessary in preparation for the crucial vote at the end of our deliberations, that is, on the definite and specific proposals we should recommend to the Plenary Assembly. If we now committed ourselves to the majority report of partition to the exclusion of all alternative plans, there would be no opportunity for consideration in detail of the various alternatives.

Palestine: The Second Phase

An eventual step was to elaborate the general propositions of the UNSCOP majority report and to come to the vote on these questions in an orderly manner and after having fully heard and examined and voted upon any proposals which could be regarded as competing with the majority plan.

I therefore proposed the appointment of a first sub-committee to submit to the full Ad Hoc Committee a detailed plan for the government of Palestine on the basis of the unanimous recommendations of UNSCOP and the majority report of UNSCOP in favour of partition.

The debate proceeded and el-Khouri of Syria submitted to me that if a sub-committee was appointed to analyse and bring forward the majority UNSCOP plan so also a sub-committee should be appointed to elaborate the proposals of Iraq, Saudi Arabia, and Syria for the creation of a unitary state of Palestine.

I immediately assented to this proposition. I pointed out that up to the present all that had been advocated by the Arab State was the general principle of a unified state and there was no constitutional proposal detailed to implement the principle.

There was opposition to the Arab proposal. I had to intervene in the interests of just procedure. I pointed out to the Committee that we were in a semi-judicial position and that it was absolutely necessary to be fully acquainted with the Arab proposal in detail so that whether it was recommended by the majority of the committee to the Plenary Assembly or not there would be available to the plenary a definite tangible scheme instead of a mere general resolution.

The delegate for El Salvador (Dr. Castro) then suggested that parallel with the work of the two proposed sub-committees, I, as Chairman, should endeavour to conciliate the opposing parties, the Jewish Agency on the one hand and the Arabs on the other, the object being to lessen the area of disagreement between them.

The discussion on procedure became more and more business-like as I ruled out any discussion whatever on the merits of the case. I was delighted to find that all members of the Committee showed a complete willingness to get on with a practical plan for completing our work.

In elaboration of what I had suggested I now proposed from the chair (1) that Sub-Committee 1 be appointed to bring back a detailed plan for the government of Palestine based on the principles of the majority report of UNSCOP, (2) that Sub-Committee 2 should be established to put forward in detail the alternative plan for unitary government on the basis of the Arab proposals, and (3) all other proposals before the committee including proposed references of legal matters to the International Court and resolutions dealing with the duty of members of the United Nations to accept a proportion of Jews as migrants could be examined by either sub-committee and recommendations brought back to the Committee.

Finally, I also proposed, following on Dr. Castro's suggestion that a sub-committee of conciliation be established consisting of myself as chairman, together with vice-chairman (Siam), and the rapporteur (Iceland).

Everything was moving steadily towards the adoption of this complete procedure when the Soviet Delegate (Tsarapkin) proposed that henceforward the Ad Hoc Committee should carry out all its work solely on the basis of the majority partition plan of UNSCOP.

To my surprise this was supported by General Hilldring of the United States. However, he was in a difficulty because if he had voted against the U.S.S.R. it would have appeared that he was voting against partition after being publicly committed to support it.

However, it would have been quite wrong for the Committee to pin itself down at that stage to the principle of partition. Indeed, while some nations might partly favour partition if the boundaries were adjusted, they might equally be forced to vote against partition as an abstract proposition if they did not know for certain what territories would be comprised in the two States.

Putting the matter very frankly, I strongly pressed on the Committee the duty of all sections to complete the preparatory and detailed work necessary before the final vote could be taken for partition and for the alternative plan.

The Russian resolution was defeated by a large majority and the Committee then adopted my proposals for procedure with practical unanimity.

Selection of Sub-committees

Next came the equally delicate question of the composition of the two committees. Here again confusion or worse threatened to spoil our work. Several countries, especially those who were endeavouring to avoid being committed either for or against partition, wanted each sub-committee to be "mixed" in the sense that it would be comprised both of supporters and critics of the plan with which it was dealing. This meant, as I pointed out, that although we were to establish a sub-committee to elaborate a detailed plan for the Palestinian government on the basis of partition, some of the sub-committee members might be altogether opposed to it. Equally in the elaboration of the competing Arab plan of unitary government, some of the members of the second sub-committee could presumably consist of those who were entirely against the Arab plan.

If this proposal was to be accepted, the whole work of the Committee would be completely stultified. We would lose all the value of the general debate and the criticisms which had already been uttered in the general debate both of those in favour of partition and of those against partition.

The truth was several delegates were hedging, trying to ascertain where the preponderance of numbers was. They therefore wished to retain an appearance of complete neutrality until the last possible moment. This was quite understandable and pardonable but it was no reason why they should serve on a sub-committee which *ex hypothesi* was committed to a definite principle.

The Soviet Union (Tsarapkin) next proposed that the partition committee should consist of fifteen members, including all the members on the Security Council. Again I felt it my duty to object otherwise the committee would have gone off the rails. Fifteen members were obviously too many for a working group and only two members of the Security Council, U.S.A. and U.S.S.R., had committed themselves in favour of partition. I said all members of a sub-committee should be prepared to accept the bare principle which the particular sub-committee was required to elaborate. The Soviet proposal was defeated on a vote.

Next the Gordian knot was cut. The Committee left both the number and the nomination of the members of the two sub-committees to my unfettered discretion.

In this way I was given a very special responsibility to discharge and I carried out this part of my work with the utmost care. I asked every member of the committee to indicate at the adjournment if they wished to serve on either sub-committee. This information was obtained and the wishes of all the delegates were ascertained during the afternoon. Finally I determined that there should be nine members both of Sub-Committee 1 (partition) and Sub-Committee 2 (unitary government). For Sub-Committee 1 I nominated countries who had spoken in favour of the principle of partition: Canada, Czechoslovakia, Guatemala, Poland, South Africa, U.S.A., U.S.S.R., Uruguay, and Venezuela.

Sub-Committee 2 I nominated to consist of: Afghanistan, Colombia (which later resigned), Egypt, Iraq, Lebanon, Pakistan, Saudi Arabia, Syria, and Yemen.

Already I could see that pressures and counter-pressures were being exerted by delegations and by interested groups, and I therefore decided to make public the names of the two Sub-

Committees as soon as possible. I did so and the names were given to the press and announced over the broadcasting stations.

That evening I was the guest of honour at a dinner given by the Australian Society of New York, and to my surprise I was repeatedly bombarded with messages from one of the delegates asking to see me in connection with the composition of one of the sub-committees. I saw this delegate at the close of the dinner party and he said that his country was dissatisfied with the composition of Sub-Committee 1 and asked me to exclude two countries and replace them with two others.

I pointed out to him that both countries whom he wished to add had expressly declared that they did not desire to serve on either Committee but that those I had nominated had both wished to serve on Sub-Committee 1, their delegates being very active supporters of partition.

I pointed out that the decision had been made, that the announcements had been given to the press and that the affair was finished.

This did not satisfy the distinguished delegate who saw me. He was very persistent and I turned him down. I flatly declined to make any change and I told him that I would not submit to any interference in the performance of my duty to the Committee. He disappeared from the scene and I heard no more about the matter. Both the delegates objected to made important contributions to the work of the Sub-Committee and Committee and certainly the two replacements suggested did not indicate to me any desire to become members of the very hard-working Sub-Committee 1.

I mention this simply to illustrate the atmosphere of brooding hostility and suspicion against which, as Chairman, I had to contend. I was determined to carry out my duty to the United Nations, which was entitled to consider the views of all its members, whether representing small powers or great.

Incidents such as this made the atmosphere of the Ad Hoc Committee very difficult. There was intrigue and rumour of intrigue, imputation and counter-imputation. I am satisfied that all this was on the fringe of the delegates' work. On both sides, many worked selflessly. For instance, John Hohenberg of the *New York Post* and Miss Schultz of the *Nation* worked indefatigably in the interests of partition, and others for the Arab view.

On looking back I am completely satisfied that the procedure which I proposed and which the Committee, in a just and business-like manner accepted, was the one method which could have enabled the Committee to reach a conclusion in a democratic manner before the end of the session. At the time the procedure was fully appreciated only by commentators like Rodgers of the *New York Herald Tribune* and Hamilton of the *New York Times*.

One other incident caused some trouble in connection with Sub-Committee 2 dealing with the Arab unitary plan. The only Latin American country which submitted its name for nomination to this particular sub-committee was Colombia. The sub-committee met and elected a delegate of Colombia as Chairman. He too desired to change the composition of his committee after the public announcement had been made and the committee duly constituted. I declined to make any change whereupon the delegate resigned from the sub-committee. But the work went on.

The Sub-committees at Work

So the two sub-committees commenced work. Both the representatives of the Jewish Agency and the Arab Higher Committee had the right to put their views before either sub-committee and this right was frequently exercised. In addition the mandatory power—United Kingdom—regularly attended meetings of both sub-committees for the purpose of assisting the deliberations and giving information.

The work of Sub-Committee 1 extended for four weeks. The broad plan for partition obtained from the UNSCOP report was analysed and amplified in considerable detail. Certain modifications were made in the proposed plan especially in connection with territories to be allocated to the proposed Jewish and Arab states in Palestine. An important feature of the work was the consideration of the means of putting the partition plan into operation. A suggestion was made that the Security Council should be requested by the General Assembly to act promptly in the event of any attempt to alter by force the settlement envisaged by the proposed Assembly resolution and to treat such attempts as a threat to the peace, breach of peace or act of aggression. I shall refer to this point again.

Sub-Committee 1, after intensive discussions with the United Kingdom representatives, succeeded in drawing up a broad schedule and time table for implementation of the partition plan by gradual stages. Provision was made for the termination of the mandate and withdrawal of the armed forces of the mandatory power by May 1, 1948 and the creation of Arab and Jewish states by July 1, 1948.

Sub-Committee 1 also proposed that the General Assembly resolution was to be brought into effect by a small commission of members to be appointed by the General Assembly but to act under the guidance of the Security Council. There was some uncertainty as to the precise meaning of an early United Kingdom statement and part of the work of the sub-committee was to clarify the position before its final report to the Ad Hoc Committee. The United Kingdom representative informed the Ad Hoc Committee that the first plan drawn up by the sub-committee contemplated that the United Kingdom, as a mandatory power, would have to perform certain functions, which involved the necessity of taking some responsibility for the establishment of the new regime despite the fact that the regime would not be established by the consent of both the Arabs and the Jews. Endeavours were made by Sub-Committee 1, which included Canada and South Africa, to meet every United Kingdom objection.

But there was a general feeling in the Ad Hoc Committee that some of these objections did not take sufficient account of the fact that the very reason why the U.N. General Assembly had been called to consider the Palestine impasse was that the Arabs and Jews could not agree upon any settlement.

Further when the declaration of the United Kingdom that it would withdraw its troops and its administration was carried into effect a vacuum of authority would be created during the transition period when British troops would be withdrawn. Sub-Committee 1 felt that the U.N. Commission could fairly look to the temporary assistance of the mandatory power, otherwise it would not be able to function at all. The sequel showed that the sub-committee's view was well founded.

The United Kingdom was saying in effect to United Nations: "We cannot obtain agreement in Palestine between Arabs and Jews. We must lay down a plan for the future government of Palestine. But, if the Arabs and Jews continue to disagree, we cannot lend our authority to active enforcement, although we will do nothing actively to impede the plan."

This attitude was completely understandable because of the great burdens and suffering of British troops. But, in application, the position was very difficult not only for the United Kingdom but for the United Nations Commission.

In Sub-Committee 2 no corresponding difficulties were met. The sub-committee based its work on the assumption of an early termination of the mandate, and the immediate transfer of full sovereignty of Palestine to a Provisional Government representing all sections of Palestine in proportion to numerical strength. Arrangements were proposed for the convening of a Constituent Assembly which would, of course, have represented all sections of Palestine in accordance with their numerical strength. In other words, the Jews would have been a permanent minority and would have been in an even worse position than they would have been under a federal scheme.

I now refer to the suggestion of settlement by conciliation of the Arab and Jewish groups. As I have explained, the Conciliation Committee, under my chairmanship, included Thor Thors, a most loyal and devoted United Nations supporter, and Prince Subha Svasti of Siam. The latter was a remarkable character. He had close associations with Britain and his military services during the war were of value to the Allies. Unfortunately for him, a revolution occurred at home just as the Palestinian committee was concluding its work.

The revolution, which seemed to terminate his authority at Lake Success, was naturally a source of considerable anxiety to Prince Subha Svasti. He was extremely puzzled as to whether he could exercise a vote in the Ad Hoc Committee. Finally, he voted against partition in the Ad Hoc Committee, but was absent when the matter was before the General Assembly.

Such a case only illustrated the ebb and flow in forecasts as to the proposed voting on partition. Every ally was a prospective enemy, every friend a potential opponent. Certainly there were some very curious changes and shifts.

On the Conciliation Committee we made a real attempt to explore the possibilities of reducing the area of disagreement. I saw Moshe Shertok, of the Jewish Agency; it was obvious that, before any agreement could be made effective, the United States would have to come in, so I also discussed the matter with Mr. Marshall, the Secretary of State. I also wrote on behalf of the Conciliation Committee to these and other powerful personages. Mr. Marshall took the simple and direct course of pointing out that the matter was before the United Nations for decision and that the best course was to go ahead and make a decision. This is the view to which I had come independently. A large majority of the delegates would have preferred agreement, but, in the atmosphere and temper of those days, the Arab states would have yielded nothing. Had they done so, they could hardly have justified their previous boycott of UNSCOP and their refusal at all stages in the Committee work to take any interest in the improvement or modification of the partition plan.

The Arabs were working with one supreme objective in view, to prevent the adoption of the partition plan, or, at any rate, to prevent its adoption by the necessary two-thirds majority. For a considerable time it seemed as though their tactics might be successful.

So far as the Jewish Agency was concerned, they took the view that, unless the United Nations decided in their favour in accordance with the general tenor of the UNSCOP report, the establishment of a Jewish State in Palestine would never be accomplished.

On the Arab side, the views hardened at Lake Success and, as I have pointed out, they did not even support in the Ad Hoc Committee the plan of federalism proposed in the minority report of UNSCOP.

Accordingly, settlement of the question by agreement turned out to be impossible, at any rate until the Plenary Assembly made its definitive recommendation. We did our utmost, but it was impossible for us to alter the foundation upon which the matter was referred to the United Nations—that is, fundamental disagreement between Arabs and Jews in relation to the government of Palestine.

XII

PALESTINE: THE THIRD PHASE

AND so, at long last, the two reports from Sub-Committee 1 and Sub-Committee 2, came back to the Ad Hoc Committee at its twenty-third meeting on 19th November.

Now there was crisis and drama in plenty. We had before us two competing plans for the future government of Palestine. The Arab plan dealt also with the general question of Jewish refugees, the objective of Sub-Committee 2 being to treat the Palestine problem as an incident of the world problem and to broaden the issue from the government of Palestine into the wider and vaguer problem of Jewish displaced persons. The Sub-Committee's report contained specific recommendations, (1) that the "countries of origin should be requested to take back these Jewish refugees and displaced persons belonging to them, and to render them all possible assistance to resettle in life," and (2) "that those Jewish refugees and displaced persons who cannot be repatriated should be absorbed in the territories of Members of the United Nations in proportion to their area, economic resources, per capita income, population and other relevant factors."

From Wednesday, 19th November, until Tuesday, 25th November, when the decision was given the proceedings of the Ad Hoc Committee were marked by mounting tension ending in a dramatic and historic climax.

Consideration of Sub-committee Reports

Before opening consideration of the report of the two Sub-Committees I carefully considered proper and just procedure. I took into account the extremely valuable work of UNSCOP and the full and unrestricted debate before the appointment of the Sub-Committees.

I therefore ruled at the outset that the reports of both Sub-Committees and the draft resolutions recommended by them should be discussed together as part of the one problem before the Assembly.

I then fixed the deadline for amendments to the draft resolutions of the two committees without prejudice to my right to admit further amendments if the circumstances warranted it. I told the Committee that the time for discussions of mere general principles was long past and that everything had to be related to one or more of the specific proposals which would soon "come to the vote."

I am afraid that the word "vote" struck a note of alarm in the case of a few delegations. They had avoided any public commitment to any view during the first general debate and by serving on neither Committee they still remained uncommitted. I at once sensed the desire of several delegates to avoid reaching a conclusion at the Second Assembly. "Why," it was said, "should we press on with this matter? After all, the struggle between the Jews and the Arabs and the problems of the Holy Land belong not to this year but to all time. Let us adjourn the Assembly and let the Ad Hoc Committee on Palestine be resumed some time in 1948."

This point of view was at first whispered but before the end of our deliberations on 25th November two delegates publicly said that we should not proceed too hastily and it was intimated to me from many other quarters that if I suggested an adjournment there would be no objection. I reminded members of the importance of action and the danger of delay.

Sometimes our Latin American colleagues are criticized for their tendency to put off until "mañana."

In this case, however, other delegates seemed to be of the same mind. I sensed the temptation and danger of delay and at one stage it was almost heartbreaking to notice the drift towards delaying manoeuvres. I opposed delay with everything I had.

I pointed out on one occasion to the Committee that the Palestine question was probably the most important question ever considered by the Assembly and that the United Nations would be judged by its capacity to recommend a solution to this problem which had so completely baffled the United Kingdom Government that they turned to the United Nations for assistance. I said it would be little short of a disgrace if we failed to come to a conclusion and that whatever the opinions of the delegates were they should be prepared to express them definitively and in the only way that really mattered, that is, by the vote.

We came to a crucial ruling. The debate on the report started. The Chairman of the Sub-Committee 2 and chief spokesman for the Arab case was Sir Zafrullah Khan of Pakistan. He had been a distinguished judge in India before the establishment of the new Pakistan. He had spoken with great eloquence and earnestness in previous stages of the debate. Equally outspoken was Mr. Chamoun the delegate for Lebanon, who, in my opinion, delivered the most eloquent speech on the Arab side. Beside him and rivalling him in the display of earnestness and energy was Jamali of Iraq. When I pointed out to the Committee a newspaper report indicating an alleged resolve on the part of the Arabs to stage a filibuster in order to prevent a vote at that session, Jamali, in the most frank and friendly manner assured me as Chairman that there was no such intention. I immediately accepted the assurance without any qualification and his colleagues acted strictly in accordance with this undertaking. No doubt at this time he was confident that it would be impossible for the partition plan to obtain the necessary two-thirds majority.

I now explain the important ruling. In these later stages the speeches commenced to reach a far higher level than was the case in the course of the general debate. The feeling was more pent up. Every word was listened to in silence. I greatly admired the restraint and dignity of Sir Zafrullah Khan. However, it became my duty to rule against him as he discussed the report of the Second Committee, and while expounding it said: "At a later stage in these proceedings I shall deal with the report of the First Committee."

Interposing at once, I ruled in accordance with what I had previously laid down, viz. that there would be no "later stage," that we were indeed approaching the final stages of debate.

Specific amendments to the resolutions contained in the two reports would be discussed but the substantial question before the Committee was to determine, first, whether as recommended by Sub-Committee 2 the International Court should be asked for legal rulings; second, whether as also recommended by Sub-Committee 2 the proposals aimed at a general acceptance by the members of the United Nations of Jewish refugees should be adopted; and, third, the main question, which of the two plans before us for the future government of Palestine should be recommended for adoption by the Plenary Assembly. I added that it was possible that the Committee might reject both plans, although that would result in utter futility. I reminded the Committee that the choice was before them and that in the Arab plan of unitary Palestine the Committee had to consider it in contrast to and competing with the rival plan of partition recommended by UNSCOP and also by Sub-Committee 1.

What I ruled in substance was that the two questions were inseparably connected as far as the debate was concerned and we could not possibly have separate debates without long and scandalous repetition. Sir Zafrullah Khan at once accepted my ruling and when, at a later stage of his lengthy address he again referred to a future debate on the rival plan and I interposed again, he at once yielded and was generous enough to pay a tribute to the great care and impartiality with which I had conducted the proceedings.

A serious hitch occurred a little later when the United Kingdom delegate indicated that under the recommended resolution of Sub-Committee 1 at least his Government would be required to perform certain functions which were incompatible with the U.K. policy—that is, withdrawing from Palestine without assuming any actual or apparent responsibility for the establishment of a new regime not based upon agreement between Arabs and Jews. As a result it became necessary for me to adjourn the Committee to allow the two sub-committees to meet immediately and to review their respective plans of implementation. Sub-Committee 2 decided not to alter its plans but certain revisions were made by Sub-Committee 1 in the light of the British statement.

A further important development took place as the representative of the Jewish Agency, Mr. Shertok, renewed the offer he had made in Sub-Committee 1 to transfer to the Arab State of Palestine certain additional territory. This offer was well received and the United States delegation proposed a consequential revision of the boundaries of the two states in conformity with the offer of Mr. Shertok.

Naturally the delay caused by the United Kingdom intervention postponed the debate in the Ad Hoc Committee. On Saturday morning, 22nd November, I was faced with the difficulty that the General Assembly was required to finish its last Plenary Session the following Saturday, 29th November.

I accordingly resolved to continue the practice I had introduced during the latter stages of the general debate, to have three meetings per day until the business was completed. No objection was raised and the Committee good-naturedly accepted the inevitable. The feeling in the Committee gradually intensified on Saturday and some hard things were said during the debate on the rival reports. It was obvious that some delegates were gradually getting final instructions from their governments as to how they should vote. Accordingly, the number of speakers on my list tended to increase.

Debate Comes to an End

At the end of the Saturday morning session I intimated that, unless objection was raised by the Committee at once, I would close the list of speakers in the debate on the rival report at three o'clock that afternoon. After that stage was reached, the only discussion which would be relevant must be directed to specific amendments to the resolutions of the two sub-committees which had to be formally put in writing that day. Stressing this note, I again repeated that the delegates could best perform their duty to the United Nations by confining themselves to relevant and reasonable discussion and by coming to an early decision.

All through Saturday afternoon and Saturday night the debate proceeded. On Saturday evening a number of delegates were the dinner guests of Nelson Rockefeller, who had played a prominent part in the making of the Charter at San Francisco, and who had continued his intense interest in the welfare of the United Nations as he and his family contributed to the generous arrangements for establishing the permanent home of the United Nations on the East Side of Manhattan. There was a large party and a great deal of good-natured chaffing. As I hurried away in order to be in time to sound the gavel for the opening of the night meeting, I laughingly said, "But, of course, I am sure you all know we will have three sittings tomorrow as well." I was not serious: still the rumour spread rapidly.

At about 11.30 p.m. on Saturday a South American delegate begged me to allow an adjournment. Everyone was becoming fatigued. I agreed to the suggestion and congratulated those who had spoken during the three long sessions of that day, upon their loyalty to the Chairman's rulings and their obvious desire to express their views succinctly. I was about to sound the gavel when Dr. Arce of Argentina interposed on the cry of "Point of order." He was at the Rockefeller party and I guessed what his concern would be; he was very afraid I would order sittings for Sunday. I at once said "Before I hear your point of order, Dr. Arce, I have an important announcement to make. In view of the excellent progress made today by the Committee and in spite of your anxiety to sit tomorrow I propose to give the Committee the special concession of a free day from sittings tomorrow, Sunday!"

Dr. Arce laughed and gesticulated in his inimitable manner but my announcement was greeted with cheers of relief. As the noise died down, I simply added "This concession is conditional upon your being here early on Monday morning because there are only eight or nine speakers left on my list, after which we will hear representatives of the Arab Higher Committee and the Jewish Agency and I shall declare the general debate on both Sub-Committees' reports finally closed." So we motored back to New York after a very heavy week.

Sunday was full of rumours as to the probability of the voting. I directed an amendment to be inserted in the name of Australia for the further protection of all religious institutions and property in both the proposed Arab and Jewish portions.

The main objective of the amendment was to prevent any form of discrimination against the church buildings and other religious institutions that were associated neither with the Arabs nor with the Jews.

I had made it my practice always to be regular in taking the chair. On the Monday morning I was twenty minutes early and many delegates informally talked to me before the necessary quorum was reached.

The Monday sittings were extraordinarily interesting. From the procedural point of view the work of the Committee was definitely on the rails. I had no intention of allowing the questions to be side-tracked by any manoeuvre. This is an important factor to note because as I have explained the question of the government of Palestine was so embedded in past and long-sustained feuds as well as in noble and legitimate ambitions that the matter was always capable of trespassing into the field of irrelevance with the probability or even certainty that the work of the committee would end with no decision except an adjournment until 1948.

But by now the situation was completely different. With the list of speakers duly closed, each delegate knew that, except for the discussion of specific amendments, his speech would be his last.

I was taken by surprise, however, when the chief representative of Egypt having spoken, his deputy claimed the right to follow him in the argument. I was disturbed by the claim but thought it best to settle the matter in the interests of free expression as both Egyptian delegates felt their position very keenly, taking the Arab view very strongly. I accordingly ruled in favour of the second delegate being permitted to supplement his leader's speech provided that the points covered were completely separated from those made by the senior delegate. The second delegate was Mr. Mahmoud Bey Fawzi who made a special feature of legal contentions and did his job well. Occasionally, however, he approached very close to the point where a legitimate warning of consequences was indistinguishable from a direct threat to the authority of the United Nations.

Some excellent speeches were delivered on the Monday and the great issue before the committee became more and more apparent, more and more stark. On several occasions I pointed out to the committee that soon they must come to the vote and that the only two real alternatives before them were the adoption of the Arab plan of unitary government for Palestine and the plan of political partition and economic union in Palestine together with a special trusteeship for Jerusalem as recommended by the majority of UNSCOP.

The result of my interventions was that all delegates could see that there was no escape from the fact that though theoretically they might vote against all proposals, in fact they could

Palestine: The Third Phase

hardly be loyal to the United Nations without making a definite choice of one or other of the alternatives before them.

In the late afternoon the spokesman for the Jewish Agency (Mr. Shertok) and for the Arab Higher Committee (Mr. Husseini) summed up their cases in the light of the speeches that had been delivered. On this occasion Mr. Shertok showed great skill in his practical attitude towards the proposals of the first committee on the alteration of boundaries.

On Monday afternoon the meeting continued until nearly seven o'clock, so I decided to resume the sitting at nine o'clock, pointing out to delegates as we adjourned that the voting would certainly commence that evening.

Delegates did not have time to take their meal in New York City with the result that the cafeteria at Lake Success was overcrowded and intense lobbying took place.

Action on Unitary Plan

At nine o'clock the sitting was resumed. I declared the debate closed and proceeded to the consideration of the specific proposals recommended by the second sub-committee for a unitary state for Palestine. These proposals came before us in the form of three specific recommendations.

The first dealt with the proposals to refer almost every aspect of the problem to the Court of International Justice. Some of the points to be referred were patently absurd, for instance the question whether or not the Balfour Declaration was a legally binding declaration. Obviously it was political in essence and character.

The only question on which there was any substantial argument was whether the United Nations itself had jurisdiction to reach a decision as to the future government of Palestine. The voting on this point was very close but the proposal for its reference to the Court was defeated.

As to the validity of the action proposed to be taken by the U.N. Assembly, I never had any doubt. The Palestine situation was obviously one likely to impair friendly relations among nations, and accordingly the Assembly was competent under Article 14 of the Charter to recommend measures for its peaceful adjustment, regardless of the origin of the situation. In addition the question also concerned the maintenance of international peace and security and accordingly the General Assembly could act under Article 11 of the Charter to call the attention of the Security Council to the position and make appropriate recommendations to all States concerned.

The United Kingdom Government, as the outgoing mandatory power, had referred the question of the Palestine Government to the Assembly. The Assembly at its Special Session earlier in the year had assumed jurisdiction over the matter by passing appropriate resolutions and by establishing a special committee to recommend to it on the whole subject of Palestine.

In these circumstances it would have been sufficient to have relied upon previous Assembly decisions and recommendations as establishing Assembly jurisdiction. But in my opinion the matter was even clearer than that. Articles 11 and 14 in the Charter, to which I have referred, gave the Assembly a clear right to make appropriate recommendations, and no legal question of interfering with the internal affairs of any country could possibly arise.

The British Government during its period as mandatory power had done a good job, and no doubt the mandate might have been confirmed and continued as a trusteeship. However, as the mandate was being surrendered, the legal vacuum thereby created had to be filled in some tangible way.

The next resolution to be put to the vote concerned the question of accepting Jewish refugees. Strictly speaking it was not entirely relevant to the question before the committee. The proposal could have been adopted without in any way determining how Palestine was to be governed in the future. In other words

Palestine: The Third Phase

the proposal was a perfect example of a side-tracking resolution which would have appeared to take action and yet would not have determined the precise and essential question before the committee.

This I felt it my duty shortly to indicate to the committee and they rejected this crucial proposal of the second committee by a substantial majority.

Accordingly we came to the primary resolution of Committee 2 favouring a plan for the unitary government of Palestine. The arguments against this plan as opposed to the plan for partition were very strong indeed. The Special Committee on Palestine had not recommended it. It would in effect have placed the Jews in Palestine entirely under the authority of the Arabs. There would have been no further Jewish immigration to Palestine on any scale. All hope of establishing a Jewish State or a national home for the Jews would have vanished, and the promises of the Balfour Declaration would have been dishonoured.

Amidst considerable excitement the resolution recommended by Committee 2 was submitted to vote by roll call.

Here I should explain my own position. I was chairman of the committee and considerable pressure was brought upon me in order that Australia should abstain on the vote. It was urged that I take advantage of my position as chairman to be so impartial as to express no opinion at all even on the final vote. No doubt it would not have been impossible for me to have abstained.

I had anticipated the situation and had been in close contact with the Australian Prime Minister, Mr. Chifley. I had pointed to the certainty of a roll-call vote in which the names of all countries are called in alphabetical order so that in a sense every country represented had to stand up and be counted. Accordingly I was authorized by the Australian Government to support the plan of partition, not because we had come to the Assembly with a preconceived view on the matter, but solely because the arguments and facts had convinced us that partition was the just solution to be adopted. Therefore Australia went on record voting against the recommendation of the second committee in favour of the unitary state.

The proposal was defeated by a majority of twenty-nine to twelve votes. The decisive vote was a great surprise to the Arab group to whom no doubt many promises and half promises had been made. It showed clearly that the strong trend in the committee was in favour of adopting the partition plan.

Final Consideration of Partition

I then said in effect: "The committee has now rejected all the proposals of the second committee, that is, reference of certain questions to the International Court; the plan for a general acceptance throughout the world of Jewish refugees; and the plan for the future government of Palestine in accordance with the principles of a unitary state. That leaves before you for consideration the plan of government recommended by Committee 1, which is a plan of partition, of economic union, and of international trusteeship for the Holy Cities of Jerusalem and Bethlehem. Before putting the vote for the plan as a whole, I shall take the amendments already submitted to the committee's report and I shall take them in the order in which they occur in the text of the recommended resolution itself."

There were nearly forty amendments to be dealt with. Some were not of great importance but many were. The hour was getting late and one or two suggestions for an adjournment were made, but I pressed on until some six or seven amendments were disposed of. In each case I permitted the proposer of the amendment to speak on it and wherever it was desired I allowed a debate, pointing out the necessity of strict adherence to the question covered by the amendment.

Here I must pay a great tribute to some of the Arab delegates. They had a perfect opportunity for filibustering and for pretending to oppose amendments merely in order to delay the proceedings of the committee. But they made no attempt to abuse the processes of the committee for this purpose.

At times I was hard-pressed myself in dealing with the amendments because some of them had been submitted tardily and they had to be arranged in the order of the very lengthy text recommended by the first committee.

In each case before putting each amendment to the vote I explained most carefully to the committee its meaning and effect in relation to the text as a whole. For this I was given generous thanks by the committee which, by this time, had been working for two months and which really needed assistance from the legal point of view in understanding the significance of each amendment.

In spite of the urgency of the matter and the very long debates which had taken place I felt I could not work the committee past 11.15 P.M. At this hour I adjourned until next morning, Tuesday. Before I did so, I indicated the procedure I would adopt next day, namely confine the debate to the specific amendments but permit a general statement either before or after taking the final vote on the partition plan as amended in any direction by the committee.

Tuesday was the day of culminating and intense excitement. Punctually at eleven o'clock we started and the committee was in a business-like mood. It was clear that the Arab group was not going to alter in principle the proposals for partition. Therefore, while some of their suggestions received a fair amount of attention, we made excellent progress.

The committee appreciated the way in which the amendments were brought to their attention. I continued to give them a careful and explicit explanation of each amendment after, and sometimes before, the speaker for the particular country sponsoring the amendment had spoken. At 12.45 P.M. it looked as though all the amendments would be disposed of before the luncheon adjournment.

However, we still had before us amendments involving reference of the Palestine question to the Security Council in the event of any attempt to alter the proposed settlement by force of arms. There appeared to be some dissent amongst the countries favouring partition as to the form of this resolution. Therefore Mr. Pearson, representing Canada, suggested an adjournment until the afternoon, and the committee accepted his suggestion. During the interval I saw Mr. Pearson and others concerned, and the apparent difficulties were soon removed.

The committee resumed punctually after lunch, everyone at last being eager for the kill, to use a phrase circulating in the lobbies at that time. The committee room was crowded. However the result turned out, history was in the making.

By ten minutes to three the last amendment was disposed of. Most of the amendments had been adopted. I told the Committee that it would now come to the crucial vote on the plan for the future government of Palestine based on partition, first recommended by UNSCOP, then elaborated and amended by Sub-Committee 1, and finally further amended by the Ad Hoc Assembly Committee now sitting.

As I had promised earlier, I permitted statements to be made both before and after the vote. The New Zealand delegate, Sir Carl Berendsen, explained that at the present time New Zealand could not support the plan but would abstain. The reason he gave was that no specific method of enforcing the Assembly's decision had been agreed upon.

Sir Carl put this case with his usual clarity and force. However, I felt that there was a great fallacy in his contention. The plain fact was that the General Assembly had no force at its disposal, and was never intended by the Charter to have any. On the contrary it was the Security Council which was intended by the Charter to have force at its disposal to deal with threats to the peace. The complete answer to Sir Carl was that the Assembly itself could and should make its recommendation, even though that recommendation might be defied by some members or non-members of the United Nations. After all the recommendation

Palestine: The Third Phase

of the Assembly had a tremendous moral force as representing the overwhelming body of opinion of the governments and peoples of the world. This moral force was the real sanction of all Assembly decisions. Physical force could be used if invoked by the Security Council. In addition the Assembly resolution expressly contemplated that the new Jewish State and the new Arab State in Palestine would each be entitled to establish its own military force.

While these facts provided in my judgment an answer to Sir Carl, the time for debate was finished and what he was doing in effect was simply giving a reason for not supporting the partition plan at that stage.

VOTE FOR PARTITION

Then we came to the vote, the three first countries being Afghanistan, Argentina and Australia—the then rules requiring alphabetical order.

Once again, as I have previously pointed out, Australia could not escape the vote and did not wish to escape it simply because I was chairman. I was finally convinced of the fairness and justice of the majority plan in favour of partition and had already prepared a short statement to explain the vote of Australia in case it should be needed. However, no one was in doubt about the correctness of my position, and I shall always remember with pride and satisfaction the tributes paid to me by several of the main Arab spokesmen for insisting on their always having a complete and adequate opportunity of presenting their case.

The question was "whether the Palestine committee approved of the plan for partition of Palestine as amended by their own series of amendments." Those in favour were to say 'yes,' those against were to say 'no,' and those abstaining were to say 'abstain.'

Afghanistan, the first country, had been closely associated

with Pakistan which had taken a leading part in supporting the Arab case, and was itself a leading Moslem state. Afghanistan therefore said 'no.'

Argentina, the second country, which had never quite committed itself, said 'abstain.'

It became my duty on behalf of Australia to vote next and Australia said 'yes.' There was an excited cheer.

So the roll call continued till the end with the voting twenty-five yes, thirteen no, and seventeen abstentions. The Assembly procedure for all its committees lays down that a simple majority is sufficient to make a recommendation to the plenary sessions of the Assembly. Accordingly I at once pronounced the recommendation in favour of the partition to be duly carried and stated that the recommendation would immediately be forwarded to the plenary session of the Assembly. I declared the business of the special Ad Hoc Committee finished, and adjourned the Committee for the last time.

It will be noticed that the vote—twenty-five–thirteen—was one short of a two-thirds majority, which in accordance with the Charter is the majority required in the plenary sessions of the Assembly for important recommendations. If New Zealand had voted 'yes' instead of abstaining, the vote would have been twenty-six–thirteen giving precisely a two-thirds majority.

I felt at once that the plenary Assembly would adopt the recommendation of the Ad Hoc Committee. For one thing, I was certain that New Zealand would support the proposal on reconsideration despite any apparent difficulties it might have. In addition I knew that one or two other countries abstaining had been on the point of voting yes and that one or two which had voted no might well reverse their attitude or abstain when the proposal went up finally.

Accordingly I felt that the proceedings of the committee would not end in futility but in success. I was particularly happy that the hard work of so many months had been crowned with a definite result. I felt the decision to be just, I felt it to be warranted

Palestine: The Third Phase

by the great principles of the United Nations Charter and its declaration in favour of self-determination.

It is true that these principles were not simple in their application to a special situation such as that of Palestine. Nonetheless great forces had been operating in favour of the decision. The merciless persecution inflicted on the Jews by the Germans under Hitler had aroused a feeling of deep compassion for the Jews, which in itself was quite consistent with and strengthened the desire for a speedy settlement of the Palestine question. The decision of Britain to surrender the mandate and in effect invite the United Nations General Assembly to offer a just solution, really imposed on the United Nations a duty to make a definite decision in the matter.

Accordingly I shared a great feeling of achievement at the result, a feeling which was heightened by the personal delight of being able to say that a job had been done successfully and that I had done my own duty to the United Nations and could proceed home after a most strenuous session. I immediately summoned a press conference which was very crowded, and summed up my views on the problem in order to explain the vote of Australia and myself, and also, frankly, to assist in securing the adoption of the recommendations by the plenary session of the Assembly.

Great emotion was shown at the end of all these proceedings. Jewish people and their supporters had struggled for years to bring about the establishment of a new State of Israel, and tears were streaming down their cheeks as the corridors were still filled. Their display of gratitude towards myself was most touching. I had only done what I believed was just and right as a good United Nations follower.

The Mayor of New York, knowing my anxiety to join the afternoon train on my way back to Australia, had provided me with an outrider escort and I had to leave the committee at Lake Success quickly, almost at once.

I was so exhausted that I could hardly speak to the large

crowd of Australian friends who had come to see my wife and myself off from Grand Central Station. However, I could not rest until I had made a report and sent a telegram to President Aranha, restating to him the issue as I saw it and expressing the hope and belief that the necessary two-thirds majority would be obtained in the plenary session of the Assembly.

The final vote of the plenary session of the General Assembly was in favour of partition, thirty-three votes against thirteen.

History was made.

XIII

PALESTINE: THE FOURTH PHASE

THE subsequent story of the State of Israel was based on the general principles of that Assembly decision.

It was always apparent to me that the economic union contemplated by the resolution of the Assembly could not be set up for some considerable time. The economic plan depended upon co-operation between Arabs and Jews.

Moreover, no sooner was the decision of the Assembly given than some of the Arab States resolved to make war against that decision. This brought into existence the very situation which the Assembly had contemplated and in relation to which the Security Council had been requested to act against those endeavouring to upset the recommendation by force of arms.

All this appears quite clearly from the report of the Commission established by the Assembly to bring into existence the partition plan.

The next step in the historical process was the calling of a special meeting of the General Assembly, described by Mr. Sumner Welles as follows:

"With each week that passed Arab aggression became more flagrant. The Arab states adjacent to Palestine permitted the enlistment and arming of Arab volunteers within their boundaries. These troops received arms from several other Moslem countries. As Arab aggression against the Jews became more serious, the Jews of Palestine undertook acts of retaliation. The Haganah which, prior to the announcement of a Palestine settlement, had been the major Jewish resistance force, and which had co-operated with the Jewish Agency, constituted itself the nucleus of the Jewish militia envisaged in the partition plan."

Mr. Welles takes the view that the Assembly in November should have made provision for enforcement of its decisions. However, the Assembly had requested the Security Council in November to regard as a breach of the peace under Article 39 of the Charter "any attempt to alter by force the settlement envisaged by this resolution."

As I have already pointed out, the Assembly itself had no jurisdiction whatever to do more than make a recommendation. Every person of common sense must have known that the danger of Arab resistance was inevitable. Certainly the Ad Hoc Committee of the Assembly had relied upon the Security Council taking up a definite stand in defence of the Assembly decision in the event which actually happened—that is, defiance by some of the Arab states of the Assembly decision.

The truth was that the three key permanent members of the Security Council—the United States, the United Kingdom, and Russia—were not in agreement as to Security Council action.

The United Kingdom had made its position clear, that it would not actively enforce any settlement unless both Jews and Arabs agreed upon the settlement. At the same time it is equally clear that the United Kingdom would not have opposed Security Council decisions enforcing the Charter against any aggressor state.

Such aggressive action was made clear by the Palestine Commission on April 14. It stated that Arab elements, both inside and outside Palestine, had exerted organized, intensive effort toward defeating the purposes of the resolution of the General Assembly. To this end, threats, acts of violence, and infiltration of organized, armed, uniformed Arab bands in Palestine territory had been employed. As early as the 16th of February the Commission, in its first special report to the Security Council, stated that "powerful Arab interests, both inside and outside Palestine, are defying the resolution of the General Assembly and are engaged in a deliberate effort to alter by force the settlement envisaged therein."

Undoubtedly it was the uncertain action of the United States before the Security Council which caused the greatest confusion. According to their distinguished delegate, the Charter of the United Nations did not empower the Security Council to enforce a political settlement, whether it was pursuant to a recommendation of the General Assembly or of the Council itself. What this meant is this: The Council under the Charter can take action to prevent aggression against Palestine from outside. The Council by these same powers can take action to prevent a threat to international peace and security from inside Palestine. But this action must be directed solely to the maintenance of international peace. The Council's action, in other words, is directed to keeping the peace and not to enforcing partition.

Mr. Sumner Welles' criticism and analysis of this statement are unanswerable. (See his book, *We Need Not Fail*, pages 98 *ff.*) The truth is that in the Charter there is a power and duty to keep the peace. If that peace is based upon a United Nations decision in favour of partition, then the duty is to protect, by force if necessary, the carrying out of the settlement made by the United Nations authorities.

Attempt to Upset Assembly Decision

I believe that Mr. Sumner Welles is right in saying that when the special Assembly, requested by the United States, met on 16th April, 1948, "the prestige of the United Nations had reached its lowest ebb." I am not able to speak from personal knowledge as to whether the organization of the session was, as Mr. Welles also says, "weighted heavily on the Arab side."

I have repeatedly emphasized that the United Nations Assembly decision was given not upon the basis of agreement between Arabs and Jews but solely on the basis of a just and impartial settlement of a dispute as to the future government of Palestine. In other words, it was because Arabs and Jews could *not* agree that the United Nations jurisdiction was invoked. However, the United States was now suggesting in fact that the settlement in November would have to be ripped up to give the Arabs and Jews an opportunity of reaching agreement, when by definition such agreement was impossible. For that purpose the United States proposed to establish a temporary trusteeship of Palestine under the Trusteeship Council of the United Nations.

It was impossible for me to attend the special Assembly, but on behalf of the Australian Government I did everything possible to make it clear that the proposed trusteeship plan was absolutely contrary to the solemn decision of the Assembly. Dean Gildersleeve who had done valuable work at the conference at San Francisco, had also put forward a proposal to the effect that some sort of compromise must be agreed to by both the Arabs and the Jews.

I was distressed and disturbed that all the work of the UNSCOP and of the Ad Hoc Committee of 1947 were in danger of being set at nought.

I could not leave Australia at that time but I sent a message which was broadcast throughout the world with the object of making it clear that the proposed trusteeship plan was not only inadmissible and indefensible in itself, but represented a complete setting aside of the decision of the previous Assembly. I attempted to lay down the following principles:

(1) Decisions of a competent international conference should be accepted after there has been full inquiry and fair debate and a just settlement has been reached.

(2) The United Nations decision was reached by more than a two-thirds majority, the only dissentients being the Arab states and certain nations associated very closely with them. The decision was a just and impartial one and must not be lightly set aside.

(3) After all that had occurred, to throw the solution into the melting pot again might be very damaging to the authority of the United Nations.

(4) It had been contended that the enforcement of the Assembly's decision was not possible. But had the great powers who supported the

proposal at Lake Success adhered firmly to it, there would have been little difficulty.

(5) In any event, under the Assembly's decisions the new Jewish state and the new Arab state was each to be entitled to establish its own military forces for the defence of the new territory, and this decision clearly carried with it the rights of Jews as well as Arabs to import arms and equipment for the purpose of defence.

(6) In my opinion the United Nations decision had been gradually undermined by intrigues directed against the Jewish people.

(7) It would be little short of a tragedy if the fundamental rights of self-government were to be denied to both the Jews and the Arabs, as it was guaranteed to them under the Assembly's decision.

(8) The only considerations that should influence the United Nations were those of justice and fair dealing to all concerned. It would be most disturbing if mere considerations of power politics or of expediency were allowed to destroy the decision.

In the above eight points I indicated my views with complete frankness and, I think, clarity. There is not the slightest doubt that many people set themselves out deliberately to destroy the Assembly decision of 1947 instead of standing up for that decision, as the Security Council was morally bound to do. Quite apart from any force, firm declarations by the Security Council in pursuance of the request of the Assembly would probably have prevented any serious combat.

I was satisfied that the expedient of trusteeship would have turned out to be little more than a device to set aside the Assembly decision and to remit the matter to where it was before the United Kingdom had referred it to the Assembly. This would have aggravated the already acute disagreement between Jews and Arabs, and would have certainly led to fighting.

One extraordinary feature of the arguments put forward at that time was the ridiculous suggestion that the Assembly decision had led to violent conflict between Arabs and Jews. This suggestion is completely foolish. If no Assembly decision had been given in November and if the United Kingdom had withdrawn from the mandate in 1948, in that event full scale war between Arabs and Jews would undoubtedly have broken out.

The truth is that the moral force of the Assembly decision daunted the Arabs to a considerable extent and equally persuaded the Jews to base their hopes of establishing the new State of Israel upon the action of the United Nations.

As it turned out the trusteeship proposal was riddled both on grounds of legality and on grounds of plain justice, and all that was done by the special Assembly was to give its blessing to the mediatory functions of the Security Council.

This left in substance the November decision of the Assembly in favour of partition still standing.

The next step in the history of Palestine is the recent General Assembly in Paris. The essence of its consideration of the Palestine question was the rejection of any attempt to alter the boundaries as determined by the Assembly resolution of November 1947, except where changes might be agreed upon between the Jews on the one hand and the neighbouring states and peoples on the other.

The basic decision in favour of political partition and the establishment of an international trusteeship for Jerusalem still remains unchallenged.

While the General Assembly at Paris was considering the question, the Security Council did not accept a proposal to admit the new state of Israel as a member of the United Nations. This decision can be explained on a number of grounds, the chief one being that an armistice had not yet been arranged in Palestine. I never doubted that Israel would soon be admitted because the 1947 Assembly resolution expressly contemplated such admission.

Recognition of Israel

At that time however quite a number of nations had not given formal recognition to the Government of Israel. In January 1948, however, de facto recognition was forthcoming from a number of states including the United Kingdom, France and New Zealand.

The Australian Government also announced *full recognition* to the Government of Israel. The Australian Prime Minister (Mr. Chifley) pointed out that it was in accordance with the policy of the Australian Government to give unwavering support of the decisions of the United Nations. Since the Assembly decision in favour of partition, the State of Israel had come into formal existence, a provisional government had been formed, and democratic elections had been conducted. It was clear that the new State had come to stay.

Mr. Chifley pointed out that, just as Israel had been created as a result of United Nations decisions, so too Israel had a role and duties to perform in fulfilment of United Nations principles and decisions. He said: "The Government of Australia believes that the new nation of Israel will be a force of special value in the world community and it confidently looks to Israel to assist in carrying out the United Nations decision declaring the special international status of Jerusalem as the Holy City. When the application of Israel comes before the General Assembly Australia will warmly support the admission of Israel to the United Nations."

Subsequently I was asked to explain whether full recognition meant *de jure* recognition as well as *de facto* recognition. My answer was in the affirmative, and was as follows:

Australia's decision to give recognition to the Government of Israel was as inevitable as it is just. As Chairman of the Special Palestine Committee of 1947, which worked for months on the problem of Palestine, I feel that a further stage has been reached in the establishment, on United Nations initiation, of a new Nation. Australia's one objective was to reach a fair and just solution, and I believe that that objective has now been satisfactorily reached.

The legal basis of Israel is unassailable. It rests on the decision of the United Nations Assembly of 1947 which contemplated the coming into existence of the new State and its subsequent recognition as a member of the United Nations. Moreover, the territorial boundaries of Israel were fixed by the decision of 1947 and these boundaries must remain until they are altered, either by the General Assembly, or by the agreement of Israel with the other states and peoples directly concerned.

The act of recognition was, therefore, a logical consequence of the basic United Nations decision of 1947, and it is the established policy of the Australian Government and of the Australian Labour Movement to give unwavering support to the decisions and principles of the United Nations. The distinction between *de facto* and *de jure* recognition which may have application in cases of Governments brought into existence as a result of internal revolution, has no application to the present case. The *de jure* or legal foundation in this case, is the Assembly decision operating in relation to the termination of the previously existing mandate.

This act does not imply anything but friendly relations with Arab States. Australia was among the first Nations to provide practical relief to Arab refugees when requested to do so last year. Moreover, we have always recognised the validity of the action taken when the State of Trans Jordania was brought into existence following upon the end of the Trans Jordania mandate.

Shortly afterwards I received a message of thanks from Mr. Shertok the Foreign Minister of Israel as follows:

On behalf of the Government of Israel I wish to convey its deep satisfaction at the full recognition extended to Israel by the Australian Government and communicated in your cable dated January 19, 1949. We gratefully recall the independent and constructive part played by Australia in shaping a United Nations solution providing for Jewish statehood and in defending that solution also the statesmanship shown by yourself personally as chairman of the ad hoc committee on Palestine in 1947 and as President of the third regular Session of the General Assembly in 1948. The Government of Israel feels heartened at the confidence expressed by your government in Israel's future and anticipates fruitful cooperation with Australia within the framework of the United Nations. The Government of Israel is seeking an early and peaceful settlement of all outstanding questions including that of Jerusalem and feels convinced that the recognition accorded by the Australian Government will materially contribute towards that end.

The Australian Government was the first of the western governments to accord full recognition to Israel. A few days later the United States Government did the same.

So far as *de facto* recognition was concerned, that merely

meant that the Government of Israel was effectively in occupation of a certain portion of territory and was exercising its governing powers in a more or less permanent manner upon that territory. Such *de facto* sovereignty of the Government of Israel was obvious for all the world to see.

It is difficult to understand the hesitations in according *de jure* recognition of Israel. That only meant that the legal basis of the Government of Israel is sound.

The legal basis of the Government and State of Israel is utterly unassailable, because it exists in the Assembly decision of November 1947. That decision addressed itself to a situation which would come into existence when the mandatory power had withdrawn from Palestine and a legal vacuum had been created. To fill this vacuum the plan of the United Nations was to sponsor and authorize the establishment of two states, one of which—the Jewish State—would be Israel.

Accordingly, it seems wrong to deny full legality to the Government of Israel, and in my opinion it is a government duly established in accordance with international law. Its boundaries are determined by the Assembly resolutions excepting so far as they may be altered by consent of all parties concerned or by the authority of the United Nations itself.

I regard the establishment of Israel as a great victory for the United Nations. The attitude of the General Assembly in the special Assembly of 1947, the regular Assembly of 1947, the special Assembly of 1948, and the regular Assembly of 1948 has been sound and just. It has sought to bring and apply the touchstone of fairness and justice to the problem before it. Even under great pressure it has not deviated from its conception of right and duty.

It is true no doubt that if the Jewish people had not stood firmly to defend the territories allocated to them by the United Nations they would probably have been overwhelmed. The new nation owes a great deal to those who fought with their bodies for its establishment. Yet in the main it is the United Nations representing the opinion of the peoples of the world, and particularly the Assembly of the United Nations, which should be given the primary credit for the establishment of Israel which will undoubtedly become a valuable member in the world community of nations.

On 4th March, 1949 the Security Council, with Egypt dissenting and the United Kingdom abstaining, decided that in its judgment Israel was a peace-loving state and was able and willing to carry out the obligations contained in the Charter. Accordingly the Council recommended to the General Assembly that it admit Israel to membership in the United Nations.

In the Assembly those who were opposed to the admission of Israel attempted in various ways to prevent a favourable decision being reached on its application. Some countries opposed admission outright, while others pressed for deferment until the fourth session. There were also attempts to have the question considered as late as possible in the agenda in the hope that the session would close before action could be taken. In accordance with our past record, Australia took the lead in defeating all attempts to dodge or postpone a decision.

All these attempts failed. In the ad hoc political committee, to which the matter was referred, Australia joined with a number of other countries in introducing a resolution admitting Israel to membership. This was later adopted by the General Assembly in plenary session by a vote of 37 in favour and 12 against.

The representative of Israel thereupon took his place in the United Nations, on 11th May. Israel has won the struggle for recognition as a member of the community of nations. This did not mean an automatic solution of all the problems connected with Palestine. But those of us who assumed leadership in the Palestinian question were convinced that the problem could be dealt with far more justly, providing Israel became a full member of the United Nations. And we look to Israel's becoming a very active member of the U.N.—having faith and confidence that outstanding questions will be handled in the spirit of the U.N.—the spirit of justice and fair play—by which alone U.N. members like Australia approached the entire problem of Palestine.

XIV

INDONESIA

THE Indonesian question is another example of the way in which the United Nations approaches situations which endanger peace. There is no doubt that if the United Nations had not intervened, there would have been much greater loss of life in Indonesia and the chances of a just settlement would have been far less.

The Dutch have governed the East Indies for over three hundred years. During that time they have made substantial contributions to the economic development of the islands and to increasing the welfare of its inhabitants. Though for several centuries it has not been self-governing, Indonesia contains many old civilizations, often with a high degree of culture and art and with complicated social structures.

Strong nationalist movements have existed in Indonesia for a long time and there have sometimes been actual uprisings. In the past, some of the Indonesian leaders were exiled and imprisoned and these included a few men who were later to occupy high office in the Republic of Indonesia.

The Birth of the Republic

The situation was drastically altered by the advent of war. The Dutch administration stood firm against the blandishments and threats of the Japanese after the fall of Holland. However, when Japan declared war against the Western powers she swept south rapidly and the Indies were soon occupied.

Japanese occupation released some of the nationalist aspirations which had been held down in the past. Several of the leaders who had been exiled were given prominent positions in the regimes set up by the military authorities. The Japanese hoped in this way to keep the Indonesian people contented and reduce the burden of supervision and government which would have otherwise fallen upon the Japanese administration. The playing up of native leaders also served to diminish the prestige and influence of the Western powers generally. It is unlikely, however, that the Japanese really intended ever to give the Indonesians any independence from Japanese dictation, and in point of fact the Indonesians often suffered from Japanese barbarities in a manner similar to the Europeans. The Japanese "new order in Asia" was really a cloak for an imperialism which was more brutal and oppressive than anything that could have been conceived.

When the occupation authorities saw the Japanese Empire crumbling around their heads, an Indonesian Republic was hastily improvised. Therefore when the British army arrived to accept the Japanese surrender and restore Netherlands sovereignty, they found themselves compelled to deal, not only with the representatives of the Dutch administration which was ready to return, but also with the new Indonesian provisional republic which was in no mood to go right back to the position which had existed up to 1941.

The British authorities had a most difficult task, which they discharged with great efficiency and humanity. It is tragic that in those early months a satisfactory solution could not have been found which would have allowed the Dutch to resume a position in the Indies but at the same time have satisfied the legitimate aspirations of the Indonesian people for self government.

The Indonesian leaders on the whole were moderate men who were realistic enough to appreciate the difficulties of establishing a new government. When we consider the extremism that marks most revolutionary movements, we can only admire the restraint which was exercised by so many of the Indonesian leaders and the skill they showed in curbing the recalcitrance of some of their followers. Even so, some excesses occurred and these hampered negotiations with the Dutch, who were naturally embittered by any reports of atrocities.

The Dutch, on their part, do not seem to have taken a sufficiently realistic view of the situation and were unduly inflexible. The pre-war conditions had disappeared forever but the Dutch seemed slow to appreciate this. They at times resented the efforts of their friends to assist them to work out an equitable solution. United Kingdom commanders in Indonesia were sometimes bitterly criticized by the Dutch. The efforts of Australia, which were not directed against the Dutch but solely in the interests of finding a solution satisfactory to both parties, were similarly misunderstood and misrepresented. As a result, the Dutch find themselves today in a position which is far worse than need have existed, or would have existed had they adopted a more conciliatory approach in the earlier years.

Yet there were not lacking statements by Dutch leaders which, if effectively translated into action, could have contributed to an early settlement. Her Majesty the Queen of the Netherlands had said in a speech on 6th December 1942, exactly a year after Japan struck: "I know that no political unity or national cohesion can endure which are not upheld by the voluntary acceptance and the faith of the great majority of the citizenry."

And much later, on 15th August 1947, the Netherlands Ministry of Foreign Affairs, was to say:

"The very early phases after the Japanese capitulation confirmed the expectations of the Netherlands Government that the war had caused such a change in outlook both in the Indies and in the Netherlands that there could be no question of a restoration, in whatever form, of the colonial relationship between the Netherlands and Indonesia."

It is not easy for a nation to accept in deed as well as in word that the old order has passed. But the British did so in India, Ceylon, and Burma, and thereby built up a new friendship which is stronger than any of the old links. But neither the Dutch nor the Indonesians really trusted one another's intentions, and so the dangerous situation drifted on without the chances of a settlement becoming any greater.

The Linggadjati Agreement

It was announced on 7th September 1946 that all British forces would be withdrawn from the Netherlands Indies by 30th November because the tasks for which they had entered the Indies, the evacuation of Allied prisoners of war and internees and the disarming of the Japanese, would be completed by that date. It was stated in London that the British Government "is anxious that an agreement may be reached by political discussion, but the future of the Netherlands Indies is not their responsibility and the Dutch and the Indonesians must work out the problem themselves."

The approaching withdrawal of British troops gave further impetus to the discussions which had been going on in an effort to reach agreement. At the beginning of 1946 Lord Inverchapel had been sent to the Indies to try to bring the parties together and at one stage seemed to be on the verge of a settlement. Later Lord Killearn attempted the same ungrateful task, and worked not only with great skill and patience but with the utmost devotion to the cause of peace and justice. He made an outstanding contribution to an ultimate solution of the Indonesian dispute.

A truce agreement was signed on 14th October between the Netherlands and the Indonesians, which was designed to put an end to all military activity on either side. Hopes were raised that clashes between the supporters of the Dutch and the Republic would henceforth cease, and the Lieutenant Governor General (Dr. H. J. van Mook) made a statement which was to read very ironically some months later, for he paid a tribute to the Indonesian leaders who, he said, had "understood that the Netherlands army does not stand ready to jump upon the young Republic and efface it from the world, but that, together with them, it will struggle for a state of affairs in which liberty and independence will be lastingly guaranteed."

Meetings continued between Dutch and Indonesian delegates in an attempt to reach a political settlement and eventually, on 15th November at a conference presided over by Lord Killearn, representatives of the Netherlands and the Republic initialled an agreement. This agreement is known as the Linggadjati Agreement, after the name of the town where it was initialled. It is also sometimes referred to as the Cheribon Agreement, after a bigger town a few miles to the north east of Linggadjati and originally designated as the meeting place.

The Linggadjati Agreement is one of the milestones in the Indonesian story. Under the first article, the Netherlands Government recognized the Government of the Republic of Indonesia as exercising *de facto* authority over Java, Madura, and Sumatra. The areas within those territories which were at that time occupied by Allied or Dutch forces were to be included gradually through mutual co-operation in Republican territory, at the latest by 1st January, 1949.

The two governments were to cooperate in the rapid formation of a sovereign democratic state on a federal basis, to be called the United States of Indonesia. This would comprise all the territories of the Netherlands Indies with the exception of those territories whose population after due consultation with the other territories should decide by a democratic process not to join.

A Netherlands-Indonesian Union was to be established consisting on the one hand of the Netherlands, Surinam, and Curaçao, and on the other hand of the United States of Indonesia. The Queen of the Netherlands was to be the head of the Netherlands-Indonesian Union. A Statute for the Union should contain provisions to safeguard the rights of both parties and to regulate the method and conditions of the assistance to be given by the Netherlands to the United States of Indonesia as long as the services of the latter were not sufficiently organized.

The two Governments were to endeavour to establish the United States of Indonesia and the Netherlands-Indonesian Union before the 1st January, 1949. Immediately after the formation of the Union, the Netherlands was to take the necessary steps to obtain admission of the United States of Indonesia to the United Nations.

The Government of the Republic recognized the claims of all non-Indonesians to the restoration of their rights and the restitution of their goods in the territory over which the Republic exercised *de facto* authority.

Article 17 provided for an organization containing representatives of the two governments to facilitate co-operation between them. It also provided that the governments should settle by arbitration any dispute which might arise from this agreement and which could not be solved by joint consultations in a conference between those delegations. In that case a chairman of another nationality, with a casting vote, was to be appointed by agreement between the delegations, or if such an agreement could not be reached, by the President of the International Court of Justice.

This Article 17 was frequently referred to later in the Security Council by the Australian representative, for the Dutch subsequently resorted to force without first attempting to carry out that provision providing for arbitration.

The Linggadjati Agreement raised great hopes of a peaceful and just settlement. These hopes however were not fulfilled. A certain amount of military activity of a rather disorganized nature continued to take place and though it did not amount to open hostilities, there were nevertheless constant friction and incidents.

The political talks also failed to reach an agreement on the carrying out of the Linggadjati Agreement. Nevertheless a lot of progress was made and the main points of dispute were narrowed down to three: the position of the representative of the Netherlands Crown in relation to the proposed interim government of the United States of Indonesia; the conduct of foreign relations of the Republic; and the question of a joint gendarmerie, for the Republic insisted that each state should be free to establish its own constabulary within its own borders. Even on these three points it seemed that an agreement could be reached. The Republican Premier, Dr. Sjahrir, went to considerable lengths in an effort to prevent a breakdown in the negotiations. In the end his moderate policy caused him to lose the confidence of some of his supporters and on 27th June he and his cabinet resigned and were replaced by Dr. Amir Sjarifoeddin. But the latter also showed himself prepared to accept a reasonable settlement and to work for an agreement, and he intimated his willingness to accept the Dutch wishes on the first two of the three disputed points.

Dr. van Mook and Dr. Sjarifoeddin accordingly reached an agreement on 15th July which provided for complete cessation of defensive preparations on both sides. At this stage only the question of the constabulary remained outstanding. The new agreement was intended to relieve tension and allow time for a search for a solution of the problem of the constabulary. But there was an absence of mutual trust and neither side appears to have been willing of its own accord to implement this agreement.

Fighting Breaks Out Again

At midnight on 20th July 1947 large-scale fighting began on Java and Sumatra between armed forces of the Netherlands and the Republic of Indonesia. In a letter to the Security Council the representative of the Netherlands described this action as "police-measures of a strictly limited character" and said they had been made necessary by the inability of the Republican Government to maintain security, law, and order in its territory. The Netherlands representative claimed that violence and destruction were occurring in the Republican and adjacent territories, that hostages were still being imprisoned and held by the Republicans, and that hostile and inflammatory propaganda was being maintained by them. The letter stated that the Netherlands "as the state with whom the sovereignty of this territory rests" was consequently ultimately responsible for maintaining law and order and could not allow these inimical actions to continue.

This development caused great concern to the Australian Government, not only because Indonesia is adjacent to our territory, but also because we are bound by the closest possible economic and commercial ties with this important area. The outbreak of fighting affected the well-being and stability of the whole of the Southwest Pacific and Southeast Asian regions.

Accordingly on 30th July the Australian Government brought the hostilities to the attention of the Security Council. It informed the Council that the Australian Government considered that these hostilities constituted a breach of the peace under Article 39 of the Charter, and urged the Council to take immediate action to restore international peace and security. Australia proposed that the Security Council, as a provisional measure and without prejudice to the rights, claims, or position of the parties concerned, should call upon the governments of the Netherlands and the Republic of Indonesia to cease hostilities forthwith and to commence arbitration in accordance with Article 17 of the Linggadjati Agreement.

In earlier disputes brought before the Security Council, Australia had pursued the course of urging investigation under Article 34 of the Charter before any decisions were reached. The situation in Indonesia, however, differed from any raised previously because hostilities were actually being carried on and it was essential that these hostilities should cease immediately, even before any investigations were undertaken. Australia's action marked the first time in the history of the Security Council that Article 39 had been invoked.

(Article 39 of the Charter comes within Chapter VII which

covers action with respect to threats to the peace, breaches of the peace, and acts of aggression. A determination under Article 39 would make it possible for the Council to order the disputing parties to comply with its decisions and in the absence of such compliance the Council could proceed with enforcement measures. Article 34 on the other hand is part of Chapter VI covering the pacific settlement of disputes and authorizes investigation and mediation but not enforcement.)

On the same day the Indian delegation also called the attention of the Security Council to the situation in Indonesia. The Government of India acted under Article 34(1) of the Charter, but in the Council debates the Indian representative supported the Australian proposal that action should be taken under Article 39.

The Security Council acted very quickly and on 1st August adopted a resolution by eight votes to none with France, the U.K., and Belgium abstaining, calling upon both parties to cease hostilities forthwith, to settle their disputes by arbitration or by other peaceful means, and to keep the Security Council informed about the progress of the settlement.

During the Council discussion the Netherlands representative maintained that the whole matter came under the domestic jurisdiction of the Netherlands and that therefore, because of Article 2(7) of the Charter, the Security Council was not competent to act. The Netherlands continued to assert that it had complete sovereignty over the Republic of Indonesia. Against this, however, other representatives pointed out that in the Linggadjati Agreement the Government of the Republic of Indonesia had been recognized by the Netherlands Government as exercising a *de facto* government over Java, Madura, and Sumatra; that the two governments had negotiated together and had reached various agreements; and that the Republic had been given *de facto* recognition by a number of other governments, including the United Kingdom, United States of America, Australia, India, and members of the Arab League.

The Council had acted very quickly up till now, but in the next stage dangers of delay appeared. Both parties complied with the request to stop fighting but there were indications that the cease-fire was not being properly observed. Moreover, the second part of the resolution providing for arbitration was not put into effect. The United States had offered to mediate in the dispute. This offer was accepted by the Netherlands, but the Republican authorities did not find mediation acceptable and did not find the good offices of only one country acceptable.

The situation was full of dangers as, while there was a truce, there was no negotiation or contact between the two parties. Incidents were likely to occur each day which might make negotiations more difficult.

The Australian Government therefore announced on 7th August that if both parties considered it would help to commence negotiations immediately, the Australian Government would be prepared to act jointly with the United States Government in the capacity of mediator and arbitrator. This offer was immediately accepted by the Indonesians, but the Netherlands authorities did not indicate their acceptance.

In the meantime discussions were continuing in the Security Council. The Australian Government was concerned at the continuing delay and kept pressing for further action in the Council. On 13th August the Australian representative presented to the Security Council a draft resolution which proposed the establishment of a commission to arbitrate. Eventually, on 25th August, the Council adopted a resolution authorizing the establishment of a committee of observers consisting of career consular representatives in Batavia (representing U.K., U.S., China, Australia, France, and Belgium) to report on the situation in the Republic, covering the observance of the cease-fire orders and conditions prevailing in the areas. The Security Council tendered its good offices to the parties in order to assist in the pacific settlement of their dispute, and offered to establish a committee of the Council consisting of three members of the

Council, each party selecting one, and the third member to be designated by the other two who had been so selected.

This resolution was accepted by both the Republic and the Netherlands. The Indonesians nominated Australia, and the Netherlands nominated Belgium. I discussed the matter in New York with the representative of the Belgian Government and we agreed on the choice of the United States of America as the third member of the Committee of Good Offices.

The American representative (Dr. Frank Graham) and the Belgian representative (Mr. Paul Van Zeeland) flew to Australia where they joined the Australian member (Mr. Justice Kirby) and held their first meeting. Then they flew on to Batavia where they arrived on 27th October.

The Good Offices Committee

The principal scene of United Nations activities was now shifted from New York to the Indies, where the Good Offices Committee and the Consular Commission laboured to carry out their mandate from the Security Council.

The Consular Commission had reported to the Council on 11th October that there was a complete absence of confidence on the part of both Dutch and Indonesians, that neither side intended to observe the order to cease hostilities, and that neither had made any move towards agreement to give effect to that order. The Dutch continued to mop up behind the lines to which they had advanced, while the Indonesians continued to resist in those areas to which both they and the Dutch laid claim.

A protracted debate ensued in the Security Council on ways of bringing hostilities to a stop. Difference of opinion appeared as to what areas the respective troops were entitled to occupy. Ultimately on 31st October the Council adopted a resolution calling upon both sides to consult one another on means of giving effect to the earlier cease-fire resolution. The Committee of Good

Offices was asked to assist the parties in reaching agreement on these arrangements, with the further aid of the Consular Commission. The Council said that its original resolution calling for a cessation of hostilities "should be interpreted as meaning that the use of armed forces of either party by hostile action to extend its control over territory not occupied by it at 4th August 1947 was inconsistent with the Council's resolution."

In this discouraging atmosphere the Committee of Good Offices began its work. Hostilities continued despite the Council's resolution, so that the Committee had to devote a great part of its efforts to ending the fighting, at the same time as it was trying to bring about a political settlement.

Their efforts were rewarded by the acceptance by both sides, on 17th January 1948, of a truce agreement and also an agreement on certain principles as a basis for subsequent political and economic discussions. This was known as the Renville Agreement, because it was reached aboard the United States naval transport *Renville*. This ship had been made available by the United States Government in order to break a deadlock between the two parties as to a meeting ground, as neither was willing for the conference to be held in the territory of the other.

The two parties agreed on twelve principles, which can be summarized as follows:

1. The Committee of Good Offices would continue to assist in securing an agreement which would carry out the Linggadjati settlement.
2. Freedom of speech and assembly should be guaranteed, but the guarantee would not include the advocacy of violence or reprisals.
3. Changes in the administration of any territory would be made only with the full and free consent of the peoples concerned and after freedom from coercion had been assured.
4. After the political agreement was signed, the armed forces of both parties should be gradually reduced.
5. Economic activity, trade, transport, and communications throughout Indonesia should be restored as soon as possible.
6. After six months of free discussion among the people and not more than twelve months after the signing of the agreement, free elections

would be held so that the people could determine for themselves their political relationship to the proposed United States of Indonesia.
7. A constitutional convention should be chosen democratically to draft a constitution for the United States of Indonesia.
8. Either party could ask the United Nations to observe conditions at any time before the transfer of sovereignty from the Netherlands to the United States of Indonesia, and the other party would take this request into serious consideration.

The last four principles were taken from the Linggadjati Agreement:

9. Independence of the Indonesian people.
10. Co-operation between the peoples of the Netherlands and Indonesia.
11. A sovereign state would be established on a federal basis under a constitution to be arrived at by democratic processes.
12. A union between the United States of Indonesia and other parts of the Kingdom of the Netherlands under the Netherlands Crown.

Two days later both parties also agreed to six additional principles which had been drawn up and submitted by the Committee of Good Offices. They were:

1. Sovereignty throughout Indonesia should remain with the Netherlands until transfer to the United States of Indonesia after a stated period.
2. All Indonesian states were to be offered fair representation in any provisional federal government created before ratification of a new constitution.
3. Either party might continue to request the assistance of the Committee of Good Offices in adjusting differences arising during the interim period.
4. A plebiscite would be held within a year to determine whether the populations of Java, Madura, and Sumatra wished to join the Republic of Indonesia or another state in the future federation.
5. Representation at the constitutional convention should be in proportion to the populations of the various states.
6. Any state unwilling to accept the constitution might negotiate a special relationship with the United States of Indonesia and the Netherlands.

The Committee of Good Offices had good reason to feel pleased with its work. Its three members flew to New York to report to the Security Council. After a long debate, the Council on 28th February adopted a resolution which noted with satisfaction the signing of the Renville Agreement; commended the members of the Committee of Good Offices for the assistance they had given the two parties in their endeavours to settle their disputes by peaceful means; maintained its offer of good offices; and requested both parties and the Committee of Good Offices to keep the Council directly informed about the progress of the political settlement in Indonesia.

During the Council's debate before it adopted that resolution, the Australian representative before the Council and also Mr. Justice Kirby pointed out that, while the conclusion of the truce agreement and the acceptance of the eighteen principles by both sides had afforded a breathing space and had improved the atmosphere, a number of controversial points would remain to be cleared away before final agreement could be reached. They argued strongly that the life of the Committee should be extended and that it should be given increased powers to enable it to play a more positive part in the conclusion of an agreement. This view came to be that of most members of the Security Council.

This was also the attitude of the Republic's own representatives. The United Nations was the main guarantee of their right to existence as an independent state. The claim of the Indonesians to self-determination was based on the Charter, and they pledged themselves unreservedly to follow United Nations decisions. Throughout the Security Council debates their concern was to secure as wide powers as possible for the Committee of Good Offices, and to give United Nations representatives the right to participate in any negotiations in the Indies. They knew that, as a young country with limited military strength, they were taking certain risks in accepting the proposals for a settlement. They were in a sense giving up part of their present powers and strength in order to achieve a greater degree of independence later on, and therefore they wanted the United Nations to be in a position to see that both sides honestly carried out their undertakings.

After Renville

Despite the Renville Agreement it was clear that many difficulties remained to be overcome, and some of them were aired during the Council's debates. Even while the Council was meeting, the Dutch were holding a conference with a view to setting up an independent state in West Java. The representatives of the Republic claimed that this action was contrary to the agreement lately achieved, whereas the Dutch maintained that they were strictly adhering to the principles laid down in that agreement, including self-determination. The Council therefore on 28th February adopted an additional resolution, which asked the Committee of Good Offices to pay particular attention to the political developments in Western Java and Madura, and to report to the Council thereon at frequent intervals.

The position of the other states in the Indies remained a constant point of dispute. The Dutch, as a preliminary step to the establishment of the United States of Indonesia, took steps towards setting up an interim Federal Government for Indonesia which, for the time being at any rate, excluded the Republic. Dutch action to organize the other states in the Indies, and particularly a conference held in Bandoeng in July, was a persistent cause of anger to the Republicans.

This, however, was not the only source of friction. The Republic's external trade was greatly impeded by what amounted to a Dutch blockade, and by the end of the year normal trade to and from the Republic had been brought almost to a standstill. Practically no progress was made in translating the Renville principles into a basis for action. Disputes on the basic question of sovereignty persisted—sometimes one or other party would refuse to agree to something because it feared it might be taken as recognition of the other's sovereignty. The Committee of Good Offices itself described the political and economic position in the most gloomy of terms in a report presented to the Security Council on 23 June 1948.

The military position was somewhat better. Thirty-five thousand Republican combatants were evacuated to Republic-controlled territory from behind forward positions of Netherlands troops. Many prisoners of war were released and returned. The Republic informed the Committee of Good Offices that it had demobilized 40,000 of its troops. But it became increasingly clear that what existed was merely a truce and not permanent peace, which still depended on a political settlement being achieved. In the words of the Committee of Good Offices in its report of 23rd June: "All in all, reviewing the present situation the Committee has the impression of two Governments eying each other across the status quo line with reserve and suspicion."

Thus once again the hopes of a just and peaceful settlement were being frustrated. It was the old story: mutual distrust, bad faith, misunderstandings, half-heartedness, divided counsels, and sometimes just plain blunders. It was in most ways a depressing picture. But there was one ray of hope. The United Nations remained seized of the question, and the Security Council and its Committee of Good Offices continued to apply the principles of the Charter to the problem. Both parties to the dispute sought to justify their actions and courses by maintaining that they conformed to the Charter.

The Indonesian leaders were constantly being faced with the problem of reconciling their followers to the concessions that had to be made. Changes in the premiership occurred at times in response to public feeling. But a remarkable consistency and moderateness of policy was maintained throughout.

On 19th September 1948, a Communist uprising occurred and a Soviet state was proclaimed. The leader of the revolt was Muso, who had just returned to Java after many years spent in Russia.

The Republican Government acted with great promptness and resoluteness. After some fighting in which Muso was killed and his second-in-command executed, the rebellion was entirely suppressed. Despite this firm action, the Republican leaders were later to be charged by the Dutch with being unable to control extremist elements!

The months passed by without a final settlement coming closer. The Australian and American members of the Committee of Good Offices prepared a working paper for an over-all settlement to be used as a basis of discussion but, though it was accepted by the Indonesians, the Dutch firmly refused to consider it. Later direct talks began between Netherlands and Republican leaders, and the Dutch Foreign Minister (Dr. Stikker) visited the Indies. This was followed by another ministerial mission led by Dr. Stikker in November, but these talks and other negotiations led to nothing.

The situation was summed up by the Committee of Good Offices on 26th November 1948 as follows:

Despite the efforts of the members of the Committee of Good Offices to find a basis for a settlement of the Indonesian dispute consistent with the Renville agreements, there has not been any progress towards such a settlement since the Third Interim Report was presented to the Security Council in June . . .
The delay in reaching a political settlement has had four important consequences:
(a) A deterioration in the economic situation within the Republic, and a delay in the economic rehabilitation of Indonesia as a whole;
(b) An increase in political difficulties within the Republic;
(c) An increase in political tension between the parties;
(d) An increasing strain on the truce, with the ever-present possibility of its general breakdown.

The truth of this last statement was proved a few days later. On 18th December 1948, the Dutch armed forces proceeded against the Republic. The Republican capital, Djockjacarta, fell within a few hours, being taken by paratroops, and most of the

Republican leaders were made prisoner, including the President (Dr. Soekarno), the Prime Minister (Dr. Hatta), and the Commander-in-Chief (General Soedirman). Taken by surprise and thus deprived of leadership, most of the Republican territory was soon occupied.

The Security Council Acts Again

At first glance it might appear that the position was similar to what had occurred eighteen months earlier, when the Dutch had previously taken "police action." Once again after agreement on general principles had been reached, the agreement had not been translated into detail and carried out, and the Dutch had resorted to force.

But this resemblance was only superficial. An important new element had now entered into the situation. The United Nations had taken up the problem, was actually seeking a solution, and had its own representative organ on the spot to handle the position. Resort to force by the Dutch was therefore completely unjustified and represented a failure to discharge the undertakings accepted under the Charter and repeated to the Security Council itself.

On 19th December, as soon as reports of the fighting had been received and confirmed, the American and Australian Governments asked the Security Council to meet as soon as possible to consider the situation. The Committee of Good Offices itself also asked the Council to consider the position as a matter of urgency.

When the Council began to discuss the substance of the question on 22nd December, it had before it a report from the Committee of Good Offices, part of which I shall quote to indicate the clear nature of its findings:

(a) In their repudiation of the Renville Truce Agreement, the Netherlands Government did not comply with the provision of Article 10 of that

Agreement." (This article provided for notice that the agreement was being terminated.)

(b) The Committee is not aware of any circumstances connected with the concentration of Republican forces or the manoeuvres of the Republican Army which would have given rise to apprehensions and alarm, leading to precipitate action on the part of the Netherlands.

(c) The tone of the Netherlands letter of 17th December to the United States representative . . . and the requirement of a reply within a time limit which was impossible of fulfilment give to this letter some features of an ultimatum." (This was a letter sent to the American representative for transmission to Dr. Hatta, the Republican Prime Minister.)

(d) Military operations of the nature carried out by the Netherlands forces must have involved considerable planning and it is difficult for the Committee not to conclude that plans for such operations were in process during the exchange of correspondence while direct negotiations were still proceeding.

(e) Not only have the possibilities of negotiations under the auspices of the Committee not been exhausted, but they have not been adequately explored. There have been no negotiations under the auspices of the Committee since 23rd July. The recent direct talks cannot be regarded as negotiations, as they took the form of Netherlands demands for the complete surrender of the Republic to the Netherlands position on all important issues.

(f) In commencing military operations on 19th December, the Netherlands Government acted in violation of its obligations under the Renville Truce Agreement.

That categorical recital gave complete refutation of the statements of Dutch representatives attempting to justify the latest action. Before the Security Council, the Dutch representative claimed that there had been repeated violations of the truce agreement by the Indonesians, often at the instigation of their leaders, and that the Republican Government had been unable to keep order or to control the Communists. He also returned to the argument that the Indonesian dispute was a matter within the domestic jurisdiction of the Netherlands, since the Republic was not a sovereign state, and that therefore the Security Council was not competent to intervene.

The issue was clear. The real matter for debate was not the

conditions existing in Indonesia or the details of the negotiations. These were admittedly important, but there were proper means for considering them. The stark point demanding immediate attention was the fact that the Netherlands had resorted to force without exhausting the means of peaceful settlement open to it, and in contradiction to its own earlier promises to co-operate with the Good Offices Committee.

This point was made by speaker after speaker. For example, the United States representative (Mr. Jessup) said: "After carefully studying the material thus far made available by the Committee, my government fails to find any justification for renewal of military operations in Indonesia. This is particularly true in the light of the fact that there has been a resort to force following a period of seven months in which the resources of the Committee of Good Offices have not been utilized. If, as alleged, the violations of the truce agreement by the Republic have been so extensive and so persistent over a period of time, then it seems to me that the Netherlands Government should have reported these violations directly to the Security Council before renouncing the truce agreement and resorting to military action by land, sea, and air against the Republic."

This was also the attitude of the Australian Government. Australia was not animated by anti-Dutch feeling; its sole desire was to secure a peaceful settlement that would be just to both parties. It was in that spirit that the Security Council had established the Committee of Good Offices. The Dutch by resort to force were ignoring and nullifying the United Nations machinery and frustrating the efforts being made towards such a solution. The general condemnation of the Netherlands on this occasion was therefore not a judging of the merits of the Indonesian question as a whole, but, on the contrary, action taken to defend the authority of the United Nations and induce the Netherlands to observe its decisions.

The Security Council on 24th December adopted a resolution based on a proposal introduced jointly by the United States, Colombia, and Syria, and incorporating amendments suggested by Australia. It called upon both parties to cease hostilities forthwith; called for the immediate release of the Republican leaders; and instructed the Committee of Good Offices to report on events in Indonesia since 19th December and to observe the compliance of the parties with this resolution. Seven countries voted for the resolution—the United States, United Kingdom, Canada, China, Colombia, Syria, and the Argentine. The other four members (France, Belgium, the U.S.S.R., and the Ukraine) abstained, the first two mainly because of doubts regarding domestic jurisdiction, the latter two because the resolution did not propose strong enough action against the Dutch.

The Council continued thereafter to keep up pressure. In the meantime, other evidence of world opinion was making itself apparent. The United States Government on 22nd December announced that the Economic Cooperation Administration (E.C.A.) had suspended the issuance of authorizations for the procurement of supplies destined to be used in Indonesia. The Indian and Pakistan Governments forbade Dutch aircraft to fly over or to land in their territories, while the Government of Ceylon announced that Dutch ships or aircraft carrying troops or war material which might be used against the Indonesian people would be denied access to Ceylon's ports and airfields.

And so the year closed with almost unanimous condemnation of the Dutch action, and with guerrilla activity growing stronger, better organized, and more effective within Indonesia itself.

Action in January

Clearly matters could not be allowed to rest where they were. In January the Security Council considered what further action should be taken. At the same time the countries of Asia and the Western Pacific met in Delhi at the invitation of the Indian Prime Minister to discuss the Indonesian question. The following countries were represented: Afghanistan, Australia, Burma, Ceylon, China, Egypt, Ethiopia, Iran, Iraq, Lebanon, Nepal, New Zealand, Pakistan, the Philippines, Saudi Arabia, Siam, Syria, and Yemen.

The conference began on 20th January. I made a statement in Sydney which outlined Australian policy, and affirmed that the conference was in accordance with the Charter and was designed to strengthen the United Nations:

The important conference on the Indonesian question which opens in New Delhi today at the invitation of India, is being attended by Australian representatives and will serve to emphasize the deep concern felt in many countries at the recent resort to force and the failure of the Dutch to carry out the Security Council's directions. This conference does not conflict in any way with the powers or the jurisdiction of the Security Council. On the contrary, it should bring home to all concerned the general opinion of the countries participating that United Nations' principles should always be observed. . . .

The New Delhi meeting may therefore be of crucial significance. Its purposes are fully in accord with the Charter of the United Nations and it is comparable to the regional meetings held in Western Europe, in Latin America, and elsewhere. Such a conference would be perfectly entitled to make suggestions and recommendations, always remembering that the Security Council is still seized of the dispute and that, especially if the Security Council is unable to recommend a definitive solution, the matter can always be brought before the General Assembly. There is a great need for close and continuing co-operation in the future between Australia, on the one hand, and the Netherlands and Indonesia on the other. Such co-operation will be facilitated and indeed guaranteed if a just settlement is peacefully worked out in accordance with the principles of the United Nations Charter and through its appropriate organs. From the very first, that has been Australia's sole objective and, because of the contribution of its servicemen to the liberation of this area, no country has a greater right to speak.

The conference was extremely successful, and revealed substantial agreement on the principles of action which the Security Council would be urged to follow. The members acted in a moderate and responsible manner, and indicated a maturity of thought and a devotion to the United Nations and its principles. They resisted the temptation to take extreme or precipitate action, but at the same time made it quite clear that they regarded the Dutch military action against the Republic as "a flagrant breach of the United Nations Charter and a defiance of the efforts of the Security Council and its Good Offices Committee to bring about a peaceful settlement."

The next big step in this story was the adoption by the Security Council on 28th January of a resolution which stated that the December resolutions of the Council had not been carried out. It called upon both parties to discontinue immediately all military operations. The Netherlands Government was called upon to release immediately and unconditionally all political prisoners arrested by them when the Republic was invaded, and to allow them to return to Djockjacarta and resume duties. It called for negotiations between representatives of the Netherlands and of the Republic, on the basis of the Linggadjati and Renville principles, to establish a United States of Indonesia according to the following timetable: an interim Federal Government to be established by 15th March 1949; elections for an Indonesian constituent assembly to be completed by 1st October 1949; and sovereignty over Indonesia to be transferred by the Netherlands to the United States of Indonesia by 1st July 1950.

The Committee of Good Offices was replaced by a United Nations Commission for Indonesia, consisting of representatives from the same three countries—Australia, Belgium, and the United States of America. The new Commission was able to act by majority vote, and was given greater powers than the former Committee of Good Offices. The Commission was instructed to assist the parties to carry out the resolution, and to assist in achieving the earliest possible restoration of the civil administration of the Republic.

This resolution was not secured without a great deal of debate. Some nations would have liked to have gone further. Others were timid, and would have preferred to evade the issue. But the resolution adopted represented a basis for a just settlement, and as such was welcomed by those who looked to the United Nations to promote peace and progress in South-East Asia.

However, the Security Council could not rest on its laurels. The resolution had to be carried out. The Commission, in a report on 1st March, said that "the Commission finds that the Netherlands Government has not complied with the basic prerequisites of further action under the resolution." It also said that "the Commission is obliged to report that as of 1st March, there has been failure of the parties to the Indonesian question to reach agreement on the establishment of an interim federal government. This situation results from the failure of the Netherlands Government to accept the procedures of the resolution of 28th January, and not from a mere difference of viewpoint on details of governmental structure and functions. If the latter were the case, the Commission would be prepared to recommend a structure for an interim federal government." The report concluded: "The Commission regrets that it has not been possible to proceed with the implementation of the resolution. It is also conscious of the progressive deterioration of the situation in Indonesia and of the augmented danger to world stability which must result." This report was unanimous.

The Security Council continued to consider the situation, and the Commission maintained its efforts on the spot where talks took place between Dutch and Indonesian representatives. In New York in April 1949, the Australian and Indian delegations placed the question of Indonesia upon the Assembly agenda. Undoubtedly the prospect of Assembly discussion had a good effect. On 7th May it was announced from Batavia that the Netherlands representatives and the leaders of the Republic of Indonesia had reached agreement on the preliminary steps to be taken. The Republican leaders were to return to Djockjacarta and the two parties would subsequently participate in a round-table conference at the Hague to accelerate the unconditional transfer of real and complete sovereignty to the United States of Indonesia.

This brought new hope. But the Australian and Indian delegations asked to defer consideration of the question until the fourth session to allow the two parties to continue their efforts to reach final agreement. The United Nations was not thereby withdrawing. The Security Council's decisions were still in force; the United Nations Commission in Indonesia continued to act both in Indonesia and at the Hague; and the General Assembly itself retained complete liberty to discuss the position at its resumed meeting.

As Australia's Foreign Minister, I fought relentlessly against any surrender by the U.N. to mere physical force—by either side to the dispute. On the contrary we fought for a just settlement, to be arrived at by agreement under the guidance of a selfless U.N. group—inspired solely by the great objective of the Charter—to substitute conciliation and justice for the arbitration of force and violence—by whomsoever employed.

It would have been easy to be discouraged. But the United Nations organs have persisted, and gradually progress has been made. The gloomy prophets who said that the United Nations would run away or fail completely have been proved false. Lives have been saved; just principles for a settlement have been asserted; public opinion has made itself known. A way to a solution is open if only goodwill and sincerity prevail.

The factual background in the whole region is one of great and dynamic change. The peoples of the region are showing a determination to take charge of their own affairs, to improve their living standards, and to take their place on an equal footing with other nations. These progressive trends cannot be arrested. Indeed, history shows that attempts at forcible repression lead almost inevitably to political extremism.

Australia's intervention and the Security Council's action were not directed against Dutch interests. Australia's one objective was to assist in a freely negotiated settlement on United Nations principles to the advantage of the Netherlands as well as all the peoples of Indonesia. The unjustified use of force in these circumstances could, in our opinion, imperil European interests and prestige throughout South East Asia and, if condoned, would severely injure the United Nations itself. On the other hand, the resolute support of United Nations principles here not only points a way to a just settlement in this region, but also strengthens the cause of peace everywhere in the world.

XV

ATOMIC ENERGY—A THREAT AND A PROMISE

THE debates on atomic energy are a good example of the role played by the middle and smaller powers at the Paris Session of the General Assembly. The first item on the agenda of the Political Committee was the reports of the Atomic Energy Commission.

Atomic energy was one of the main subjects to which the United Nations addressed itself when it assembled for the first time in London in January 1946. The dropping of the atomic bombs at Hiroshima and Nagasaki had made a profound impression upon all men. Public imagination quickly grasped the enormous devastation, destruction, and death which the atomic bomb could bring about in another war, and the threat which it represented to all free peoples if it came into the hands of an aggressor. At the same time it was hoped that atomic energy had equally great potentialities for peace and that with wise handling it would be possible to raise the standards of living and welfare of all mankind.

The General Assembly, at the beginning of 1946, acting on a recommendation by the five permanent members of the Security Council and Canada, asked the Security Council to establish an Atomic Energy Commission composed of representatives of the eleven members of the Council. This Commission assembled for the first time in June of that year. I had the honour of presiding as the first Chairman of that body, and submitted the following basic points in the initial discussions:

1. The international authority should be vested with control of all rights in the raw materials, plants, and processes, leaving as much freedom as possible to national and private interests in the non-dangerous field.
2. There must be a system of effective control and inspection.
3. When, and only when, controls and safeguards are effectively organized, the manufacture of atomic weapons should be prohibited and stock piling cease.
4. Information as to the beneficial uses of atomic energy should be made available to all nations.
5. Research and development for peaceful purposes should be accelerated.
6. A just and equitable sequence for the implementation of the foregoing must be designed.

These principles have in no way been invalidated by later technical developments or by the work of the Atomic Energy Commission. Indeed they form part of the framework of the structure elaborated by the majority of the Commission in the plans set out in its reports.

The Commission worked very hard over the past three years but it has been unable to reach agreement. On essential points the only dissentient countries are the Soviet Union and the Ukraine.

At the very beginning of the discussions in 1946 the United States made a most striking offer to surrender its technical information and secrets as soon as an international system of inspection and control was established which would guarantee that no country could develop and make atomic bombs without detection and measures being taken to stop it. This offer to give up the monopoly of the bomb and to prescribe this weapon if all countries would co-operate in a plan of effective control and safeguard was epic-making and unparalleled in history, and I immediately welcomed it as such when Mr. Baruch first put it forward in the Atomic Energy Commission on behalf of the United States. Since then the United States has co-operated fully in giving technical information and advice to the Commission, and progress would have been far less had it not been for this assistance.

When the Third Session of the General Assembly met, it was confronted by failure of the Commission to agree, principally on three points. The Soviet Union insisted that a convention should be concluded outlawing atomic weapons before consideration was given to the control of atomic energy. Secondly, there were differences as to the powers of the proposed international agency, the Soviet Union opposing all but the most limited powers. The third point in dispute was the use of enforcement action in the event of breaches of the control system. The Soviet Union insisted that all enforcement action, even for minor violations, should be undertaken only by the Security Council itself, thus conceding the right of five powers to exercise an individual veto over all actions taken in this field of enforcement.

The Atomic Energy Commission presented a report to the Paris Assembly stating that the Commission had reached an impasse because of difficulties caused by the attitude of the Soviet Union, whose co-operation was necessary for an effective control system. In the opinion of the majority of the Commission the counter-proposals submitted by the Soviet Union were completely inadequate. The functions and powers so far elaborated by the majority of the Commission for the international control agency provided in its opinion the technically necessary basis for an effective control of atomic energy, irrespective of whether they were politically acceptable or not.

The majority of the Commission believed that the deadlock could not be broken at the Commission level and in view of these considerations concluded that no useful purpose could be served by carrying on negotiations at that level. The Commission therefore suspended its work until the General Assembly otherwise directed or until the permanent members reached agreement on the question of control.

Third Assembly Action on Atomic Energy

Early in the debate on the Atomic Energy Commission's report in the Political Committee, the Canadian representative introduced a resolution which was strongly supported by the United States Government. It approved the findings and recommendations of the Atomic Energy Commission as constituting the necessary basis for establishing an effective system of international control of atomic energy. One essential point about the Canadian resolution, however, was that it would have suspended all further work of the Commission on the ground that no basis of agreement at present existed. Each member of the United Nations was, in effect, to be left to his own devices on matters relating to atomic energy, at least as far as the United Nations was concerned.

This resolution was strongly attacked by the Soviet Union which had been throughout in the minority in the Atomic Energy Commission and which was specifically referred to with condemnation in the Canadian proposal. Soviet opposition was only to be expected in view of that country's policy on atomic energy as previously expressed in the United Nations.

But the resolution was also criticized by the representatives of many countries which could in no way be regarded as communist or in sympathy with communism, but which were appalled at the prospect of the United Nations, in effect, washing its hands of the whole problem. The lead in urging that something further be done was taken by Australia, India, and Syria who quickly obtained wide support among Latin American states and some of the Western European states such as Belgium.

Of the great powers, France came out in support of continuing United Nations work in this field. Her representative, M. Ramadier (a former premier and now Minister of National

Defence) made a very moving speech, in which he pictured the terrible consequences of an atomic war resulting from failure to agree in this field, and he pleaded with delegates never to abandon the search for agreement so long as even the faintest hope remained.

As a result of these expressions of opinion, which soon came to reflect that of the majority of the committee, a sub-committee was established to examine the various proposals which had been submitted to the Committee and to attempt to reach agreement on a resolution. The sub-committee was ably presided over by Sir Narsing Rau of India, whose delegation throughout the session played a notable role in working for agreement among members. The sub-committee moderated some of the original Canadian proposal, eliminating the provocative references to the Soviet Union. It also called upon the five great powers and Canada, who are the permanent members of the Atomic Energy Commission, to meet together to determine when a basis of agreement existed on the international control of atomic energy to ensure its use only for peaceful purposes and for the elimination from national armaments of atomic weapons.

But these concessions in the sub-committee did not prove sufficient to satisfy the committee itself. Consequently the proposal had to be further amended so that, in addition to the consultations between the six countries already mentioned, the Atomic Energy Commission was instructed also to survey its programme of work and proceed to further study of those subjects remaining in its programme of work which it considered to be practicable and useful.

The resolution in this form was eventually adopted by a plenary session of the Assembly itself, where discussion showed that members would not be satisfied if the Commission sat down on its new work in a perfunctory manner. The Assembly clearly expected that a sincere and concerted attempt should be made to find an agreement.

The debates were very useful and informative. They showed that, with the exception of the Soviet group of states, almost every member of the United Nations was in favour of the principles contained in the recommendations of the Atomic Energy Commission.

In the course of the debate, when the Soviet Union in common with all other states round the table was called upon to justify its attitude publicly before the world, Mr. Vyshinsky seems to have made certain concessions. Previously, for example, the Soviet Union had insisted that a convention could not be drawn up—indeed that discussions could not even take place—on the control of atomic energy for peaceful purposes until a convention had been adopted prohibiting the use of the atomic weapon. This had hitherto been a stumbling block, because the United States, not unnaturally, was not prepared to destroy its stocks of atomic bombs until it had an effective assurance that no other country would be able to manufacture atomic bombs of its own without the knowledge of the rest of the world. But during the debate Mr. Vyshinsky said that the Soviet Union was now prepared to modify its earlier stand and would agree to a convention on the control of atomic energy being concluded simultaneously with a convention outlawing the atomic weapon.

There were some who claimed this concession was more apparent than real. There were also others who pointed out the very real practical obstacles which still existed and also the difficulties in defining exactly what Mr. Vyshinsky's concession really meant. But the overwhelming consensus of the Committee was that some new hope of agreement had been given and that the matter should be further examined in detail, with the Soviet Union and all other countries given full opportunity to explain and to examine the issues involved. Obviously the Atomic Energy Commission was the body to do this.

Thus the General Assembly was able to ensure continuance of the United Nations work on atomic energy, and provided a debate which illuminated some of the issues involved and may have led to real and important concessions. The Assembly did not secure agreement. Great difficulties still remain. But the Assembly did ensure that the search for agreement was not abandoned.

XVI

PEACE AND WELFARE—
A COMMON INTEREST

IN 1943 Mr. Wendell Willkie published a book entitled *One World*. This book had remarkable sales throughout America and also in other countries. Its success was partly due to its author's own personality and record. He was probably the most colourful and popular personality nominated by the Republican Party for the Presidency since Teddy Roosevelt, whom he resembled in some ways.

But a great deal of the book's appeal lay in its message, which was so succinctly summed up in its title. Wendell Willkie preached the doctrine that we all belong to one world and are interdependent, that we can not isolate ourselves from other peoples and from events in other countries, and that in turn our own actions affect other people.

This doctrine was in some ways contrary to traditional American belief in the efficacy and desirability of isolationism. Nor is isolationism confined to the United States. Everyone would find it comforting to think that he could bury his head in the sand like an ostrich and not have to worry about distant events in faraway lands about which he knows comparatively little and for which he does not want to accept any responsibilities or burdens.

It is a tribute to the common sense and insight of the people of the world that they did not choose this easy course and that in so many cases they were ahead of their leaders, as the enormous sales of Wendell Willkie's book testified—and as election results in so many countries also proved. I have always believed that you can and must trust the people, that their instincts are fundamentally sound, and that they are often closer to the truth than the experts who know the details but sometimes forget the great purposes of life. The general public may not always be able to appreciate the refinements of argument or the minutiae of fact, but if they are told the facts they can usually grasp the basic issues involved and they know what the right course should be.

Wendell Willkie travelled right around the world, visiting the Middle East, Russia, and China. He summarized his conclusions as follows: "The net impression of my trip was not one of distance from other peoples, but of closeness to them. If I had ever had any doubts that the world has become small and completely interdependent, this trip would have dispelled them altogether."

He was also convinced that the secret of progress and peace lay in mutual aid among all countries, and that it was vital to help devasted and under-capitalized countries like the Soviet Union, China, and the Middle East to develop their resources and raise their standards of living. He saw that low standards of living and unrest in these countries threatened the standards of living and tranquility of the United States itself.

Universal Nature of Charter

The principles and purposes of the United Nations Charter are universal in character. They must be enforced impartially everywhere, even when it may not always seem in our immediate interests to do so. In the world today each country finds protection in the fact that it can point to a set of principles for fair international dealing which have been accepted by fifty-eight nations, including all the great powers.

If, however, these principles are violated with impunity in some cases they will cease to have general application. The country which violates these principles today in its own interests cannot complain or be surprised if later on some other country also violates them, possibly against the interests of the first country. A blow at the Charter in one place is a blow everywhere. An action cannot be right when it suits yourself, and wrong when it suits someone else but not you.

That is why every country must take a stand against aggression wherever it occurs, even though the immediate consequences of such a stand may not be altogether palatable and the victim of aggression may be remote. Aggression anywhere tends to become aggression everywhere. If it occurs successfully in one part of the world it will spread in time to other parts, either by involving other countries in a great war resulting from that aggression or by setting precedents and undermining the authority and unity of the United Nations which is the only body which can prevent such aggression.

The record of the years 1918-1939 proves this point. The three totalitarian states of Germany, Italy, and Japan could have been stopped if early action had been taken when they first began their careers of open aggression. Manchuria was the first big test. The League of Nations was well served by an international commission of inquiry under the late Lord Lytton, which presented a clear and frank factual report definitely establishing Japanese aggression. But the governments of the world were not prepared to take the necessary enforcement action which would have restrained and repelled Japan. For reasons of expediency or weakness of heart, they shuffled and temporized, and Japan was allowed to consolidate her position in Manchuria and gird herself for fresh aggression against the countries of East Asia and the Western Pacific.

Heartened by this experience, which showed the weakness of the League so long as the member governments would not support it, Mussolini with the encouragement of Hitler began his adventures in Abyssinia. There was still time then to check this fresh example of aggression but once again the governments of the world were not prepared to do so.

From then on, events moved inexorably and swiftly to the

Second World War. Mr. Chamberlain made some sporadic attempts to preserve peace but his efforts failed, partly because the forces of aggression had been allowed to go too far and were now strong and insatiable, and partly because his policies did not take account of vital features of the situation, such as the position of the Soviet Union and the importance of securing just treatment for those who were threatened with German aggression and of supporting the League of Nations.

Before the Second World War Mr. Litvinov, the Soviet Foreign Minister, preached the doctrine that peace is indivisible. Events have shown the truth of that statement. They have also shown that the principles on which such peace must be based are indivisible—that peace must always be based on justice, not on expediency or the dictates of power. That is the distinction between efforts at mediation and settlement made within the United Nations Charter, and "appeasement." It is always proper and right to seek to preserve or secure peace, as long as one's vital principles and the interests of justice are not sacrificed.

The nations of the world are interdependent economically no less than politically and in the field of international security. Poverty and unemployment in one country are a threat to the economic well-being of every other country in the world. A country which has a low standard of living, and a high rate of unemployment is a source of constant unrest and contagion to its neighbours. It is a breeding ground for extreme political philosophies and warlike doctrines, a stamping ground for dictators and militarists.

Economic disturbances often lie at the bottom of, or at least contribute to, political tensions, internally and in international relations. Trade disputes, economic expansionism, and denial of access to raw materials on equitable terms can lead to political action and retaliation and even to war. As Mr. Charles Malik of Lebanon said in his Presidential statement to the Economic and Social Council in July 1948, the work of the Security Council will decrease proportionally to the success of the Economic and

Social Council in promoting solutions to economic and social problems.

ECONOMIC DEVELOPMENT

We should try to raise standards everywhere in order to practise the simple humanitarian doctrine which is the basis of all morality, namely that we should help our neighbour and relieve misery and suffering. The Charter itself imposes on us individually and collectively the obligation to combat poverty, hunger, and ignorance.

No one can look unmoved at the destitution of millions of people in the Far East, and the scarcely less happy conditions of vast numbers in Africa and some of the underdeveloped portions of Latin America. Those who live in the more wealthy and developed countries of Europe, North America, and Australasia, can hardly imagine the low standards which are the common lot of so many of mankind—disease, low expectation of life, and unrelieved pain; flood, famine, and epidemics which have come to be regarded in those countries as almost seasonal and quite uncontrollable; inability to increase production or improve its quality because of lack of equipment and technical training. These wrongs cry out for redress, and can and must be righted by co-operative international effort.

That is the human side of the problem. It is a challenge to the sense of justice and service of all men, and our common humanity bids us lend a hand.

Assistance to these countries is worth while even on selfish grounds. Their development helps everyone. An increased standard of living in one country means greater purchasing power for imports and thereby affords a bigger market for other countries. At the same time a new source of materials and goods is opened up, and the world as a whole benefits as well as the country concerned.

The biggest need in the Far East and other greatly underdeveloped countries is capital equipment and training in industrial techniques and skills.

Economic development has attracted increasing attention from the United Nations. The General Assembly at its Paris session recommended that the Economic and Social Council and the specialized agencies give further and urgent consideration to the whole problem of the economic development of underdeveloped countries. The Council was asked to report on the measures already devised and to make other proposals for promoting economic development and raising the standards of living of underdeveloped countries.

The problem of economic development was the "fourth point" in President Truman's inaugural address on 20th January, 1949. The President advocated a "bold new programme" under which the United States would make available to peace-loving peoples the benefits of its store of technical knowledge. In co-operation with other nations, he said, the United States should foster capital investment in areas needing development. President Truman invited other countries to pool their technological resources in this undertaking, in a co-operative enterprise in which all nations would work together through the United Nations and its specialized agencies whenever practicable.

Under the double impetus of the Assembly resolution and President Truman's speech, the Economic and Social Council gave particular and prolonged attention to the question of economic development during its Eighth Session which began in New York in February 1949. The Council discussed the question generally and arranged that a detailed plan for technical assistance in economic development should be prepared for consideration by the Council in July.

It would be foolish and misleading to underestimate the immensity of the task. Capital equipment cannot be produced overnight, and technical training and education also take time. The capacity of the developed countries to assist others is also limited.

Practical results can only be accomplished if realistic account is taken of the limited nature of the resources and skill available.

The bulk of the necessary capital must come from the under-developed countries themselves. External assistance can be useful and significant, but in the long run the countries which develop most will be those that do most to help themselves. The biggest assistance which can be given by the United Nations and by other countries is to advise and assist development along the right lines and by providing for certain specific needs (such as technical advice) which will enable countries to make the most use of their own resources.

It would be wrong to think of economic development exclusively in terms of industrialization. A great deal needs to be done to improve methods of agriculture, expand food production, and improve health standards and facilities. It is natural for countries to be attracted by the glamour of having large-scale industrial works, but often their present degree of economic development and their available natural resources may not warrant this.

At the same time, we should not go to the other extreme and maintain that there should be no industrial development. No one should wish to keep the under-developed countries in the status of mere producers of raw materials. There are strong social arguments in favour of diversifying the economy as much as possible, and in working towards a degree of economic independence. It is a question of striking a balance. In general, the soundest course is for development to proceed along lines which will employ a country's labour and resources in the most productive manner.

Economic development is not a new problem. The United Kingdom has for a long while been developing its dependent areas and fitting them for self-government. It is doing so today on possibly a greater scale than ever before. Australia is undertaking the development of New Guinea and its own resources, and has also given economic assistance to countries in South East Asia. The United States has in the past also given considerable economic assistance, both public and private, towards the development and rehabilitation of all countries of the world. The United Nations and the specialized agencies can develop and supplement the work that has been done already, and can bring all countries—developed and under-developed alike—into a great international drive against poverty and ill-health. Unemployment, which is so great a problem in more developed countries, is hardly a problem in most of the undeveloped areas. The battle for life is so intense and so many people are living at subsistence level that there is no unemployment in the western sense of the word. Vast numbers are engaged in tasks that would simply not be considered worth while in a more highly developed community because their return is so small. Unemployment at home is therefore of minor interest to these countries. But to the world as a whole unemployment is of profound importance, and deserves major attention from the United Nations.

Unemployment

The Charter of the United Nations contains a pledge by each member to take joint and separate action in co-operation with the Organization to promote higher standards of living, full employment, and conditions of economic and social progress and development. This is a most important pledge, which was only inserted in the Charter by Australia and some other delegations at San Francisco after a long fight against great opposition.

Many people were terrified of the words "full employment" at that time. When they saw that some reference was unavoidable, they tried to obtain less positive phrases such as "a high level of employment." They did not consider *full* employment practicable and felt that attempts to secure it might necessitate too much state interference and state planning. There may even have been some who thought that a certain measure of unemployment was desirable as a means of disciplining labour and

Peace and Welfare

promoting technical efficiency. However, this fight was won and the pledge was given.

At that time Australia and several other countries were basing their policies upon a belief in the necessity and practicability of ensuring full employment. During the depression of the Thirties, the unemployed throughout the world totalled many millions and great misery was caused, not only to the unemployed themselves and their families, but also to those countless numbers who suffered greatly reduced incomes as a result of the depression.

In addition great wastage was caused; the world is paying dearly today for its failure to use those men and resources when they were available. All countries have a shortage of housing and of capital equipment which is now needed to increase production and raise standards of living. The Thirties were a decade of lost opportunity, and that failure then made its contribution to bringing about the Second World War.

Unemployment is not just a material loss or a period of physical suffering. Prolonged unemployment has grave psychological effects and tends to produce moral inertia and degradation on those who suffer it. When men and women came to feel that society had no use for them, their skill and experience withered away through disuse so that when later on they were given fresh opportunities they were no longer capable of using them. Some educated men, particularly from middle-class families, often felt that there was no niche for them in the existing structure of the nation and sought to bring about a new order which unfortunately often took a fascist, totalitarian form. It was such dissatisfied young men, backed by large numbers of the unemployed, who formed the core of Hitler's rise to power in Germany.

It may therefore be no exaggeration to say that western democracy could not survive another great depression which involved unemployment over a long period of many millions of men. Whatever the technical arguments against full employment—and there are some—the overwhelming fact is that on social, humanitarian, and even political grounds mass unemployment is a bad thing and must be overcome at all costs if society itself is to survive. If unemployment is not overcome in the democratic way, an effort will be made by extremists to overcome it with a dictatorship.

Unemployment is the most exportable of all products. The last world depression first manifested itself in an Austrian bank failure, and for the world at large it was symbolized by the Wall Street crash of late 1929. Yet within a short time its repercussions had spread from the Wall Street market to the rubber tapper of Malaya who had never even heard of a ticker-tape.

Australia is a country which depends for a significant proportion of its national income on its exports of wool, wheat, and other primary products. The depression first hit Australia through a slump overseas in the price of these products. Consequently Australia, the Argentine, and other great exporting countries, including Great Britain herself, are very conscious that the inability of countries to buy one's own products has sharp and immediate repercussions on one's own economy and the economy of the rest of the world.

Even a country like the United States, which is wealthy beyond all others and which devotes on an average only ten per cent of its activity to foreign trade, is also closely interested in the world economic situation. Ten per cent is a not insignificant proportion of any country's economy, and in the United States provides employment and incomes for several million people. In many important American industries, the export market provides that margin which means for them the difference between prosperity and depression. We saw only too well in 1929 and 1930 how a small economic setback can snowball and by action and reaction turn into a great depression.

In this connexion some of the Soviet Union's attacks on the Marshall Plan have made great play of the allegation that one of its purposes is to provide markets for American businessmen and to avoid what might otherwise be a slump at home. A blunt statement of this nature does not give sufficient credit to the fact that Marshall aid has meant a real sacrifice by the American people, not simply in increased budgetary costs but in actual loss of goods which would otherwise be available for home consumption. At the same time it is obvious that the United States also gains from this great plan. It is evidence of the truth that no country can afford to see depression and poverty in other regions without facing repercussions at home. It is both the duty and self-interest of wealthier nations to assist those who are less well-off.

Therefore one of the most important tasks of the United Nations is to study the problem of unemployment and to plan effective international action. This is primarily the responsibility of the Economic and Social Council, which has established a special commission charged with the task. So far, unfortunately, progress has been disappointing. This is not the fault of the members of the commission who have worked hard and are well qualified. The slow progress appears to have been caused chiefly by the intrusion of political differences into discussions that should have been primarily technical in nature. At the meeting of the Economic and Social Council last August, I drew attention to the slow rate of progress in this field and as a result of the discussion the Council proposes to review the whole situation at its second meeting in 1949.

What the world needs first is accurate information on world economic conditions which will form a basis for decisions in these matters and, secondly, a concrete programme of action which each country can put into effect if occasion arises.

The need for factual information in the economic field as a basis for policy and action is similar to the need for factual studies in the political field as a basis for decisions on disputes. In neither case can just and effective decisions be made without a knowledge of the relevant facts. Australian delegations have taken a lead in urging this course in both economic and political fields.

In the economic committee at the Second Session of the General Assembly of 1947, during the general debate on the annual report of the Economic and Social Council, I advocated two courses: that the Council should consider regularly a survey of current world conditions and trends; and that the secretariat should be used to a greater extent and in particular should be encouraged to collect and analyse factual information for the Council's work.

The Polish delegate, Dr. Oscar Lange, also made some valuable suggestions to the same end. The Australian and Polish delegations got together and discussed the whole matter informally between themselves and as a result joined in sponsoring a resolution which was adopted by the Assembly.

This resolution has been put into effect in a most satisfactory manner. An annual survey of the whole world economic situation has been undertaken by the secretariat, and appears on the agenda of the Economic and Social Council once a year. Other economic reports, some of them related to regions and some relating to particular topics such as public debt, are also appearing. Their standard is very high and will become even better as gaps in statistics are filled and experience in preparation and collation is gained. This is another of those aspects of United Nations work which attracts very little public attention but is of outstanding importance and quality. It is moreover something in which all nations join without strong differences impeding most of the work.

The second need is for a concrete programme of action to prevent or counteract major depressions and mass unemployment. Australia has already prepared a programme for action of its own to overcome these forces, and so have many other countries. It is important that the plans of the various nations should dovetail. During the last great depression, for example, many countries attempted to protect their own foreign exchange position by cutting down their imports, which meant that further unemployment was caused to other countries, who in turn took similar measures with repercussions again in other countries. Again, serious monetary and foreign-exchange difficulties can be caused by one country's pursuing a deflationary policy in a depression while some other countries are pursuing an inflationary policy with the same objects in view. Co-ordination of policy and, just as important, co-ordination of timing are vital.

For this purpose it is necessary that the Economic and Social Council should try to develop procedures to give general guidance. In particular the Council should see that necessary studies and plans are prepared now so that they can be thoroughly analysed by the individual governments and will be ready to be put into effect at short notice.

The actual carrying out of the policies will depend upon the government concerned and upon the specialized agencies. For example, the International Bank and the International Monetary Fund have perhaps the chief role to play in foreign-exchange problems. One of the major functions conferred upon the Economic and Social Council by the Charter is to co-ordinate the policies of these agencies and also to give guidance in the co-ordination of governmental policies too.

Over-concentration on Europe

The fifty-nine countries which comprise the United Nations are drawn from all six continents. In the old League of Nations the European states held the dominating position, but increasingly it is becoming clearer in the new organization that Europe is not the only region of significance and that events and problems in other regions are often of equal or greater importance.

During the past thirty years and particularly since the end of the war, new states have arisen in the Far East and the Middle

East which now exercise an independent voice. The old dominance of Europe in the world has been diminished by such factors as the great devastation on that continent; the weariness resulting from years of occupation; the defeat of two former great powers there; the rise to still-increasing world stature by America and Russia; and the granting of independence to territories which were formerly dependent on European powers. The number of European states who are members of the United Nations is also much smaller than in the League, because the ex-enemy nations and Portugal and Ireland have not yet been admitted to membership.

Nevertheless many still have almost an obsession with European problems. It is comparable to the wartime policy of "Beat Hitler first" which, if carried out in its original extreme form, would have had disastrous effects in the Pacific, led to the overrunning of several key nations, and possibly have cost the democracies the war.

One would not wish to disparage or underrate Europe. It still has a standard of education and skill which is greater than that of any other continent. The great contributions of Europe to civilization which have marked the past will, we hope, be continued for a long time to come to the advantage of the whole world. It is therefore proper that European recovery and reconstruction should attract a lot of attention.

But the problems of the Far East are, from a historical point of view, possibly of even greater importance than what is happening in Europe at present. In the Far East are old civilizations with a high standard of culture, and enormous and rapidly growing populations. The twin forces of nationalism and industrialization are forming powerful new states bound in the future to exercise a great influence.

The future of the whole world will be shaped in part by the changes in this region. The United Nations Charter did not contemplate a static world. It realized that change was inevitable and desirable. The preamble of the Charter specifically states that the peoples of the United Nations are determined to employ international machinery to promote the economic and social advancement of all peoples, which implies continual change and improvement. It is the task of the United Nations and of all its members to see that these changes are brought about in a just, democratic, and peaceful manner.

Another region of the world which so far has attracted too little attention is Latin America. This is a vast continent, much of which is still underdeveloped. The United Nations has established an economic commission for this area but the tasks before it are enormous and are not fully appreciated in other countries.

A healthy world requires all regions to prosper and work towards common standards of welfare and peace. The task is enormous, and we must not expect miracles. Capital equipment takes a long time to build, and technical skill and experience are slow to be acquired. But the immensity of the task should be a challenge to us, not an excuse for shirking. In a deep sense we are bound together in one world brotherhood.

World Government

THE interdependence of all countries in political and economic relationships is reinforced by technical progress in communication. One can fly from Sydney to New York in less than three days, and from New York to London in twelve hours. The wireless has made it possible for people in distant countries to speak together.

This has led many people to the conclusion that the idea of one world implies also a single world government, and a submerging of existing state sovereignties into the sovereignty of one world government. This conception attracted some public attention in Paris because of the activities of Mr. Garry Davis, a young American ex-serviceman who, just before the Assembly convened in September, publicly renounced his American citizenship and proclaimed himself a "citizen of the world." For a while he camped outside the Paris buildings of the United Nations and claimed to be the Organization's first citizen.

Later he attracted further attention by interrupting a public plenary session of the General Assembly and haranguing the delegates from the gallery on the need for a world government until the police put a stop to his speech. He had timed his intervention for four o'clock in the afternoon, but by a coincidence I had just adjourned the session temporarily when the interruption occurred. Later on I discovered that his intention had been known beforehand to some newspaper and newsreel companies, who had no doubt encouraged him, and that they had arranged for photographers to be ready at the time fixed for the interruption. They had also arranged privately with some of the staff of the United Nations who controlled the lighting system so that spotlights would be focussed at the proper spot when the time came. Such is the extent to which our information agencies are prepared to go in order to give the public service!

Mr. Davis's activities were thus sufficiently spectacular and colourful to gain the publicity which he sought for his ideas of a world government. However, they led many people to write him off as a crank and his influence was therefore rather limited.

Later on he addressed a public meeting in Paris to further his ideas and wrote to me beforehand asking me to support his conception and let him have my views on it. I sent him a courteous reply in which I conceded that there was a great deal of substance in what he wanted and that a world government might some day come. It was, however, I said, not yet within the bounds of practical possibilities and it was the duty of everyone to rally around the United Nations which was the existing organization and the one on which future development could and should be built.

The idea of a world government is attractive and many tidy schemes have been worked out on paper. Bodies to propagate the schemes exist in several countries, including the United

States, where several eminent men with experience in political and international affairs are associated with them. These bodies often perform a valuable service in stimulating and educating the public. They are undoubtedly ahead of their time and are none the less influential for that.

The fact is that at present no nation is prepared to surrender its sovereignty completely. Even in federal systems like the United States, Australia, and Canada it is difficult to get the states or provinces to concede greater powers to the central government. This is even more true of nations which do not have the homogeneity of American and Australian states. The five central American republics, for example, have never got far in their discussions on some form of federation or association. If closer links are to be sought it is probably best to proceed first among kindred states and even then perhaps only in regard to specified functions, as the Benelux and Western Union associations have done.

Indeed in some countries the value attached to sovereignty is greater now than it used to be. Representatives of the Soviet Union for example have laid great stress on preserving sovereign rights. Mr. Vyshinsky has said that sovereignty is the protection which the Soviet state has against encroachments of the capitalist world seeking to break down its system of life. While that attitude prevails, there are many limitations to any subordination of the state to a world system.

However, the very act of entering into a treaty implies some limitation of the exercise of sovereignty. The United Nations Charter itself is a great multilateral treaty. Under a treaty each signatory undertakes to limit his sovereignty in so far as he will not do certain things except under specified conditions, and undertakes to perform certain acts in consideration of certain conduct by another country.

A treaty is thus in one sense a surrender of sovereignty. But in another sense it is an exercise of sovereignty. It is the supreme mark of the sovereign independence of a state to be able to undertake obligations or to exact undertakings from other states. Historically one of the first indications of the sovereign independence of the British dominions was their acquisition of the right to enter into treaties on their own account without any intervention or concurrence by the United Kingdom.

The United Nations therefore in all its acts, even those of the most routine nature, is to some extent limiting the sovereignty of its members. More and more countries are agreeing to co-ordinate their policies and actions and to consult with one another on matters of common concern. Thereby they are accepting obligations, but at the same time they are extending the sphere of their international activities and influence. Except when these agreements take the form of definite conventions, treaties, or binding agreement they are not normally enforceable but this does not in any way weaken their significance. New habits of international conduct based on co-operation and interdependence are being built.

The destruction or dissolution of the United Nations would not lead to its replacement by a world government. On the contrary, it would be succeeded by a number of antagonistic groupings of states. So far from having a world-wide sovereign state, there would no longer be even the present degree of subordination of national sovereignty represented by acceptance of the United Nations Charter and reflected in the working of the Organization.

I do not want here to discuss the theoretical or moral advantages of world government. The objections which I am putting forward are practical ones. Whatever we may think of the desirability of world government, it just could not be secured at present. My concern is lest those who advocate world government help to destroy or impede the only world-wide body we have working for world-wide peace, justice, and welfare—which is, moreover, gradually inducing governments to subordinate national sovereignty in certain matters.

XVII

CHURCHILL'S LETTER TO STALIN

IN the House of Commons debate of 10th December 1948 Mr. Churchill quoted from what he called "a private personal communication" sent by him to Marshall Stalin on 29th April 1945.

The date of the letter is not without significance. The conference at Yalta between Roosevelt, Stalin, and Churchill had taken place in February, and Russia had agreed to enter the war against Japan upon the basis that the Kuriles and Southern Sakhalin would be ceded to Russia by Japan together with vital concessions in relation to Port Arthur and Dairen and control of southern Manchurian and Chinese eastern railway systems. This had been done without the prior consent of China but Churchill, Stalin, and Roosevelt undertook that the Russian terms would be "unquestionably fulfilled after Japan has been defeated." (See *Roosevelt and Hopkins* page 867)

President Roosevelt's death occurred early in April and the San Francisco conference which formulated the Charter of the United Nations began on 25th April.

It was in these circumstances that Churchill wrote to Stalin. The fighting in Germany was practically completed but it was by no means certain how long the struggle against Japan would continue. U. S. and Australian forces had already been allocated for vital offensives to take place against the mainland of Japan late in 1945. The decision to use the atomic bomb on Hiroshima and Nagasaki had, of course, not been taken.

The Churchill letter is extremely important and there are three parts of it which he quoted.

First of all Churchill dealt with Poland. In his letter he wrote:—

Side by side with our strong sentiment for the rights of Poland, which I believe is shared in at least as strong a degree throughout the United States, there has grown up throughout the English-speaking world a very warm, deep desire to be friends on equal and honourable terms with the mighty Russian, Soviet Republic, and to work with you, making allowances for our different systems and thought and government in long and bright years for all the world, which we three Powers alone can make together. I, who in my years of great responsibility, have worked faithfully for this unity, will certainly continue to do so with every means in my power, and, in particular, I can assure you that we in Great Britain would not work for, or tolerate, a Polish Government unfriendly to Russia. Neither could we recognize a Polish Government that did not truly correspond to the description in our joint declaration at Yalta, with proper regard for the rights of the individual as we understand these matters in the western world.

The essence of this letter was the expression of "very warm, deep desire to be friends on equal and honourable terms with the mighty Russian, Soviet Republic." This was a true expression of the feeling of the English-speaking world at the time of the San Francisco conference. It was evident on all sides in America as Mr. Molotov appeared from time to time, not only in San Francisco, but in other places. So far as warmth of feelings is concerned, undoubtedly the Russians had the ball at their feet.

In the British Commonwealth the feeling towards Russia was even warmer, always remembering that until June 1941 the British Commonwealth was fighting practically alone against Hitler.

The second point I want to make is Churchill's expression of the desire "to work with you, making allowances for our different systems and thought and government in long and bright years for all the world, which we three Powers alone can make together."

These are very telling words and said very eloquently. It has been frequently said by Stalin that his country desires to work with the west despite the differences in the internal social and economic system between Russia and other countries who do not necessarily have the same system. Marshal Stalin spoke in this strain to Mr. Stassen. Molotov and Vyshinsky have repeatedly spoken in the same way.

Churchill's letter then indicated that he had worked faithfully as Prime Minister for this unity of the three Powers and would "certainly continue to do so with every means in my power."

Here we see the basic principle, stating not so much a method of co-operation as a determined will to co-operate, even though the three countries concerned would not have changed their own social and economic systems or attempt to change the others.

But Churchill did not leave the matter here. He went on stating "in particular, I can assure you that we in Great Britain would not work for, or *tolerate,* a Polish Government unfriendly to Russia." Churchill added another sentence on Poland as to not being able to recognize a new Polish Government system that did not correspond to the Yalta declaration with due regard to individual rights "as we understand these matters in the western world." At once we see a possibility of contradiction in these two statements because full application of the doctrines of the Atlantic Charter to Poland might, theoretically at any rate, have resulted in the establishment of a government that would be hostile to Russia. At the same time Churchill makes it clear that he would not even tolerate a Polish Government unfriendly to Russia.

The matter need not proceed further. The whole basis of Russian policy in relation to Poland and other countries now behind what is called "the iron curtain" is based upon the footing that they were part and parcel of Russia's security zone. In two world wars the uncertainties caused by the presence of fascist or dictatorial governments in Poland, Hungary, Bulgaria, Roumania, and Yugoslavia had made it axiomatic in Russian policy that they too would not in future "tolerate" unfriendly governments in these areas of vital strategic import.

When you say you will not "tolerate" a government that is unfriendly, that must mean that the electoral or democratic freedoms given to the people of that country are subject to some qualification. If that qualification is not satisfied, the possibility of intervention from outside to prevent the government from acting in a certain way must always be taken into account.

Churchill's letter then dealt with the subject of Greece. It read as follows:—

In Greece we seek nothing but her friendship, which is of long duration, and desire only her independence and integrity, but we have no intention to try to decide whether she is to be a monarchy or a republic. Our only policy is to restore matters to the normal as quickly as possible, and to hold fair and free elections, I hope within the next four or five months. These elections will decide the regime and later the constitution. The will of the people expressed under conditions of freedom and universal franchise must prevail. That is our root principle. If the Greeks were to decide for a republic it would not affect our relations with them. We will use our influence with the Greek Government to invite Russian representatives to come to see freely what is going on in Greece, and at the elections I hope that there will be Russian, American, and British commissioners at large in the country to make sure there is no intimidation or other frustration to the free choice of the people between the parties contending.

This expressed in impeccable terms the proper attitude towards Greece. None the less, from the point of view of vital British interests in the Mediterranean, a Greek Government unfriendly to Britain might have presented a grave menace. It would have been quite reasonable therefore for Churchill to claim he could not tolerate a Greek Government unfriendly to Britain since this would involve very serious consequences, and that Russia should take this into account.

Churchill's letter then faced the spectre which haunts so many people today. Taking a broad view of the relationships of the United States and Britain to Russia he says:—

There is not much comfort in looking into a future where you and the countries you dominate, plus the Communist parties in many other States, are all drawn up on one side, and those who rally to the English-speaking nations, with their associates and dominions are on the other. It is quite obvious that their quarrel would tear the world to pieces, and all of us, leading men on either side, who had anything to do with that would be shamed before history. Even embarking on long periods of suspicion, or abuse and counterabuse, and of opposing policies, would be a disaster, hampering great development of world prosperity for the masses, which are attainable only by our trinity.

I hope there is no word or phrase in this out-pouring of my heart to you which unwittingly gives offence. If there is let me know. But do not, I beg of you, my friend Stalin, underrate the divergences which are opening up about matters, which you may think small but which are symbolic of the way the English-speaking democracies look at life.

What does this all add up to? He refers in the clearest terms to the division between east and west—with Russia, the satellites of Russia, and the communist forces throughout the world, on one side, and the group described by Churchill as "English-speaking nations with their associates and dominions" on the other. He says that the struggle between east and west obviously "will tear the world to pieces" and that leaders on either side having anything to do with that catastrophe would be "shamed before history."

Churchill, on a second point, says that short of a quarrel, long periods of suspicion, abuse, and counter-abuse of opposing policies would hamper world prosperity for the masses and "would be a disaster." It should be noted that Churchill states that world prosperity is attainable only by "our trinity." There is no doubt that Churchill regarded himself as certain to continue as Prime Minister of Great Britain for some years, at least, after 1945. As it was, his term of office was destined to last only three months longer, before his overwhelming defeat at the hands of the Labour Party as a result of a general election forced on the people before the war could be regarded even as nearly won. Churchill's sentiment in this letter must be regarded as being utterly sincere and genuine in every respect. He and Roosevelt had made concessions to Russia not only in the Far East but in Europe which had caused special difficulties for their successors who were honourably bound to carry out these territorial and other post-war arrangements. Their justification before history is based upon two facts: all the arrangements were necessary to obtain Russia as an active ally, and Russian assistance was absolutely vital in their supreme objective of overthrowing Hitler.

Differences with Russia which had arisen during the war had sometimes been acute. Nowhere is this better evidenced than in relation to the second front which Roosvelt had half-promised for 1942, the performance being, for practical reasons of overwhelming weight, deferred until 1944. Other even more acute difficulties were to arise over the atomic bomb.

Nonetheless, Churchill had supreme self-confidence that, with the government of Britain in his hands and despite the tragic death of Roosevelt he could co-operate with Russia and other communist-controlled countries for the improvement of economic standards of living. For him, at any rate, the word "impossible" did not exist.

But the very situation which Churchill described as a possibility has come into existence even though there are in fact some exceptions and qualifications to two blocs. There was abuse and certainly vituperation by Mr. Vyshinsky at Lake Success in 1947 and to a lesser extent in Paris recently, of remarkable force and duration; and the counter-abuse evident in quite a few of the speeches of western leaders in Paris was of equal vehemence.

So the stage has been reached where suspicion has come into existence, has lasted for a long period, has been followed by abuse and counter-abuse and acutely different policies. Till recently the trend was to go still further towards the "fatal quarrel" which, in Mr. Churchill's opinion in 1945, would tear the world to pieces and cause everlasting shame to leaders responsible for such a dire consequence. And when I speak of opposing policies and of Vyshinsky, one should not overlook the very frank speeches of Churchill in 1946 at Fulton and more recently in Llandudno.

In 1945 Churchill postulated that the quarrel could be avoided and that east and west, without surrendering what they regarded as very vital principles, could sufficiently co-operate to prevent the unspeakable disaster of armed conflict, and could also improve standards of living throughout the world. Why can't the frank, sincere, impressive thesis of Churchill in 1945 be revived again?

It is as convincing today as in 1945. It is more necessary today than in 1945. Difficulties abound and suspicion is still very great. But the Berlin situation has eased, and the New York Assembly provided important instances of United Nations co-operation and United Nations principles of conciliation and justice triumphing in the end. For my part, I regard Mr. Churchill as pointing out in his letter the true approach—not surrender or appeasement, but frankness, directness, conciliation, and justice. Acting on these principles we can and must succeed.

XVIII

ONE WORLD—THE TASK OF ALL NATIONS AND ALL PEOPLE

ONE world is still possible. If peace is to be preserved and if mankind is to progress to new heights, "one world" can be approached. What is needed is a positive policy based on the principles and purposes of the United Nations Charter.

Our aim must be to build and sustain a world in which each individual can live a peaceful life with a decent standard of living and freedom to develop his talents and express himself as he chooses. It is a world in which the Four Freedoms of President Roosevelt would be a reality.

Freedom of the Individual

Democracy is based upon the great principle of freedom of the individual. Arising out of Christian teaching and tradition, democracy regards each individual as an end in himself, and society should be designed to give the fullest possible expression to the individual's desires and needs. Government is based on the freely expressed will of the people.

This in turn implies obligations on the part of the individual towards society. But regimentation is something to be avoided except in an emergency such as war. It is a test of the political maturity of a democratic country if its citizens willingly carry out their obligations to the rest of the community out of a sense of duty and an appreciation of the interdependence of all its members, and not because they are forced by law to do so.

In a true democracy each citizen can sleep peacefully at night, unafraid of a knock on his door by the police; he is not spied upon by agents of the state in his ordinary business of life; he is free to speak and read and write and publish as he pleases and to assemble at public meetings; he is not accountable to any state official for his personal conduct or for his political beliefs.

But freedom of the individual, though it is a noble and attractive principle and basic to democracy, is not enough by itself. Positive efforts are also needed to increase standards of living and to reduce inequality.

Higher Living Standards

The ability of the individual to express himself and exercise his rights may be severely limited if he is hungry, ill-clothed, or badly housed. Unemployment is a most deadly disease for the individual no less than for the state. A healthy society with contented citizens can only exist when the economic and social system is looking after the needs of all members of the community and giving each his opportunity to play a full role.

This means a steadily rising standard of living for everyone, based on increased national production. It also means adequate social services to take care of those who, usually through no fault of their own, are faced with the burdens of unemployment, illness, or other disaster. Enlightened thought regards this aid as the right of every citizen, and not as a gracious bounty given as a mere favour.

Notable work in this direction has already been done and is being done in many countries. In earlier centuries the church was the main source of relief. Later liberal and socialist movements in Western Europe paved the way for the State itself to assume greater responsibilities aided by private benevolence whose contribution, even today, should be neither overlooked nor deprecated.

One World—The Task of All Nations

Over the past fifty years great pioneering work has been done in Australia and New Zealand in the fields of social services and fair labour legislation. In Great Britain the achievements of the Attlee Labour Government in combining state planning with parliamentary democracy provide great hope for the future.

The United States of America was formerly in a rather different position. It is a land of immense wealth, high standards of living, and still untapped resources. Until recently there was an immense inflow of immigrants. Consequently private capitalism tended for a long while to rule without restraint, and the great energy of American frontier and industrial pioneers developed its resources at a great pace. But during the present century, under the inspiration and drive of T. R. Roosevelt, Woodrow Wilson, and particularly Franklin D. Roosevelt, curbs have been placed on the abuse of power by capital and big business, and social services have been established and extended.

It is true to say that in most countries today there is no longer any dispute as to whether the State shall intervene in economic and business matters and undertake some degree of planning. That battle has been won. The State cannot be indifferent to mass unemployment and huge depressions, for these not only cause immense human misery but threaten the whole structure of society. The economic dependence of every country on every other has also become clearer during the present century. Consequently, even the most conservative and capitalistic of Governments now accepts a degree of State interference which would have seemed revolutionary in the time of Gladstone and Cleveland.

Intervention by the State is therefore no longer a question of principle but a question of degree to be decided on its merits for each country and each industry. Some of the present controls may be temporary and are forced on us for the time being by the world shortage of dollars and the scarcity of certain materials for reconstruction. Other controls are necessary to limit major economic fluctuations or to secure an equitable distribution of limited resources.

The problem is to choose and apply the controls in a manner that will not injure personal freedom; will not impose the petty pinpricks which are so often harder to bear than more sweeping restrictions; will not curb enterprise and initiative; and will not bog life down in a mass of red tape and bureaucratic delay.

THE QUEST FOR EQUALITY

Democracy must also answer the challenge of other political creeds which claim to offer equality to all men irrespective of colour, race, or class. Their claims may not be true in practice. Moreover, most of us would feel that equality without personal freedom is hardly worth having. But the dissatisfaction which results from resentment and discrimination on grounds of colour or class is a fundamental weakness in the structure of western civilization, particularly in countries where there are substantial minorities and where whole races feel themselves looked on as inferiors.

This problem must be faced squarely. It is true that it is difficult to proceed overnight with sweeping remedies. The prejudices of mankind, irrational though they may be, are deep rooted in the tradition of each country and in the teaching which each child absorbs, often unconsciously. These prejudices cannot be easily overturned.

We must therefore first seek the betterment of conditions through education and through the pressure of world opinion. In this respect the United Nations is performing a great service by setting out in an international declaration of human rights a detailed statement of what everyone in every country should be entitled to receive.

The practical difficulties in the way of reform should not, however, be regarded as due cause for protracted delay. If we delay too long, the remedies may be found in violence, as has already occurred in some countries. Revolutions may break out which will not only destroy all the bad paraphernalia of the past, but also the good.

The British Commonwealth has set one example by giving India, Pakistan, Ceylon, and Burma complete independence. Burma unfortunately chose to leave the Commonwealth. But the other three states, of their own free will, became independent sovereign Dominions, and twice their representatives have sat in London at a conference of the Commonwealth Prime Ministers as equal partners in that great brotherhood.

It must be realized that the days of old-time imperialism and exploitation in Asia are over. The Western Powers, it is true, gave much to the countries of Asia in the way of capital development. They also helped—the British in particular—to give them some appreciation of the democratic values of western civilization, including the very idea of national independence and the dignity of the individual. These are exactly the things which the peoples of these regions are now demanding.

So too in other underdeveloped territories of the world. The Charter of the United Nations covers all non-self-governing territories, with a special category of trust territories. The Charter provides that in these territories the welfare of the inhabitants shall be the paramount consideration and that the aim of the administering powers shall be the full participation of the inhabitants in their own government.

These purposes and principles are set out clearly in the Charter—fundamental freedoms, rising standards of living, peace based on justice. Probably in no country does practice correspond in every point to our professions in the Charter. But every member nation has subscribed to the Charter, and pursuit of its principles provides a common aim and connecting link for the nations.

War Is Not Inevitable

It is tragic to hear some people glibly talking of "the next war," thereby helping to bring one about by accustoming people to the idea of it. War is not inevitable. Mr. Churchill's letter shows the way.

Countries can differ on basic matters and yet continue to live in peace. For example, British and Russian policies before 1914 were on many matters opposed to one another for over a century and some of their vital interests clashed in almost all regions where they came in contact, yet there was no war between the two nations except for the brief period of the Crimean campaign. Different political and economic systems can exist side by side without war arising.

The interests of all countries will be better served by peace than by war. The peoples of all countries abhor war and sincerely desire a long period of peace in which they can mend their wounds and repair the devastation which has laid waste their cities and countryside.

Fortunately there are leaders all over the world working for peace. The representatives of Governments who gather at meetings of the United Nations are gradually developing mutual understanding and fellowship. The groups of citizens who discuss these matters together and work for the cause of the United Nations are playing their part too.

Our four great foes are: Tyranny, Poverty, Injustice, and War. They are the foes of all mankind, not just of one or two nations. The one world, which is still possible, will be a reality if we all join in the great and inspiring task of overcoming all the foes, guided by the Charter of the United Nations and working within the great Organization which it has established.

Preserving Peace

The achievement of these aims requires a long period of peace—not peace at any price, but peace based on justice. The United Nations provides the machinery to discuss international disputes, remove causes of friction, and settle differences. The Charter sets out the principles.

The United Nations requires the support of all the members who compose it. They must approach each question on its merits, judging it honestly. Power politics is sometimes defended as being realistic, but it is a realism which takes account of certain facts only—the facts of naked power—and neglects other facts which are no less real—justice and welfare. A state which bases its policy on power alone is like a rudderless ship, floundering through converging currents, unable to pierce for any distance ahead the fog that surrounds it. Properly used, power is an instrument, not a criterion of action.

Only policies aiming at serving the ends of justice can hope to have permanence and consistency, because the only conditions which people will accept and support permanently are those which serve the ends of justice and welfare.

Responsibilities of Each Citizen

I have said a great deal about what the United Nations can do. But there is one thing it cannot do. It cannot absolve the individual from the duties and responsibilities of facing the problems of life and shouldering his share of its burdens.

Some people hailed the establishment of the United Nations in 1945 as something that was going to solve automatically all international questions. Now, they seemed to say, we have nothing to do but sit back and relax, and the Organization will settle everything. These feckless escapists are often the very ones who turn round now and charge the United Nations with failure. Having set their hopes absurdly high, they are naturally disappointed to find that international problems can be solved only by patience, understanding, and friendship.

The process of change and progress in itself involves problems of adjustment. Honest differences of opinion always exist as to what adjustments should be made. Many differences which confront us are the legacy of history and, even when irrational, cannot be exorcised by pretending they do not exist. The United Nations does not prevent problems from arising: it provides machinery for handling them, and principles according to which they should be handled.

The United Nations is therefore not a super-government. Everyone has a part to play. He has an obligation to familiarize himself with the organization of the United Nations and the problems it is tackling. He must throw his full support behind those leaders who stand for the United Nations and its purposes and principles. He should not follow those who fail to give the United Nations "unwavering" and "unfaltering" support. The United Nations will surely win out in its great struggle against tyranny, poverty, injustice, and war.

THE UNITED NATIONS CHARTER

THE UNITED NATIONS CHARTER

The text of the final draft of the United Nations Conference as adopted at the Security Conference at San Francisco, June 26, 1945, is as follows:

We, the peoples of the United Nations, determined:
—To save succeeding generations from the scourge of war, which twice in our lifetime has brought untold sorrow to mankind, and
—To reaffirm faith in fundamental human rights, in the dignity and worth of the human person, in the equal rights of men and women and of nations large and small, and
—To establish conditions under which justice and respect for the obligations arising from treaties and other sources of international law can be maintained, and
—To promote social progress and better standards of life in larger freedom,
And for these ends
—To practice tolerance and live together in peace with one another as good neighbors, and
—To unite our strength to maintain international peace and security, and
—To insure, by the acceptance of principles and the institution of methods, that armed force shall not be used, save in the common interest, and
—To employ international machinery for the promotion of the economic and social advancement of all peoples,
Have resolved to combine our efforts to accomplish these aims.

Accordingly, our respective governments, through representatives assembled in the city of San Francisco, who have exhibited their full powers found to be in good and due form, have agreed to the present charter of the United Nations and do hereby establish an international organization to be known as the United Nations.

CHAPTER I

PURPOSES AND PRINCIPLES

Article 1

The purposes of the United Nations are:

1. To maintain international peace and security, and to that end: to take effective collective measures for the prevention and removal of threats to the peace and for the suppression of acts of aggression or other breaches of the peace, and to bring about by peaceful means, and in conformity with the principles of justice and international law, adjustment or settlement of international disputes or situations which might lead to a breach of the peace;

2. To develop friendly relations among nations based on respect for the principle of equal rights and self-determination of peoples, and to take other appropriate measures to strengthen universal peace;

3. To achieve international cooperation in solving international problems of an economic, social, cultural, or humanitarian character, and in promoting and encouraging respect for human rights and for fundamental freedoms for all without distinction as to race, sex, language, or religion; and

4. To be a center for harmonizing the actions of nations in the attainment of these common ends.

Article 2

The organization and its members, in pursuit of the purposes stated in Article 1, shall act in accordance with the following principles:

1. The organization is based on the principle of the sovereign equality of all its members.

2. All members, in order to insure to all of them the rights and benefits resulting from membership, shall fulfill in good faith the obligations assumed by them in accordance with the present charter.

3. All members shall settle their international disputes by peaceful means in such a manner that international peace and security, and justice, are not endangered.

4. All members shall refrain in their international relations from the threat or use of force against the territorial integrity or political independence of any state, or in any other manner inconsistent with the purposes of the United Nations.

5. All members shall give the United Nations every assistance in any

action it takes in accordance with the present charter, and shall refrain from giving assistance to any state against which the United Nations is taking preventive or enforcement action.

6. The organization shall insure that states which are not members of the United Nations act in accordance with these Principles so far as may be necessary for the maintenance of international peace and security.

7. Nothing contained in the present charter shall authorize the United Nations to intervene in matters which are essentially within the domestic jurisdiction of any state or shall require the members to submit such matters to settlement under the present charter; but this principle shall not prejudice the application of enforcement measures under Chapter VII.

CHAPTER II

MEMBERSHIP

Article 3

The original members of the United Nations shall be the states which, having participated in the United Nations Conference on International Organization at San Francisco or having previously signed the Declaration by United Nations of January 1, 1942, sign the present charter and ratify it in accordance with Article 110.

Article 4

1. Membership in the United Nations is open to all other peace-loving states which accept the obligations contained in the present charter and, in the judgment of the organization, are able and willing to carry out these obligations.

2. The admission of any such state to membership in the United Nations will be effected by a decision of the General Assembly upon the recommendation of the Security Council.

Article 5

A member of the United Nations against which preventive or enforcement action has been taken by the Security Council may be suspended from the exercise of the rights and privileges of membership by the General Assembly upon the recommendation of the Security Council. The exercise of these rights and privileges may be restored by the Security Council.

Article 6

A member of the United Nations which has persistently violated the principles contained in the present charter may be expelled from the organization by the General Assembly upon the recommendation of the Security Council.

CHAPTER III

ORGANS

Article 7

1. There are established as the principal organs of the United Nations: a General Assembly, a Security Council, an Economic and Social Council, a Trusteeship Council, an International Court of Justice, and a Secretariat.

2. Such subsidiary organs as may be found necessary may be established in accordance with the present charter.

Article 8

The United Nations shall place no restrictions on the eligibility of men and women to participate in any capacity and under conditions of equality in its principal and subsidiary organs.

CHAPTER IV

THE GENERAL ASSEMBLY

COMPOSITION

Article 9

1. The General Assembly shall consist of all the members of the United Nations.

2. Each member shall have not more than five representatives in the General Assembly.

FUNCTIONS AND POWERS

Article 10

The General Assembly may discuss any questions or any matters within the scope of the present charter or relating to the powers and functions of any organs provided in the present charter, and, except as provided for in Article 12, may make recommendations to the members of the United Nations or to the Security Council or to both on any such questions or matters.

Article 11

1. The General Assembly may consider the general principles of cooperation in the maintenance of international peace and security, including the principles governing disarmament and the regulation of armaments, and may make recommendations with regard to such principles to the members or to the Security Council or to both.

2. The General Assembly may discuss any questions relating to the maintenance of international peace and security brought before it by any member of the United Nations, or by the Security Council, or by a state which is not a member of the United Nations in accordance with Article 35, paragraph 2, and, except as provided in Article 12, may make recommendations with regard to any such questions to the state or states concerned or to the Security Council or to both. Any such question on which action is necessary shall be referred to the Security Council by the General Assembly either before or after discussion.

3. The General Assembly may call the attention of the Security Council to situations which are likely to endanger international peace and security.

4. The powers of the General Assembly set out in this article shall not limit the general scope of Article 10.

Article 12

1. While the Security Council is exercising in respect of any dispute or situation the functions assigned to it in the present charter, the General Assembly shall not make any recommendation with regard to that dispute or situation unless the Security Council so requests.

2. The Secretary-General, with the consent of the Security Council, shall notify the General Assembly at each session of any matters relative to the maintenance of international peace and security which are being dealt with by the Security Council and shall similarly notify the General Assembly, or the members of the United Nations if the General Assembly is not in session, immediately the Security Council ceases to deal with such matters.

Article 13

1. The General Assembly shall initiate studies and make recommendations for the purpose of:

(a) Promoting international cooperation in the political field and encouraging the progressive development of international law and its codification;

(b) Promoting international cooperation in the economic, social, cultural, educational, and health fields, and assisting in the realization of human rights and fundamental freedoms for all without distinction as to race, sex, language, or religion.

2. The further responsibilities, functions, and powers of the General Assembly with respect to matters mentioned in paragraph 1 (b) above are set forth in Chapters IX and X.

Article 14

Subject to the provisions of Article 12, the General Assembly may recommend measures for the peaceful adjustment of any situation, regardless of origin, which it deems likely to impair the general welfare or friendly relations among nations, including situations resulting from a violation of the provisions of the present charter setting forth the purposes and principles of the United Nations.

Article 15

1. The General Assembly shall receive and consider annual and special reports from the Security Council; these reports shall include an account of the measures that the Security Council has decided upon or taken to maintain international peace and security.

2. The General Assembly shall receive and consider reports from the other organs of the United Nations.

Article 16

The General Assembly shall perform such functions with respect to the international trusteeship system as are assigned to it under Chapters XII and XIII, including the approval of the trusteeship agreements for areas not designated as strategic.

Article 17

1. The General Assembly shall consider and approve the budget of the organization.

2. The expenses of the organization shall be borne by the members as apportioned by the General Assembly.

3. The General Assembly shall consider and approve any financial and budgetary arrangements with specialized agencies referred to in Article 57 and shall examine the administrative budgets of such special-

ized agencies with a view to making recommendations to the agencies concerned.

VOTING

Article 18

1. Each member of the General Assembly shall have one vote.
2. Decisions of the General Assembly on important questions shall be made by a two-thirds majority of the members present and voting. These questions shall include: recommendations with respect to the maintenance of international peace and security, the election of the non-permanent members of the Security Council, the election of the members of the Economic and Social Council, the election of the members of the Trusteeship Council in accordance with paragraph 1 (c) of Article 86, the admission of new members to the United Nations, the suspension of the rights and privileges of membership, the expulsion of members, questions relating to the operation of the trusteeship system, and budgetary questions.
3. Decisions on other questions, including the determination of additional categories of questions to be decided by a two-thirds majority, shall be made by a majority of the members present and voting.

Article 19

A member of the United Nations which is in arrears in the payment of its financial contributions to the organization shall have no vote in the General Assembly if the amount of its arrears equals or exceeds the amount of the contributions due from it for the preceding two full years. The General Assembly may, nevertheless, permit such a member to vote if it is satisfied that the failure to pay is due to conditions beyond the control of the member.

PROCEDURE

Article 20

The General Assembly shall meet in regular annual sessions and in such special sessions as occasion may require. Special sessions shall be convoked by the Secretary-General at the request of the Security Council or of a majority of the members of the United Nations.

Article 21

The General Assembly shall adopt its own rules of procedure. It shall elect its President for each session.

Article 22

The General Assembly may establish such subsidiary organs as it deems necessary for the performance of its functions.

CHAPTER V

THE SECURITY COUNCIL

COMPOSITION

Article 23

1. The Security Council shall consist of eleven members of the United Nations. The Republic of China, France, The Union of Soviet Socialist Republics, The United Kingdom of Great Britain and Northern Ireland, and The United States of America shall be permanent members of the Security Council. The General Assembly shall elect six other members of the United Nations to be non-permanent members of the Security Council, due regard being specially paid, in the first instance to the contribution of members of the United Nations to the maintenance of international peace and security and to the other purposes of the organization, and also to equitable geographical distribution.

2. The non-permanent members of the Security Council shall be elected for a term of two years. In the first election of the non-permanent members, however, three shall be chosen for a term of one year. A retiring member shall not be eligible for immediate re-election.

3. Each member of the Security Council shall have one representative.

FUNCTIONS AND POWERS

Article 24

1. In order to insure prompt and effective action by the United Nations, its members confer on the Security Council primary responsibility for the maintenance of international peace and security, and agree that in carrying out its duties under this responsibility the Security Council acts on their behalf.

2. In discharging these duties the Security Council shall act in accordance with the purposes and principles of the United Nations. The specific powers granted to the Security Council for the discharge of these duties are laid down in Chapters VI, VII, VIII, and XII.

3. The Security Council shall submit annual and, when necessary, special reports to the General Assembly for its consideration.

Article 25

The members of the United Nations agree to accept and carry out the decisions of the Security Council in accordance with the present charter.

Article 26

In order to promote the establishment and maintenance of international peace and security with the least diversion for armaments of the world's human and economic resources, the Security Council shall be responsible for formulating, with the assistance of the military staff committee referred to in Article 47, plans to be submitted to the members of the United Nations for the establishment of a system for the regulation of armaments.

VOTING

Article 27

1. Each member of the Security Council shall have one vote.
2. Decisions of the Security Council on procedural matters shall be made by an affirmative vote of seven members.
3. Decisions of the Security Council on all other matters shall be made by an affirmative vote of seven members including the concurring votes of the permanent members; provided that, in decisions under Chapter VI, and under paragraph 3 of Article 52, a party to a dispute shall abstain from voting.

PROCEDURE

Article 28

1. The Security Council shall be so organized as to be able to function continuously. Each member of the Security Council shall for this purpose be represented at all times at the seat of the organization.
2. The Security Council shall hold periodic meetings at which each of its members may, if it so desires, be represented by a member of the government or by some other specially designated representative.
3. The Security Council may hold meetings at such places other than the seat of the organization as in its judgment will best facilitate its work.

Article 29

The Security Council may establish such subsidiary organs as it deems necessary for the performance of its functions.

The United Nations Charter

Article 30

The Security Council shall adopt its own rules of procedure, including the method of selecting its President.

Article 31

Any member of the United Nations which is not a member of the Security Council may participate, without vote, in the discussion of any question brought before the Security Council whenever the latter considers that the interests of that member are specially affected.

Article 32

Any member of the United Nations which is not a member of the Security Council or any state which is not a member of the United Nations, if it is a party to a dispute under consideration by the Security Council, shall be invited to participate, without vote, in the discussion relating to the dispute. The Security Council shall lay down such conditions as it deems just for the participation of a state which is not a member of the United Nations.

CHAPTER VI

Pacific Settlement of Disputes

Article 33

1. The parties to any dispute, the continuance of which is likely to endanger the maintenance of international peace and security, shall, first of all, seek a solution by negotiation, inquiry, mediation, conciliation, arbitration, judicial settlement, resort to regional agencies or arrangements, or other peaceful means of their own choice.

2. The Security Council shall, when it deems necessary, call upon the parties to settle their dispute by such means.

Article 34

The Security Council may investigate any dispute, or any situation which might lead to international friction or give rise to a dispute, in order to determine whether the continuance of the dispute or situation is likely to endanger the maintenance of international peace and security.

Article 35

1. Any member of the United Nations may bring any dispute or any situation of the nature referred to in Article 34 to the attention of the Security Council, or of the General Assembly.

2. A state which is not a member of the United Nations may bring to the attention of the Security Council or of the General Assembly any dispute to which it is a party if it accepts in advance, for the purposes of the dispute, the obligations of pacific settlement provided in the present charter.

3. The proceedings of the General Assembly in respect of matters brought to its attention under this article will be subject to the provisions of Articles 11 and 12.

Article 36

1. The Security Council may, at any stage of a dispute of the nature referred to in Article 33 or of a situation of like nature, recommend appropriate procedures or methods of adjustment.

2. The Security Council should take into consideration any procedures for the settlement of the dispute which have already been adopted by the parties.

3. In making recommendations under this article the Security Council should also take into consideration that legal disputes should as a general rule be referred by the parties to the International Court of Justice in accordance with the provisions of the Statute of the Court.

Article 37

1. Should the parties to a dispute of the nature referred to in Article 33 fail to settle it by the means indicated in that Article, they shall refer it to the Security Council.

2. If the Security Council deems that the continuance of the dispute is in fact likely to endanger the maintenance of international peace and security, it shall decide whether to take action under Article 36 or to recommend such terms of settlement as it may consider appropriate.

Article 38

Without prejudice to the provisions of Articles 33-37 the Security Council may, if all the parties to any dispute so request, make recommendations to the parties with a view to a pacific settlement of the dispute.

CHAPTER VII

Action with Respect to Threats to the Peace, Breaches of the Peace, and Acts of Aggression

Article 39

The Security Council shall determine the existence of any threat to the peace, breach of the peace, or act of aggression and shall make recommendations, or decide what measures shall be taken in accordance with Articles 41 and 42, to maintain or restore international peace and security.

Article 40

In order to prevent an aggravation of the situation, the Security Council may, before making the recommendations or deciding upon the measures provided for in Article 41, call upon the parties concerned to comply with such provisional measures as it deems necessary or desirable. Such provisional measures shall be without prejudice to the rights, claims, or position of the parties concerned. The Security Council shall duly take account of failure to comply with such provisional measures.

Article 41

The Security Council may decide what measures not involving the use of armed force are to be employed to give effect to its decisions, and it may call upon the members of the United Nations to apply such measures. These may include complete or partial interruption of economic relations and of rail, sea, air, postal, telegraphic, radio, and other means of communications, and the severance of diplomatic relations.

Article 42

Should the Security Council consider that measures provided for in Article 41 should be inadequate or have proved to be inadequate, it may take such action by air, sea, or land forces as may be necessary to maintain or restore international peace and security. Such action may include demonstrations, blockade, and other operations by air, sea, or land forces of members of the United Nations.

Article 43

1. All members of the United Nations, in order to contribute to the maintenance of international peace and security, undertake to make available to the Security Council, on its call and in accordance with a

special agreement or agreements, armed forces, assistance, and facilities, including rights of passage, necessary for the purpose of maintaining international peace and security.

2. Such agreement or agreements shall govern the numbers and types of forces, their degree of readiness and general location, and the nature of the facilities and assistance to be provided.

3. The agreement or agreements shall be negotiated as soon as possible on the initiative of the Security Council. They shall be concluded between the Security Council and members or between the Security Council and groups of members and shall be subject to ratification by the signatory states in accordance with their constitutional processes.

Article 44

When the Security Council has decided to use force it shall before calling upon a member not represented on it to provide armed forces in fulfillment of the obligations assumed under Article 43, invite that member, if the member so desires, to participate in the decisions of the Security Council concerning the employment of contingents of that member's armed forces.

Article 45

In order to enable the United Nations to take urgent military measures, members shall hold immediately available national air-force contingents for combined international enforcement action. The strength and degree of readiness of these contingents and plans for their combined action shall be determined, within the limits laid down in the special agreement or agreements referred to in Article 43, by the Security Council with the assistance of the Military Staff Committee.

Article 46

Plans for the application of armed force shall be made by the Security Council with the assistance of the Military Staff Committee.

Article 47

1. There shall be established a military staff committee to advise and assist the Security Council's military requirements for the maintenance of international peace and security, the employment and command of forces placed at its disposal, the regulation of armaments, and possible disarmament.

2. The Military Staff Committee shall consist of the Chiefs of Staff of the permanent members of the Security Council or their representatives. Any member of the United Nations not permanently repre-

sented on the Committee shall be invited by the Committee to be associated with it when the efficient discharge of the Committee's responsibilities requires the participation of that member in its work.

3. The Military Staff Committee shall be responsible under the Security Council for the strategic direction of any armed forces placed at the disposal of the Security Council. Questions relating to the command of such forces shall be worked out subsequently.

4. The Military Staff Committee, with the authorization of the Security Council and after consultation with appropriate regional agencies, may establish regional sub-committees.

Article 48

1. The action required to carry out the decisions of the Security Council for the maintenance of international peace and security shall be taken by all the members of the United Nations or by some of them, as the Security Council may determine.

2. Such decisions shall be carried out by the members of the United Nations directly and through their action in the appropriate international agencies of which they are members.

Article 49

The members of the United Nations shall join in affording mutual assistance in carrying out the measures decided upon by the Security Council.

Article 50

If preventive or enforcement measures against any state are taken by the Security Council, any other state whether a member of the United Nations or not, which finds itself confronted with special economic problems arising from the carrying out of those measures shall have the right to consult the Security Council with regard to a solution of those problems.

Article 51

Nothing in the present charter shall impair the inherent right of individual or collective self-defense if an armed attack occurs against a member of the United Nations, until the Security Council has taken the measures necessary to maintain international peace and security. Measures taken by members in the exercise of this right of self-defense shall be immediately reported to the Security Council and shall not in any way affect the authority and responsibility of the Security Council under the present charter to take at any time such action as it deems necessary in order to maintain or restore international peace and security.

CHAPTER VIII

REGIONAL ARRANGEMENTS

Article 52

1. Nothing in the present charter precludes the existence of regional arrangements or agencies for dealing with such matters relating to the maintenance of international peace and security as are appropriate for regional action, provided that such arrangements or agencies and their activities are consistent with the purposes and principles of the United Nations.

2. The members of the United Nations entering into such arrangements or constituting such agencies shall make every effort to achieve pacific settlement of local disputes through such regional arrangements or by such regional agencies before referring them to the Security Council.

3. The Security Council shall encourage the development of pacific settlement of local disputes through such regional arrangements or by such regional agencies either on the initiative of the states concerned or by reference from the Security Council.

4. This article in no way impairs the application of Articles 34 and 35.

Article 53

1. The Security Council shall, where appropriate, utilize such regional arrangements or agencies for enforcement action under its authority. But no enforcement action shall be taken under regional arrangements or by regional agencies without the authorization of the Security Council, with the exception of measures against any enemy state, as defined in paragraph 2 of this article, provided for pursuant to Article 107 or in regional arrangements directed against renewal of aggressive policy on the part of any such state, until such time as the organization may, on request of the governments concerned, be charged with the responsibility for preventing further aggression by such a state.

2. The term "enemy state" as used in paragraph 1 of this article applies to any state which during the Second World War has been an enemy of any signatory of the present charter.

Article 54

The Security Council shall at all times be kept fully informed of activities undertaken or in contemplation under regional arrangements or by regional agencies for the maintenance of international peace and security.

CHAPTER IX

INTERNATIONAL ECONOMIC AND SOCIAL COOPERATION

Article 55

With a view to the creation of conditions of stability and well-being which are necessary for peaceful and friendly relations among nations based on respect for the principle of equal rights and self-determination of peoples, the United Nations shall promote:

A. Higher standards of living, full employment, and conditions of economic and social progress and development;

B. Solutions of international economic, social, health, and related problems; and international cultural and educational cooperation; and

C. Universal respect for, and observance of, human rights and fundamental freedoms for all without distinction as to race, sex, language, or religion.

Article 56

All members pledge themselves to take joint and separate action in cooperation with the organization for the achievement of the purposes set forth in Article 55.

Article 57

1. The various specialized agencies, established by inter-governmental agreement and having wide international responsibilities, as defined in their basic instruments, in economic, social, cultural, educational, health, and related fields, shall be brought into relationship with the United Nations in accordance with the provision of Article 63.

2. Such Agencies thus brought into relationship with the United Nations are hereinafter referred to as "specialized agencies."

Article 58

The organization shall make recommendations for the coordination of the policies and activities of the specialized agencies.

Article 59

The organization shall, where appropriate, initiate negotiations among the states concerned for the creation of any new specialized agencies required for the accomplishment of the purposes set forth in Article 55.

Article 60

Responsibility for the discharge of the functions of the organization set forth in this chapter shall be vested in the General Assembly and, under the authority of the General Assembly, in the Economic and Social Council, which shall have for this purpose the powers set forth in Chapter X.

CHAPTER X

THE ECONOMIC AND SOCIAL COUNCIL

COMPOSITION

Article 61

1. The Economic and Social Council shall consist of eighteen members of the United Nations elected by the General Assembly.

2. Subject to the provisions of paragraph 3, six members of the Economic and Social Council shall be elected each year for a term of three years. A retiring member shall be eligible for immediate re-election.

3. At the first election, eighteen members of the Economic and Social Council shall be chosen. The term of office of six members so chosen shall expire at the end of one year, and of six other members at the end of two years, in accordance with arrangements made by the General Assembly.

4. Each member of the Economic and Social Council shall have one representative.

FUNCTIONS AND POWERS

Article 62

1. The Economic and Social Council may make or initiate studies and reports with respect to international economic, social, cultural, educational, health, and related matters and may make recommendations with respect to any such matters to the General Assembly, to the members of the United Nations, and to the specialized agencies concerned.

2. It may make recommendations for the purpose of promoting

respect for, and observance of, human rights and fundamental freedoms for all.

3. It may prepare draft conventions for submission to the General Assembly, with respect to matters falling within its competence.

4. It may call, in accordance with the rules prescribed by the United Nations, international conferences on matters falling within its competence.

Article 63

1. The Economic and Social Council may enter into agreements with any of the agencies referred to in Article 57, defining the terms on which the agency concerned shall be brought into relationship with the United Nations. Such agreements shall be subject to approval by the General Assembly.

2. It may coordinate the activities of the specialized agencies through consultation with the recommendations to such agencies and through recommendations to the General Assembly and to the members of the United Nations.

Article 64

1. The Economic and Social Council may take appropriate steps to obtain regular reports from the specialized agencies. It may make arrangements with the members of the United Nations and with the specialized agencies to obtain reports on the steps taken to give effect to its own recommendations and to recommendations on matters falling within its competence made by the General Assembly.

2. It may communicate its observations on these reports to the General Assembly.

Article 65

The Economic and Social Council may furnish information to the Security Council and shall assist the Security Council upon its request.

Article 66

1. The Economic and Social Council shall perform such functions as fall within its competence in connection with the carrying out of the recommendations of the General Assembly.

2. It may, with the approval of the General Assembly, perform services at the request of members of the United Nations and at the request of specialized agencies.

3. It shall perform such other functions as are specified elsewhere in the present charter or as may be assigned to it by the General Assembly.

VOTING

Article 67

1. Each member of the Economic and Social Council shall have one vote.
2. Decisions of the Economic and Social Council shall be made by a majority of the members present and voting.

PROCEDURE

Article 68

The Economic and Social Council shall set up commissions in economic and social fields and for the promotion of human rights, and such other commissions as may be required for the performance of its functions.

Article 69

The Economic and Social Council shall invite any member of the United Nations to participate, without vote, in its deliberations on any matter of particular concern to that member.

Article 70

The Economic and Social Council may make arrangements for representatives of the specialized agencies to participate, without vote, in its deliberations and in those of the commissions established by it, and for its representatives to participate in deliberations of the specialized agencies.

Article 71

The Economic and Social Council may make suitable arrangements for consultation with non-governmental organizations which are concerned with matters within its competence. Such arrangements may be made with international organizations and, where appropriate, with national organizations after consultation with the member of the United Nations concerned.

Article 72

1. The Economic and Social Council shall adopt its own rules of procedure, including the method of selecting its president.
2. The Economic and Social Council shall meet as required in accordance with its rules, which shall include provision for the convening of meetings on request of a majority of its members.

CHAPTER XI

DECLARATION REGARDING NON-SELF-GOVERNING TERRITORIES

Article 73

Members of the United Nations which have or assume responsibilities for the administration of territories whose peoples have not yet attained a full measure of self-government recognize the principle that the interests of the inhabitants of these territories are paramount, and accept as a sacred trust the obligation to promote to the utmost, within the system of international peace and security established by the present charter, the well-being of the inhabitants of these territories, and, to this end:

A. To insure, with due respect for the culture of the peoples concerned, their political, economic, social and educational advancement, their just treatment, and their protection against abuses;

B. To develop self-government, to take due account of the political aspirations of the peoples, and to assist them in the progressive development of their free political institutions, according to the particular circumstances of each territory and its peoples and their varying stages of advancement;

C. To further international peace and security;

D. To promote constructive measures of development, to encourage research, and to cooperate with one another and, when and where appropriate, with specialized international bodies with a view to the practical achievement of the social, economic, and scientific purposes set forth in this article; and

E. To transmit regularly to the Secretary-General for information purposes, subject to such limitation as security and constitutional considerations may require, statistical and other information of a technical nature relating to economic, social, and educational conditions in the territories for which they are respectively responsible other than those territories to which Chapters XII and XIII apply.

Article 74

Members of the United Nations also agree that their policy in respect of the territories to which this chapter applies, no less than in respect of their metropolitan areas, must be based on the general principle of good-neighborliness, due account being taken of the interests and well-being of the rest of the world, in social, economic, and commercial matters.

CHAPTER XII

INTERNATIONAL TRUSTEESHIP SYSTEM

Article 75

The United Nations shall establish under its authority an international trusteeship system for the administration and supervision of such territories as may be placed thereunder by subsequent individual agreements. These territories are hereinafter referred to as trust territories.

Article 76

The basic objectives of the trusteeship system, in accordance with the purposes of the United Nations laid down in Article 1 of the present charter, shall be:

A. To further international peace and security;

B. To promote the political, economic, social, and educational advancement of the inhabitants of the trust territories, and their progressive development towards self-government or independence as may be appropriate to the particular circumstances of each territory and its peoples and the freely expressed wishes of the peoples concerned, and as may be provided by the terms of each trusteeship agreement;

C. To encourage respect for human rights and for fundamental freedoms for all without distinction as to race, sex, language, or religion, and to encourage recognition of the interdependence of the peoples of the world; and

D. To insure equal treatment in social, economic, and commercial matters for all members of the United Nations and their nationals, and also equal treatment for the latter in the administration of justice, without prejudice to the attainment of the foregoing objectives and subject to the provisions of Article 80.

Article 77

1. The trusteeship system shall apply to such territories in the following categories as may be placed thereunder by means of trusteeship agreements:

(a) Territories now held under mandate;

(b) Territories which may be detached from enemy states as a result of the Second World War; and

(c) Territories voluntarily placed under the system by states responsible for their administration.

2. It will be a matter for subsequent agreement as to which territories in the foregoing categories will be brought under the trusteeship system and upon what terms.

Article 78

The trusteeship system shall not apply to territories which have become members of the United Nations, relationship among which shall be based on respect for the principle of sovereign equality.

Article 79

The terms of trusteeship for each territory to be placed under the trusteeship system, including any alterations or amendment, shall be agreed upon by the states directly concerned, including the mandatory power in the case of territories held under mandate by a member of the United Nations, and shall be approved as provided for in Articles 83 and 85.

Article 80

1. Except as may be agreed upon in individual trusteeship agreements, made under Articles 77, 79 and 81, placing each territory under the trusteeship system, and until such agreements have been concluded, nothing in this chapter shall be construed in or of itself to alter in any manner the rights whatsoever of any states or any peoples or the terms of existing international instruments to which members of the United Nations may respectively be parties.

2. Paragraph 1 of this article shall not be interpreted as giving grounds for delay or postponement of the negotiation and conclusion of agreements for placing mandated and other territories under the trusteeship system as provided for in Article 77.

Article 81

The trusteeship agreement shall in each case include the terms under which the trust territory will be administered and designate the authority which will exercise the administration of the trust territory. Such authority, hereinafter called the administering authority, may be one or more states or the organization itself.

Article 82

There may be designated, in any trusteeship agreement, a strategic area or areas which may include part or all of the trust territory to which the agreement applies, without prejudice to any special agreement or agreements made under Article 43.

Article 83

1. All functions of the United Nations relating to strategic areas, including the approval of the terms of the trusteeship agreements and of their alteration or amendment, shall be exercised by the Security Council.

2. The basic objectives set forth in Article 76 shall be applicable to the people of each strategic area.

3. The Security Council shall, subject to the provisions of the trusteeship agreements and without prejudice to security considerations, avail itself of the assistance of the Trusteeship Council to perform those functions of the United Nations under the trusteeship system relating to political, economic, social, and educational matters in the strategic areas.

Article 84

It shall be the duty of the administering authority to insure that the trust territory shall play its part in the maintenance of international peace and security. To this end the administering authority may make use of volunteer forces, facilities, and assistance from the trust territory in carrying out the obligations towards the Security Council undertaken in this regard by the administering authority, as well as for local defense and the maintenance of law and order within the trust territory.

Article 85

1. The functions of the United Nations with regard to trusteeship agreements for all areas not designated as strategic, including the approval of the terms of the trusteeship agreements and of their alteration or amendment, shall be exercised by the General Assembly.

2. The Trusteeship Council, operating under the authority of the General Assembly, shall assist the General Assembly in carrying out these functions.

CHAPTER XIII

THE TRUSTEESHIP COUNCIL

COMPOSITION

Article 86

1. The Trusteeship Council shall consist of the following members of the United Nations:

(a) Those members administering trust territories;

(b) Such of those members mentioned by name in Article 23 as are not administering trust territories; and

(c) As many other members elected for three-year terms by the General Assembly as may be necessary to insure that the total number of members of the Trusteeship Council is equally divided between those members of the United Nations which administer trust territories and those which do not.

2. Each member of the Trusteeship Council shall designate one specially qualified person to represent it therein.

FUNCTIONS AND POWERS

Article 87

The General Assembly and, under its authority, the Trusteeship Council, in carrying out their functions, may:

A. Consider reports submitted by the administering authority;

B. Accept petitions and examine them in consultation with the administering authority.

C. Provide for periodic visits to the respective trust territories at times agreed upon with the administering authority; and

D. Take these and other actions in conformity with the terms of the trusteeship agreements.

Article 88

The Trusteeship Council shall formulate a questionnaire on the political, economic, social, and educational advancement of the inhabitants of each trust territory, and the administering authority for each trust territory within the competence of the General Assembly shall make an annual report to the General Assembly upon the basis of such questionnaire.

VOTING

Article 89

1. Each member of the Trusteeship Council shall have one vote.

2. Decisions of the Trusteeship Council shall be made by a majority of the members present and voting.

PROCEDURE

Article 90

1. The Trusteeship Council shall adopt its own rules of procedure, including the method of selecting its president.

2. The Trusteeship Council shall meet as required in accordance with its rules, which shall include provision for the convening of meetings on the request of a majority of its members.

Article 91

The Trusteeship Council shall, when appropriate, avail itself of the assistance of the Economic and Social Council and of the specialized agencies in regard to matters with which they are respectively concerned.

CHAPTER XIV

THE INTERNATIONAL COURT OF JUSTICE

Article 92

The International Court of Justice shall be the principal judicial organ of the United Nations. It shall function in accordance with the annexed statute, which is based upon the Statute of the Permanent Court of International Justice and forms an integral part of the present charter.

Article 93

1. All members of the United Nations are ipso facto parties to the Statute of the International Court of Justice.

2. A state which is not a member of the United Nations may become a party to the Statute of the International Court of Justice on conditions to be determined in each case by the General Assembly upon the recommendation of the Security Council.

Article 94

1. Each member of the United Nations undertakes to comply with the decision of the International Court of Justice in any case to which it is a party.

2. If any party to a case fails to perform the obligations incumbent upon it under a judgment rendered by the Court, the other party may have recourse to the Security Council, which may, if it deems necessary,

make recommendations or decide upon measures to be taken to give effect to the judgment.

Article 95

Nothing in the present charter shall prevent members of the United Nations from entrusting the solution of their differences to other tribunals by virtue of agreements already in existence or which may be concluded in the future.

Article 96

1. The General Assembly or the Security Council may request the International Court of Justice to give an advisory opinion on any legal question.

2. Other organs of the United Nations and specialized agencies, which may at any time be so authorized by the General Assembly, may also request advisory opinions of the Court on legal questions arising within the scope of their activities.

CHAPTER XV

THE SECRETARIAT

Article 97

The Secretariat shall comprise a Secretary-General and such staff as the organization may require. The Secretary-General shall be appointed by the General Assembly upon the recommendation of the Security Council. He shall be the chief administrative officer of the organization.

Article 98

The Secretary-General shall act in that capacity in all meetings of the General Assembly, or the Security Council, of the Economic and Social Council, and of the Trusteeship Council, and shall perform such other functions as are entrusted to him by these organs. The Secretary-General shall make an annual report to the General Assembly on the work of the organization.

Article 99

The Secretary-General may bring to the attention of the Security Council any matter which in his opinion may threaten the maintenance of international peace and security.

Article 100

1. In the performance of their duties the Secretary-General and the staff shall not seek or receive instructions from any government or from

any other authority external to the organization. They shall refrain from any action which might reflect on their position as international officials responsible only to the organization.

2. Each member of the United Nations undertakes to respect the exclusively international character of the responsibilities of the Secretary-General and the staff and not to seek to influence them in the discharge of their responsibilities.

Article 101

1. The staff shall be appointed by the Secretary-General under regulations established by the General Assembly.

2. Appropriate staffs shall be permanently assigned to the Economic and Social Council, the Trusteeship Council, and, as required, to other organs of the United Nations. These staffs shall form a part of the Secretariat.

3. The paramount consideration in the employment of the staff and in the determination of the conditions of service shall be the necessity of securing the highest standards of efficiency, competence, and integrity. Due regard shall be paid to the importance of recruiting the staff on as wide a geographical basis as possible.

CHAPTER XVI

MISCELLANEOUS PROVISIONS

Article 102

1. Every treaty and every international agreement entered into by any member of the United Nations after the present charter comes into force shall as soon as possible be registered with the Secretariat and published by it.

2. No party to any such treaty or international agreement which has not been registered in accordance with the provisions of paragraph 1 of this article may invoke that treaty or agreement before any organ of the United Nations.

Article 103

In the event of a conflict between the obligation of the members of the United Nations under the present charter and obligations under any other international agreement, their obligations under the present charter shall prevail.

Article 104

The organization shall enjoy in the territory of each of its members such legal capacity as may be necessary for the exercise of its functions and the fulfillment of its purposes.

Article 105

1. The organization shall enjoy in the territory of each of its members such privileges and immunities as are necessary for the fulfillment of its purposes.

2. Representatives of the members of the United Nations and officials of the organization shall similarly enjoy such privileges and immunities as are necessary for the independent exercise of their functions in connection with the organization.

3. The General Assembly may make recommendations with a view to determining the details of the application of paragraphs 1 and 2 of this article or may propose conventions to the members of the United Nations for this purpose.

CHAPTER XVII

TRANSITIONAL SECURITY ARRANGEMENTS

Article 106

Pending the coming into force of such special agreements referred to in Article 43 as in the opinion of the Security Council enable it to begin the exercise of its responsibilities under Article 42 the parties to the four-nation declaration, signed at Moscow, October 30, 1943, and France, shall, in accordance with the provisions of paragraph 5 of that declaration, consult with one another and as occasion requires with other members of the United Nations with a view to such joint action on behalf of the organization as may be necessary for the purpose of maintaining international peace and security.

Article 107

Nothing in the present charter shall invalidate or preclude action, in relation to any state which during the Second World War has been an enemy of any signatory to the present charter, taken or authorized as a result of that war by the governments having responsibility for such action.

CHAPTER XVIII

Amendments

Article 108

Amendments to the present charter shall come into force for all members of the United Nations when they have been adopted by a vote of two-thirds of the members of the General Assembly and ratified in accordance with their respective constitutional processes by two-thirds of the members of the United Nations, including all the permanent members of the Security Council.

Article 109

1. A general conference of the members of the United Nations for the purpose of reviewing the present charter may be held at a date and place to be fixed by a two-thirds vote of the members of the General Assembly and by a vote of any seven members of the Security Council. Each member of the United Nations shall have one vote in the conference.

2. Any alteration of the present charter recommended by a two-thirds vote of the conference shall take effect when ratified in accordance with their respective constitutional processes by two-thirds of the members of the United Nations including all the permanent members of the Security Council.

3. If such a conference has not been held before the tenth annual session of the General Assembly following the coming into force of the present charter, the proposal to call such a conference shall be placed on the agenda of that session of the General Assembly, and the conference shall be held if so decided by a majority vote of the members of the General Assembly and by a vote of any seven members of the Security Council.

CHAPTER XIX

Ratification and Signature

Article 110

1. The present charter shall be ratified by the signatory states in accordance with their respective constitutional processes.

2. The ratifications shall be deposited with the Government of the United States of America, which shall notify all the signatory states of

each deposit as well as the Secretary-General of the organization when he has been appointed.

3. The present charter shall come into force upon the deposit of ratifications by the Republic of China, France, the Union of Soviet Socialist Republics, the United Kingdom of Great Britain and Northern Ireland, and the United States of America, and by a majority of the other signatory states. A protocol of the ratifications deposited shall thereupon be drawn up by the Government of the United States of America which shall communicate copies thereof to all the signatory states.

4. The states signatory to the present charter which ratify it after it has come into force will become original members of the United Nations on the date of the deposit of their respective ratifications.

Article 111

The present charter, of which the Chinese, English, French, Russian, and Spanish texts are equally authentic, shall remain deposited in the archives of the Government of the United States of America. Duly certified copies thereof shall be transmitted by that government to the governments of the other signatory states.

In faith whereof the representatives of the United Nations have signed the present charter.

Done at the city of San Francisco the twenty-sixth day of June, one thousand nine hundred and forty-five.

INDEX

Afghanistan 6, 140, 161, 162, 195
Albania 55, 57, 58, 59, 62, 63, 65, 69, 70, 71, 72
Alfaro, Ricardo J. 17
Amendment of Charter 30
American States, Organization of 34
Arab Higher Committee 125, 132, 142, 153, 155
Arab League 126, 183
Arab States 14-15, 38, 99, 121-174, 183
Aranha, Oswaldo 14, 15, 129, 130, 131, 164
Arce, Jose 12, 15, 152, 153
Argentina 6, 12, 15, 30, 76, 152, 161, 162, 195, 218
Atomic energy 3, 201-207
Attlee, C. R. 237
Atyeo, S. L. 131
Austin, Warren R. 7
Australia 6, 13, 27, 30, 33, 39, 40, 43, 46, 51, 52, 56, 57, 60, 61, 62, 63, 64, 87, 88, 93, 95, 98, 104, 106, 107, 108, 114, 115, 123, 124, 125, 129, 130, 131, 153, 157, 161, 162, 163, 168, 171, 172, 174, 180, 182, 183, 184, 185, 188, 191, 192, 194, 195, 196, 197, 198, 204, 215, 217, 218, 220, 225, 227, 237
Austria 84, 89, 90
Azerbaijan 23-24

Balfour Declaration 123, 124, 133, 155, 157
Balkan dispute *see* Greek question
Baruch, Bernard M. 202
Bebler, Ales 60, 61, 64, 69
Bech, Joseph 12, 16

Belgium 6, 11, 63, 73, 76, 183, 184, 185, 195, 197, 204
Belt, Guillermo 17
Benelux 34, 45, 225
Berendsen, Sir Carl 9, 160-161
Berlin 16, 28-29, 73-85, 92
Bernadotte, Count 122
Bethlehem 121, 158
Bevin, Ernest 98
Bloc voting 38
Bludan decisions 126
Bramuglia, Juan A. 15-17, 28, 81, 83, 84
Brazil 14, 15, 129
British Commonwealth 9-11, 37, 38, 43, 107, 111, 228, 239
Bulgaria 55, 57, 58, 59, 62, 63, 69-72, 89, 229
Bunche, Ralph 122
Burma 12, 177, 195, 239
Byelorussia 19

Cadogan, Sir Alexander 46
Cairo Declaration 92
Campbell, Eric 118
Canada 9, 10, 13, 44, 76, 106, 107, 125, 140, 143, 160, 195, 201, 204, 225
Castro, H. D. 137, 138
Ceylon 27, 177, 195, 239
Chamberlain, Neville 212
Chamoun, Camille 149
Chang, P. C. 112
Charter of UN: 29-31, 33-34, 43, 111, 114, 167, 210, 216, 222, 225, 235
Article 2(7) 66, 183
Article 4 30
Article 7 12
Article 10 49

275

Article 11 50, 156
Article 14 49, 156
Article 27 46-47, 51, 78
Article 34 182, 183
Article 39 76, 166, 182, 183
Article 103 33
Chapter VI 77-78, 183
Chapter VII 76, 77-78, 182
Chapter VIII 33
Cheribon Agreement *see* Linggadjati
Chifley, J. B. 157, 171
Children's Appeal 105-109
Children's Fund 105-109
Chile 17, 108
China 19, 46, 62, 76, 92, 95, 96, 184, 195, 210, 227
Churchill, Winston S. 47, 80, 227-233
Cleveland, Grover 237
Colombia 76, 140, 142, 195
Committees of General Assembly 101-102
Connally, Senator T. 46
Conventional Armaments, Commission on 3
Cordier, Andrew W. 5
Council of Foreign Ministers 73, 76, 79, 82, 84, 85
Cuba 17
Curacao 179
Cyrenaica 98, 99
Czechoslovakia 67, 125, 129, 140

Dairen 227
Davis, Garry 223-224
Denmark 108
Djockjacarta 191, 197, 198
Domestic jurisdiction 65-67, 183, 193
Dominican Republic 62
Dulles, John Foster 7-8, 58, 93
Dumbarton Oaks proposals 27, 34, 47, 48, 51

Economic and Social Council 12, 17, 27, 49, 103, 104, 106, 107-109, 111, 112, 118, 212, 214, 219-221
Economic Co-operation Administration (E.C.A.) 195
Economic development 213-216
Egypt 122, 140, 154, 174, 195
el-Khouri, Faris 11, 137
El Salvador 62, 137

Epiris 65, 70-72
Eritrea 96-99
Ethiopia 26, 98, 99, 195

Fawzi, Mahmoud Bey 154
Fezzan 98, 99
Finland 89
Food and Agriculture Organization 27
France 13, 19, 46, 59, 62, 73, 76, 89, 97, 99, 170, 183, 184, 195
Fraser, Peter 10
Freedom of Information 117-118

Genocide 101, 102-105
Germany 26, 57, 73-85, 89, 90, 103, 105, 163, 211, 217, 227
Gildersleeve, Virginia C. 168
Gladstone, W. E. 237
Graham, Frank P. 185
Granados, J. G. 129
Greece 62, 230
Greek children 25, 63, 64-65, 70
Greek question 3, 24-25, 39, 40, 55-72, 130, 131, 230
Greek trade unionists 67-69
Gromyko, Andrei 9
Guatemala 125, 129, 140

Hamilton, T. J. 142
Hatta, Mohammed 192, 193
Heba, Theodor 69
Hilldring, Maj.-Gen. J. H. 138
Hitler, Adolph 56, 77, 103, 133, 163, 211, 217, 222, 228
Hohenberg, John 142
Hood, J. D. L. 131
Hopkins, Harry L. 20, 227
Human Rights, Commission on 111-113, 115, 117
Human Rights, Covenant of 115
Human Rights, Universal Declaration of 5, 21, 111-119
Hungary 89, 229
Husseini, Jamel 133, 155

Iceland 138
India 9, 10, 44, 45, 125, 149, 177, 183, 195, 198, 204, 205, 239
Indonesia 25, 51, 175-199
Information, freedom of 117-118
Interim committee of General Assembly 40, 79, 130

Index

International Bank 27, 221
International Children's Emergency Fund 105-109
International Civil Aviation Organization 27
International Court of Justice 133, 138, 155, 158, 180
International Labour Office 27
International Law Commission 105
International Monetary Fund 27, 221
International Trade Organization 27
Inverchapel, Lord 178
Investigation, method of 38-39
Iran 125, 195
Iranian question 23-24, 131
Iraq 99, 126, 127, 132, 137, 140, 149, 195
Ireland 222
Israel 24, 122, 133, 163, 165, 170, 174
Israel, recognition of 170-174
Italian colonies 92, 96-99
Italy 26, 57, 89, 211

Jamali, M. F. 149
Japan, 26, 84, 89, 90, 92, 93, 175, 176, 177, 178, 211, 227
Java 179, 181, 183, 187, 189, 190
Jerusalem 121, 154, 158, 171
Jessup, Philip C. 85, 194
Jewish Agency 125, 132, 137, 142, 145, 146, 151, 153, 155
Jordan 172

Kashmir 25
Killearn, Lord 178, 179
King, W. Mackenzie 10
Kirby, Mr. Justice R. C. 185, 188
Korea 3, 18, 19, 40, 91, 92-96, 130
Kuriles 227

Lange, Oscar R. 11, 220
Latin American states 14-17, 34, 38, 97, 104, 129, 130, 204
League of Nations 26, 27, 31, 90, 91, 122, 133, 211, 212, 221, 222
Lebanon 62, 112, 118, 140, 149, 195, 212
Lemkin, Raphael 103
Libya 96-99
Lie, Trygve 5, 17, 81-84
Limitation of speeches 17-20
Linggadjati agreement 178-181, 182, 183, 186, 187, 197

Litvinov, Maxim 212
Louw, Eric H. 11
Luxemburg 12, 16, 73
Lytton, Earl of 211

McNeil, Hector 9

Madura 179, 183, 187, 189
Malik, Charles 112, 118, 212
Malik, Yakov A. 9, 85
Manchuria 211, 227
Manuilsky, D. Z. 76
Marshall, George C. 7, 145
Marshall Plan 45, 218-219
Masaryk, Jan 129
Mechanical majorities 42, 52
Membership of United Nations 26-27, 30, 130, 174, 180
Mexico 17, 79, 80, 87, 89
Modzelewski, Zygmunt 16
Molotov, V. M. 228, 229
Montgomery of Alamein, Field-Marshal Viscount 44
Mook, H. J. van 178, 181
Mudaliar, Sir Ramaswami 9
Muso 190, 191
Mussolini, Benito 56, 211

Nehru, Pandit Jawaharlal 10, 195
Nepal 195
Netherlands 73, 103, 108, 125, 175-199
New Guinea 215
New Zealand 9, 10, 44, 56, 57, 103, 107, 160, 162, 170, 195, 237
Norway 106
Nuremberg judgment 103, 104

Ording, Aake 106

Padilla Nervo, Luis 17, 79, 80, 83, 87
Pakistan 10, 140, 149, 162, 195, 196, 239
Palais de Chaillot 3, 4
Palestine 15, 24, 25, 36, 39, 51, 101, 121-174
Panama 17
Pandit, Mrs. 10
Paris peace conference 89, 114, 115
Peace settlements 81, 87-99
Pearson, L. B. 160
Peru 108, 125
Philippines 196

Index

Pipinelis, P. 68, 69
Poland 11, 16, 44, 55, 59, 103, 108, 140, 220, 227-230
Port Arthur 227
Portugal 222
Potsdam agreements 73, 74, 76, 92
Presidential elections of General Assembly 1947 129
    1948 14-16

Ramadier, Paul 204
Rau, Sir Benegal Narsing 205
Red Cross 64-65
Regional arrangements 33-34
Renville agreement 186-188, 189, 191, 192, 193, 197
Robertson, General Sir Brian 74
Rockefeller, Nelson A. 152
Rodgers, John G. 142
Roosevelt, Mrs Eleanor 8, 112
Roosevelt, F. D. 8, 47, 80, 90, 91, 227, 231, 232, 237
Roosevelt, T. R. 209, 237
Roumania 89, 229

Sakhalin 227
San Francisco Conference 12, 16, 27, 29, 33, 34, 43, 45, 46, 47, 48, 49, 51, 52, 77, 90, 123, 129, 130, 152, 168, 216, 227, 228
Santa Cruz, Herman 17, 108
Sarper, Selim 63
Saudi Arabia 132, 137, 140, 196
Scandinavia 38, 107
Schultz, Lillie 142
Secretary-General 12, 82
Security Council 12, 16, 17, 23-24, 27, 28, 30, 31, 39, 40, 46-52, 55-57, 59, 60, 73, 76-79, 81, 82, 84, 122, 140, 143, 156, 160, 165-167, 169, 180, 181-185, 188, 192-195, 196, 197-199, 212
Sforza, Count 98
Shertok (now Sharret), Moshe 133, 145, 151, 155, 172
Siam 138, 145, 196
Silver, A. H. 133
Sjahrir, Soetan 181
Sjarifoeddin, Amir 181
Smith, Kingsbury 85
Soedirman, General 192

Soekarno 192
Sokolovsky, Marshal V. D. 74, 75, 76
Somaliland 96-99
South Africa 11, 44, 62, 107, 140, 143
South Pacific Commission 34
Spaak, Paul-Henri 11, 63, 64
Spain 39, 48
Specialized agencies 27
Stalin, Marshal J. V. 47, 80, 85, 227-233
Stassen, H. E. 229
Stikker, D. U. 191
Sudan 99
Sumatra 179, 181, 183, 187
Surinam 179
Svasti Svastivat, Prince Subha 145
Sweden 125
Switzerland 106, 107
Syria 11, 76, 137, 140, 195, 196, 204

Thors, Thor 145
Transjordan 172
Tripolitania 98, 99
Truman, H. S. 214
Trusteeship Council 12, 49
Tsarapkin, S. K. 138, 140
Turkey 63, 122, 123, 133

Ukraine 19, 76, 77, 78, 79, 195, 202
Unemployment 119, 216-221, 236
U. K. 6, 9, 24, 25, 39, 43, 46, 52, 57, 62, 66, 67, 73-76, 89, 92, 97, 99, 103, 107, 122-128, 131, 133, 142, 143, 144, 149, 151, 156, 166, 169, 170, 174, 176, 177, 183, 184, 191, 195, 215, 218, 226, 227-230, 237, 240
UNRRA 106
USA 3, 5, 7, 25, 26, 29, 30, 36, 43-46, 52, 59, 62, 66, 67, 73, 75, 76, 85, 89, 92-97, 99, 106, 109, 126, 138, 140, 145, 166, 167, 172, 183-185, 192, 194, 195, 197, 202, 203, 204, 206, 209, 210, 215, 218, 219, 222, 225, 227, 228, 230, 237
USSR 3, 5, 8-9, 13, 14, 18, 23-24, 25, 26, 28-30, 38, 40, 43-46, 48, 51, 52, 55, 57-59, 66, 73-79, 82, 83, 85, 89, 92-95, 97, 104, 113, 118, 138, 139, 140, 166, 195, 203-206, 210, 212, 218, 222, 228-232, 240
Uruguay 106, 125, 140

Index

Vandenberg, Arthur H. 8
Venezuela 108, 140
Veto 30, 31, 38, 41-42, 46-52, 56, 77
Vladigherov, Theodor 69
Vyshinsky, Andrei Y. 8-9, 13, 18, 28, 58, 76, 93, 206, 225, 229, 232

Warmongering, resolution on 13, 130
Webster, Sir Charles 46
Weizmann, Chaim 133
Welles, Sumner 165-7
Western Union 225
Wilgress, L. Dana 9
Wilhelmina, Queen 177

Willkie, Wendell 209, 210
Wilson, T. Woodrow 90, 91, 237
World government 223-226
World Health Organization 27

Yalta agreement 47, 73, 74, 80, 227, 228
Yemen 140, 196
Yugoslavia 25, 55, 57, 58, 59, 60, 61, 62, 63, 69, 70, 71, 72, 125, 229

Zafrullah Khan, Sir Muhammad 10, 149, 150
Zeeland, Paul van 185